Loïs Bates

**Kindergarten guide**

Loïs Bates

**Kindergarten guide**

ISBN/EAN: 9783337131364

Printed in Europe, USA, Canada, Australia, Japan

Cover: Foto ©Paul-Georg Meister /pixelio.de

More available books at **www.hansebooks.com**

*HANDBOOKS for Students and General Readers.*

# HISTORY OF
# AMERICAN POLITICS

BY
ALEXANDER JOHNSTON, A.M.

*SECOND EDITION, REVISED, AND ENLARGED*

(EIGHTEENTH THOUSAND)

NEW YORK
HENRY HOLT AND COMPANY
1889

COPYRIGHT, 1879, 1882,
BY HENRY HOLT & CO.

TROW'S
PRINTING AND BOOKBINDING COMPANY,
NEW YORK.

# PREFACE TO THE SECOND EDITION.

THIS book was first published in March, 1879. Since that time corrections have been made for each of the eight times that the book has been put to press, but these have been comparatively so unimportant that it has not at any time seemed fitting to call the result a new edition. It would hardly be proper, however, to allow this issue to go out except as a new edition. In it the whole book has been carefully revised and brought down to date; detached portions have been rewritten; the whole outline history from 1868 until 1881 has been given very much more fully than was possible while events were still uncertain; and a new appendix, called for by many correspondents, has been added in the form of a list of the cabinets of the successive administrations, with the dates of appointment.

For the guidance of readers who desire to study more fully the history of which this is an outline, a classified list of authorities is given below.

The scope of the book will be sufficiently indicated by repeating the last paragraph of the preface to the first edition:

"The design of the book is not to present the politics of the States, or to criticise party management, but to make our *national* political history easily available to young men. It is of interest to the whole republic that young citizens should be able to learn that true national party differences have a history and a recognized basis of existence, and should be prevented from following factitious party differences, contrived for personal objects by selfish men. If, for this purpose, this book shall be considered worthy to serve as an introduction to the larger works already in existence, its object will be accomplished."

NORWALK, CONN., *January* 2, 1882.

## AUTHORITIES.

HISTORICAL.—Bancroft's *United States* (to 1782); Pitkin's *United States* (to 1797); Hildreth's *United States* (to 1820); Hamilton's *Republic of the United States;* Tucker's *United States* (to 1840); Hammond's *Political History of New York* (to 1840); von Holst's *United States* (vol. 3, to 1850); Spencer's *United States* (to 1856); Benton's *Debates of Congress* (1789-1850); Appleton's *Annual Cyclopædia* (1861-1880); *Statutes at Large; Electoral Count;* Benton's *Thirty Years*

*View* (1820-50); *North American Review*, January, 1876 ("Politics in America"); Draper's *Civil War in America;* Greeley's *American Conflict* (to 1865); *Statesman's Manual* (to 1858); Wilson's *Rise and Fall of the Slave Power;* Lunt's *Origin of the Late War;* Giddings's *Rebellion*.

BIOGRAPHICAL.—Marshall's *Life of Washington;* Randall's *Life of Jefferson;* Adams's *Life of John Adams* and *Life of John Quincy Adams;* Rives's *Life of Madison;* Jay's *Life of John Jay;* Sparks's *Life of Gouverneur Morris;* Austin's *Life of Gerry;* Parton's *Life of Burr* and *Life of Jackson;* Hammond's *Life of Wright;* Garland's *Life of Randolph;* Colton's *Life of Clay;* Curtis's *Life of Webster;* Schuckers's *Life of Chase;* Pollard's *Life of Jefferson Davis;* Raymond's *Life of Lincoln;* Tyler's *Life of Taney;* Barnes's *Thirty-ninth and Fortieth Congresses;* Spencer's *Life of T. F. Bayard;* Poore's *Political Register.*

HISTORICAL (SPECIAL PERIODS).—Lodge's *English Colonies;* Frothingham's *Rise of the Republic;* Curtis's *History of the Constitution;* Jameson's *Constitutional Convention;* H. Adams's *Documents Relating to New England Federalism;* Dwight's *Hartford Convention;* Carey's *Olive Branch;* Ingersoll's *Second War with Great Britain;* Peters's *Cherokee Case;* Gouge's *Banking in the United States;* Stryker's *American Register* (1849-51); Cairnes's *Slave Power;* Greeley's *Slavery Restriction;* Chittenden's *Peace Conference;* McPherson's *History of the Rebellion* and *History of the Reconstruction;* Putnam's *Rebellion Record;* Whiting's *War Powers;* Callan's *Military Laws;* Eaton's *Civil Service in Great Britain;* *The Nation* (1865-81).

STRICT CONSTRUCTION.—Van Buren's *Origin of Political Parties;* Capen's *Democracy;* Gillet's *Democracy in the United States;* Jefferson's *Writings;* Madison's *Writings;* Woodbury's *Writings;* Calhoun's *Works;* Hunt's *Life of Livingston;* Sedgwick's *Political Writings of William Leggett;* Byrdsall's *Loco-Foco Party;* Hamilton's *Memoir of*

*Rantoul;* *Democratic Review;* Harris's *Political Conflict;* Buchanan's *Administration;* A. H. Stephens' *War Between the States;* Centz's *Republic of Republics.*

LOOSE, OR BROAD, CONSTRUCTION.—Hamilton's *Works;* John Adams's *Works;* Webster's *Works;* Clay's *Speeches;* Story's *Commentaries;* *Whig Review;* Ormsby's *Whig Party;* Seward's *Works;* Sumner's *Works;* Creswell's *Speeches of Henry Winter Davis;* Mulford's *The Nation;* Andrews's *Handbook of the Constitution;* Farrar's *Manual;* Tiffany's *Constitutional Law;* Hurd's *Theory of the United States Government.*

MISCELLANEOUS.—*Tribune Almanac* (1838–81); Cluskey's *Political Text-book;* Greeley's *Political Text-book of* 1860; *Congressional Reports* (particularly those on *Kansas, Harper's Ferry, Covode Investigation, Impeachment of President Johnson, Reconstruction, Ku-Klux Conspiracy, Credit Mobilier, Louisiana*); Poore's *Federal and State Constitution;* Appendix *D* is to be credited to Spofford's *American Almanac;* Appendix *H* has been furnished by the various Departments.

# CONTENTS.

PREFACE AND AUTHORITIES, . . . . iii
INTRODUCTION, . . . . . . 1

## CHAPTER I.
Origin of Political Parties in the United States. Formation of the Constitution of 1787, under the guidance of the Federal Party, . . . . . 3

## CHAPTER II.
FIRST ADMINISTRATION, 1789–1793. Settlement of the government, and rise of the Republican Party, . 18

## CHAPTER III.
SECOND ADMINISTRATION, 1793–1797. The political contests of Europe transferred to America. Success of the Federalists in the first national party contest, . 28

## CHAPTER IV.
THIRD ADMINISTRATION, 1797–1801. Continued success of the Federalists. Alien and Sedition Laws. Defeat of the Federalists. The disputed election of 1800, 41

## CHAPTER V.
FOURTH ADMINISTRATION, 1801–1805. The Republican Party in power. Purchase of Louisiana, . . 52

## CHAPTER VI.

FIFTH ADMINISTRATION, 1805-1809. Continued decline of the Federal Party. The Napoleonic Wars. The Embargo, . . . . . . . 60

## CHAPTER VII.

SIXTH ADMINISTRATION, 1809-1813. War with England. Opposition to it by the Federalists, . . 69

## CHAPTER VIII.

SEVENTH ADMINISTRATION, 1813-1817. Discontent in New England. The Hartford Convention. Peace, 76

## CHAPTER IX.

EIGHTH ADMINISTRATION, 1817-1821. Disappearance of the Federal Party. Appearance of loose constructionist Republicans. Purchase of Florida. The Slavery Question, and the Missouri Compromise of 1820, . 83

## CHAPTER X.

NINTH ADMINISTRATION, 1821-1825. The Era of Good Feeling. Real existence of Parties. The disputed election of 1824, . . . . . . 93

## CHAPTER XI.

TENTH ADMINISTRATION, 1825-1829. Formation of the National Republican and Democratic Parties. Success of the Democrats, . . . . 96

## CHAPTER XII.

ELEVENTH ADMINISTRATION, 1829-1833. The Opposition. Rotation in office. Nullification. The National Bank, . . . . . . . 102

## CHAPTER XIII.

TWELFTH ADMINISTRATION, 1833-1837. Removal of the Deposits. Success of the President. Slavery and the Anti-Slavery Society, . . . . 115

## CHAPTER XIV.

THIRTEENTH ADMINISTRATION, 1837–1841. Panic of 1837. Defeat of the Democrats. Appearance of an Abolition Party, . . . . . 125

## CHAPTER XV.

FOURTEENTH ADMINISTRATION, 1841–1845. The Whig Party in power. Its disagreement with President Tyler. Success of the Democrats, and Annexation of Texas, . . . . . . 132

## CHAPTER XVI.

FIFTEENTH ADMINISTRATION, 1845–1849. The Democratic Party in power. War with Mexico. The Slavery Question revived as to territory acquired from Mexico. The Wilmot Proviso. The Formation of the Free Soil Party. The Whig Party evades the Slavery Question, . . . . . . 141

## CHAPTER XVII.

SIXTEENTH ADMINISTRATION, 1849–1853. The Whig Party in power. Adoption of Squatter Sovereignty by the Democrats. California. The Compromise of 1850. Its acceptance by the Whig Convention, . 151

## CHAPTER XVIII.

SEVENTEENTH ADMINISTRATION, 1853–1857. The Democratic Party in power. The Kansas-Nebraska Bill, and the Repeal of the Compromise of 1820. Division of the Whig Party. Rise of the Republican and American Parties. Kansas, . . . 158

## CHAPTER XIX.

EIGHTEENTH ADMINISTRATION, 1857–1861. The Dred Scott Decision, and its Consequences. Southern Democrats reject Squatter Sovereignty. Division of the Democratic Party. Success of the Republicans. Secession, Conciliation, and attempted Compromise, 170

## CHAPTER XX.

NINETEENTH ADMINISTRATION, 1861-1865. The Republican Party in Power. Civil War. Loose Constructionist Measures. The Democratic Party opposes the War and is defeated. Abolition of Slavery, . . 186

## CHAPTER XXI.

TWENTIETH ADMINISTRATION, 1865-1869. Return of the seceding States to the Union. Reconstruction. Disagreement between Congress and the President. The Democratic Party opposes Reconstruction by Congress and is defeated, . . . . . . . . 196

## CHAPTER XXII.

TWENTY-FIRST ADMINISTRATION, 1869-1873. Reconstruction by Congress accomplished, and the results of the War finally accepted by the Democratic Party. The "Liberal Movement." Success of the Republican Party, . . . . . . . . . . 209

## CHAPTER XXIII.

TWENTY-SECOND ADMINISTRATION, 1873-1877. Disturbances in the South. The enforcement of Reconstruction. The disputed Presidential Election of 1876, . 223

## CHAPTER XXIV.

TWENTY-THIRD ADMINISTRATION, 1877-1881. Questions of Currency and Financial Legislation. The condition of the Civil Service, . . . . . . . . 238

APPENDIX A. Articles of Confederation, . . . . 248
APPENDIX B. The Constitution, . . . . . . 262
APPENDIX C. Admission of the States, . . . . 289
APPENDIX D. Summary of Popular and Electoral Votes in Presidential Elections, 1789-1880, . . . . . 290
APPENDIX E. Population of the Sections, 1790-1860, . . 297
APPENDIX F. Congressional Representation of the Sections, 1790-1860, . . . . . . . . . . 298
APPENDIX G. The Sections in 1870 and 1880, . . . 299
APPENDIX H. Cabinet Officers of the Administrations, . 300
INDEX, . . . . . . . . . . . 309

# INTRODUCTION.

1. THE government of the United States, in its original form (in 1777), was an extreme Democracy, whose controlling principle was the complete independence of separate communities. Those who opposed its change to a Representative Republic (in 1787) were generally distinguished afterwards by a desire that the Constitution then adopted should be construed or interpreted strictly according to its terms, and that ingenious interpretations of its provisions should not give the Federal Government any further stretch of power. The party which was thus founded, and which has retained the name of Democratic-Republican even to our own day, has therefore usually been called the **Strict Constructionist** party.

2. On the other hand the successive parties which have opposed the Strict Constructionist view, and have endeavored to carry the government still further from its originally extreme democratic form, have generally been distinguished by a desire that the Constitution should be interpreted loosely and broadly, so as to give the

Federal Government increased power in various objects of national importance. They have therefore usually been called **Loose Constructionist,** or **Broad Constructionist,** parties.[1] Their policy has necessarily been one of attack, and each of them has, in the main, been successful in securing a general acceptance by the whole country of the principle upon which its formation was based.[2]

3. This question of a strict or a loose construction of the Constitution has always been at the root of legitimate national party differences in the United States. All other pretended distinctions have been either local and temporary, or selfish and misleading, and the general acceptance of any such party difference would mark an unfortunate decline in the political intelligence of the people.

---

[1] It must not be imagined, however, that any party has ever called itself "The Strict Constructionist Party," or "The Loose Constructionist Party." These names are used as descriptions, not as titles.

[2] The Federalists succeeded in forming a stronger Central Government; the Whigs in maintaining for the Central Government the power of making certain Internal Improvements at national expense; and the Republicans in maintaining for the Central Government the power of abolishing Slavery (first in the Territories, and afterwards in the States also), of coercing a rebellious State, and of protecting the slaves when set free. The power of the Central Government to lay Protective Duties on imports, and to organize a national banking system, was maintained for a time by the Whigs, and revived and carried into effect by the Republicans.

# CHAPTER I.

### ORIGIN OF POLITICAL PARTIES IN THE UNITED STATES

1. **Political Parties** in the United States had no real existence until the revolution which dissolved allegiance to Great Britain. Most of the colonies were under royal or proprietary governments, in some of which there was a deliberative assembly. But in none of these did the people have such an influence upon the government as would have given to their differences of political opinion the distinction of party membership. In the **New England Colonies** the opportunities for the formation of parties were greater. The immigrants in this section of America had brought with hem the town system of local government, and had left behind them the strong central power which had held it in check in England. They had also the good fortune, or the political foresight, to obtain charters from the king, by which they were allowed to exercise powers of government denied to the other colonies To these charters they clung with tenacity, and their distance from England made it difficult for the king to

overcome their stubborn resistance to his endeavors to withdraw the gift, when its results had roused his suspicion and dislike. The consequence was the establishment in New England of a multitude of petty towns, each a pure democracy. In these were put in practice without question the principles of personal liberty, trial by jury, the voting of taxes by the people, and the responsibility of public officials to the people, for which all the succeeding years, and a great expenditure of blood and money, have hardly been able to secure recognition elsewhere. But the questions debated and decided in these petty democracies, or even in the larger colonial assemblies, were not such as give rise to settled differences of opinion and political parties. For these a broader field was necessary.

2. This principle of **Popular Sovereignty** had spread rapidly from the townships to the collective New England colonies. but was longer in influencing the colonies to the southward. It was not until about the year 1760 that this work can be considered accomplished. By that time most of the thinking men in the colonies agreed in believing that in the colonies rested the right to govern themselves. The principle had been repeatedly announced in theory before revolution was thought of, but personal loyalty to the king, pride in the name of Englishman, and the infrequent exercise by England of her asserted rights of absolute dominion over her colonies, permitted it to lie dormant. In the year 1760 the financial necessities of England drove her into a fifteen years' intermittent endeavor to govern the

colonies without their consent. The attempt at once awakened the principle of popular sovereignty, and the continuing contest increased the extent of its acceptance, until it became strong enough to overcome the forces which had hitherto held it in check.

3. During this period of contest the English party names, **Whig and Tory**, became naturalized in America. Their use at first was only nominal, for those who claimed them had no power to influence the course of government. Lord North and his Tory ministry and party, being in power and in need of money, advocated repressive and coercive measures toward the insubordinate colonies, and these were naturally opposed by the Whigs, the party in opposition. The name of Whig, therefore, became more popular yearly in the colonies, and was the boast of thousands whose only claim to it lay in their gratitude to the real Whigs in England.

4. The successive Congresses of delegates from the different colonies, which gradually learned to exercise all the functions of government, to form an army and navy, to organize a post-office department, and to raise money for national purposes, were recognized and attended only by the so-called **American Whigs**. Therefore, although they offered no opportunity for party contests, they at least gave the American Whigs an influence, whether rightful or usurped, upon the course of government, and thus made them the first American political party. As soon as independence was announced, in 1776, to be the final object of the

contest, the names Whig and Tory lost, in America, whatever of British significance they had ever possessed. One who espoused the cause of the revolted colonies was called a **Whig**, and one who still clung to the mother country and the crown was called a **Tory**. Th Tory party was finally abolished at the close of the Rev olution, when the triumphant Whigs confiscated th estates of its more active members, and compelled their owners to emigrate.

5. Before the end of the year 1776 most of the States had settled their forms of State government. These were generally such adaptations of the old colonial governments as the altered condition of affairs seemed to demand. But there was greater difficulty in settling a collective government for all the States. The idea of popular sovereignty, of local government, had spread from the township to the county, and from the county to the colony, without evil results. But the difficulty of intercommunication, and the diversity of local interests, caused each State to regard the others as, in great measure, foreign soil. And, now that a Confederacy was to be formed, the determination of each State to allow no dictation from its neighbors, or from the new Federal Government, was found to be an insuperable barrier against the formation of a close union In their anxiety to be without a master the States left themselves without a government.

6. The form of government for the new **Confeder acy**[1] was agreed upon in November, 1777. The **Con**

---

[1] See Appendix A.

gress was to be composed of not more than seven, or less than two, delegates from each State, to be chosen by the Legislature. The States were to be equal in power, each having but one vote, no matter how great its population or wealth. There was to be no President or other Executive power, except committees of Congress. Important measures required the votes of nine of the thirteen States, and amendments required the votes of *all*. Congress had hardly more than an advisory power at the best. It had no power to prevent or punish offenses against its own laws, or even to perform effectively the duties enjoined upon it by the Articles of Confederation. It alone could declare war, but it had no power to compel the enlistment, arming, or support of an army. It alone could fix the needed amount of revenue, but the taxes could only be collected by the States at their own pleasure. It alone could decide disputes between the States, but it had no power to compel either disputant to respect or obey its decisions. It alone could make treaties with foreign nations, but it had no power to prevent individual States from violating them. Even commerce, foreign and domestic, was to be regulated entirely by the States. and it was not long before State selfishness began to show itself in the regulation of duties on imports. In everything the States were to be sovereign, and their creature, the Federal Government, was to have only strength enough to bind the States into nominal unity, and only life enough to assure it of its own practical impotence. The jealous States then felt, with considerable satisfaction, that their liberties were reasonably secure.

7. A human society bound together by no stronger ties than those provided by the **Articles of Confederation** must tend naturally to anarchy. Even during the War of Revolution the weakness of the government seemed to many to portend financial ruin and a speedy dissolution of the Union. As soon as the pressure of war was removed the symptoms of disintegration grew alarmingly worse. Congress had become a mere Rump, without dignity, without power, and without a home. It was compelled to appeal repeatedly to the States before it could obtain a quorum of members to ratify the treaty of peace. Many of the States refused or neglected to pay even their allotted shares of interest upon the public debt, and there was no power in Congress to compel payment. Eighteen months were required to collect only one-fifth of the taxes assigned to the States in 1783. The national credit became worthless. Foreign nations refused to make commercial treaties with the United States, preferring a condition of affairs in which they could lay any desired burden upon American commerce without fear of retaliation by an impotent Congress. The national standing army had dwindled to a corps of eighty men. In 1785 Algiers declared war against the United States. Congress recommended the building of five 40-gun ships of war. But Congress had only power to recommend. The ships were not built, and the Algerines were permitted to prey on American commerce

with impunity. England still refused to carry out the Treaty of 1783, or to send a Minister to the United States. The Federal Government, in short, was despised abroad, and disobeyed at home.

8. The apparent remedy was the possession by Congress of the power of levying and collecting internal taxes and duties on imports, but, after long urging, it was found impossible to gain the necessary consent of *all* the States to the article of taxation by Congress. In 1786, therefore, this was abandoned, and, as a last resort, the States were asked to pass an Amendment intrusting to Congress the collection of a revenue from imports. This Amendment was agreed to by all the States but one. New York alone rejected it, after long debate, and her veto seemed to destroy the last hope of a continuance of national union in America. Perhaps the dismay caused by the action of New York was the most powerful argument in the minds of many for an immediate and complete revision of the government.

9. The first step to **Revision** was not so designed. In 1785 the Legislatures of Maryland and Virginia, in pursuance of their right to regulate commerce, had appointed Commissioners to decide on some method of doing away with interruptions to the navigation of Chesapeake Bay. The Commissioners reported their inability to agree, except in condemning the Articles of Confederation. The Legislature of Virginia followed the report by a resolution, inviting the other States to meet at Annapolis, consider the defects of the government, and suggest some remedy. In September, 1786,

delegates from five of the Middle States assembled, but confined themselves to discussion, since a majority of the States were not represented. The general conclusion was that the government, as it then stood, was inadequate for the protection, prosperity, or comfort of the people, and that some immediate and thorough reform was needed. After drawing up a report for their States and for Congress, recommending another convention, to be held at Philadelphia, in May, 1787, they adjourned. Congress, by resolution, approved their report and the proposed Convention.

10. **The Convention** met as proposed, May 14th, 1787, being composed of delegates from all the States, with the exception of Rhode Island. Its proceedings were secret, but an account of them was afterwards drawn up from Mr. Madison's notes. Washington, who was a delegate from Virginia, was chosen as presiding officer, and the Convention decided to transcend the instructions given to the delegates, and form an entirely new Constitution, on the ground that the work must finally be submitted to, and approved by, the people, before it could go into effect. May 29th, Randolph, of Virginia, offered the so-called "Virginia plan" for a new government. It consisted of fifteen points, of which the most important were that representation in the new Congress should be proportional to population and that Congress should have power to compel the States to fulfill their obligations. These provisions were particularly distasteful to the smaller States, who preferred the "New Jersey plan," offered by Patterson, of

New Jersey, which continued the old Confederation, but with the additional power to regulate commerce, and to raise a revenue. By this plan the smaller and larger States would still have been equal in power. June 19th the Convention rejected the New Jersey plan, and took up that of Virginia for consideration. After long debate a compromise was made. The smaller States agreed to take a proportional share in the lower of *two* Houses of Congress, in return for an equal share in an upper House. The question of omitting or including slaves in reckoning population as a basis for representation was compromised by agreeing to estimate them as equal to three-fifths of the same number of whites. The friends and enemies of the slave-trade agreed not to prohibit it until 1808. Other debatable questions were adjusted in the same spirit, and in September, 1787, the Constitution of the United States was completed,[1] being, like all other sound and lasting political works, the result of wise, judicious, and even-handed compromise.

11. Any full discussion of **The Constitution of 1787** must be left to the treatises upon it. But there are some points which require notice, in view of party action upon them. Unquestionably the most important creation of the Constitution was **The Federal Judiciary**. It will be seen that the only guarantee for the observance of the Articles of Confederation was the naked *promise* of the States. This had been found to be utterly worthless. The creation of a system of

---

[1] See Appendix B, where the Confederation is compared with it.

United States Courts, extending throughout the States, and empowered to define the boundaries of Federal authority, and to enforce its decisions by Federal power, supplied the element needed to bring order out of chaos. Without it the Constitution might easily have proved a more disheartening and complete failure than the Articles of Confederation.

12. How far **The New Federal Government** succeeded to the sovereign rights of the States and formed a centralized government in their place each must decide for himself by a study of the Constitution, and on his decision will depend generally his party membership. All agree that the new Federal Government succeeded to at least a part of the sovereign rights previously vested in the States, that the Federal Government thus obtained what it had previously lacked, the power over individuals, and that, within the sphere abandoned to it, the Federal Government is supreme. How far that sphere extends is, and it is to be hoped always will be, a great party question. The very **Preamble**, "we, the people of the United States," has been construed by one party as an assertion that the Constitution was adopted by the people *of each State for itself*, and by the opposite party as announcing th consolidation of discordant states into one powerful nation, not a mere league. All agree that it was intended "to form a more perfect union," but all do not agree as to how nearly perfect that union was to be.

13. **The Powers Granted to Congress** in Article I, § 8, should be carefully studied, for the antago

nistic views of the Strict Constructionist and Loose Constructionist parties have always been most clearly shown in interpreting them. For instance, under the clauses which give Congress the power to establish post-roads, and to provide for the common defense, Loose Constructionists have claimed, and Strict Constructionists have denied, that Congress has power to appropriate public money for the building of roads, and for general internal improvements. There is hardly a clause in this whole section upon whose interpretation and application the members of opposite parties agree, except when impelled to do so by selfish interests.

14. Is the Union a federal, or league, government, as claimed by the Strict Constructionists, or a centralized national government, as claimed by the Loose Constructionists? The question may best be answered in the words of Mr. Madison: "The Constitution is, in strictness, neither a national nor a federal constitution, but a composition of both. In its *foundation* it is federal, not national; in the *sources* from which the ordinary powers of the government are drawn it is partly federal and partly national; in the *operation* of these powers it is national, not federal; in the *extent* of them, again, it is federal, not national; and, finally, in the authoritative mode of introducing *Amendments* it is neither wholly federal, nor wholly national."

15. Only thirty-nine of the fifty-five delegates to the Convention signed the Constitution, and it cannot truly be said that it really satisfied any one. Had it been entirely satisfactory to one great party, it would have

been intolerable to the other. But it was a compromise in every important particular, and each party, while lamenting its own concessions, could derive some satisfaction from considering those of its adversaries. For, on the question of its adoption, the people of the United States had at last divided into opposing parties, Federalists and Anti-federalists, though both parties varied these formal titles by the use of such spiteful and opprobrious epithets as party hatred so well knows how to invent and apply.

16. The extreme **Federalists** were anxious for a strong government, and, if possible, for a monarchy. During the secret proceedings of the Convention the report was common that the "high-flying" Federalists had induced it to call an English prince to the throne of the United States. The great mass of the party however, had no such desire. They despised the Confederacy as a mere "rope of sand," which would fall apart at the first shock, and leave the separate States to become the successive prey of a foreign enemy, or of each other. In place of it they wished to see a strong republican government, fitted to make itself respected abroad, and obeyed at home. In supporting the new Constitution the Federalists were aided by many who were their natural opponents, but who either despaired of anything better, or were influenced by respect for the great names appended to or favoring it.

17. The extreme **Anti-federalists** wished for no Federal Government whatever, but for a continuance of the league between thirteen independent republics

The great mass of the party were united only in opposing the new Constitution, which seemed to them fantastic and experimental, and a fit instrument to deprive he States of the liberties which they had gained by the sword. But no definite and united line of action was taken by the Anti-federalists. Many of them united with the Federalists in accepting and voting for the Constitution, but with the hope and expectation of future amendments. The whole party in a few years became a Strict Constructionist party, accepting the Constitution unreservedly, but aiming to confine the powers of the Federal Government to the letter of its terms.

18. September 17th, 1787, the new Constitution was transmitted to Congress and thence referred to **Conventions** of the several States for adoption or rejection. The opposition was chiefly in the great States of New York, Virginia, and Massachusetts, but was shown in varying degrees in all the Conventions. Many of the States followed the "Massachusetts plan," adopting the Constitution, but strongly recommending amendments to it. Even with this expedient, it was only adopted by votes of 31 to 29 in New York, 88 to 80 in Virginia, and 187 to 168 in Massachusetts. North Carolina and Rhode Island at first rejected, but more than a year afterward adopted it, their ratifications only reaching Congress in 1790.

19. According to the terms of the Constitution, it was to go into effect as soon as adopted by nine States. The contest between Federalists and Anti-federalists lasted for months. A noble relic of the controversy is

the series of papers written by Hamilton, Jay, and Madison, over the joint signature of *Publius*, explaining and defending the Constitution. They are known collectively as *The Federalist.* It was not until June 21st, 1788, that the ninth State ratified the Constitution, and it became an accomplished fact. New York and Virginia soon afterwards ratified it, and only North Carolina and Rhode Island refused. July 14th, 1788, the Congress of the Confederacy, which was in session, referred the ratifications received from nine States to a committee which reported a resolution for carrying the new government into effect. There was some difficulty in deciding upon a time and place of meeting for the new Congress, but it was finally fixed at New York, March 4th, 1789. The first Wednesday of January, 1789, was appointed for the choice of electors for President and Vice-President, and the first Wednesday in February for the voting of the electors.

20. **The Constitution** has always been plain enough to guide the policy of the statesman and the decisions of the judge, and yet elastic enough to give full play to honest differences of opinion and party contest, and to fit the body politic at any time during its growth from 3,000,000 to 40,000,000 inhabitants. The first eleven Amendments were added so soon after its adoption that they may fairly be considered a part of the original instrument. It was then complete, and, with the exception of the change in the manner of voting for President and Vice-President, after the disputed election of 1800, no further alteration was found neces-

sary until the extirpation of Slavery introduced three Amendments which would have been impracticable in 1787. Even now, with the exception of the old torment of the Presidential election, there is seldom any serious suggestion of a point in which the Constitution would be benefited by a revision. Its wheels move as smoothly to-day as at any time since the inauguration of the first President. Their motion is so quiet that we are usually unconscious of our own comfort. The tests of foreign and civil war, of bitter party and personal contests, of financial convulsion and an unparalleled prosperity, have tried and approved it. The stability of our own government, compared with the radical changes in those of every other civilized nation during the past ninety years, is an honorable memorial of the political wisdom of the men who framed the Constitution of 1787, and of their descendants who have expounded and obeyed it.

# CHAPTER II.

### FIRST ADMINISTRATION, 1789-1793.

**George Washington, President.   John Adams, Vice-President.**
**1st and IId Congresses.**

1. MARCH 4th, 1789, had been appointed for the formal inauguration of the new Government, but the members elect had not yet unlearned the Confederacy's slovenly habits. It was not until April 6th that a sufficient number of members of Congress arrived in New York to form a quorum and count the electoral votes. At that time, and until 1805, no electoral votes were cast distinctively for President and Vice-President. Each elector voted by ballot for two persons. If a majority of all the votes were cast for any person, he who received the greatest number of votes became President, and he who received the next greatest number became Vice-President. When the votes were counted in 1789 they were found to be, for **George Washington**, of Virginia, 69 (each of the electors having given him one vote), for **John Adams**, of Massachusetts, 34

*1st Congress, Extra Session.*

and 35 for various other candidates. Washington received notice of his election, and, after a triumphal progress northward from his home at Mount Vernon, was sworn into office April 30th. The Vice-President had taken his place as presiding officer of the Senate a few days before.

2. Frederick A. Muhlenberg, of Pennsylvania, was chosen Speaker of the House, but the vote had no party divisions, for **Parties** were still in a state of utter confusion. Between the extreme Anti-federalists, who considered the Constitution a long step toward a despotism, and the extreme Federalists, who desired a monarchy modeled on that of England, there were all varieties of political opinion. The union between the moderate members of both parties in support of the new form of government still existed. The extreme importance of Washington lay in his ability, through the universal confidence in his integrity and good judgment, to hold together this alliance of moderate men for a time, and to prevent party contest upon the interpretation of Federal powers until the Constitution should show its merit and be assured of existence.

3. The President selected his **Cabinet** with a careful regard to the opposite opinions of his supporters. The Treasury Department was given to Alexander Hamilton, of New York, a Federalist, and a lawyer of distinguished ability, who had served with credit in the Revolutionary War, and was considered the ablest man of his party. The War Department was given to General Henry Knox, of Massachusetts, also a Fed-

eralist. The State Department was given to Thomas Jefferson, of Virginia, an Anti-federalist. He was the author of the Declaration of Independence, and had the confidence of all the factions of his divided party. Edmund Randolph, of Virginia, also an Anti-federalist, was appointed Attorney-General, and John Jay, of New York, a Federalist, Chief Justice of the Supreme Court.

4. Twelve **Amendments** were adopted by this Session of Congress, in order to meet the conscientious objections of many moderate Anti-federalists, and to take the place of a "Bill of Rights." Ten of these, having received the assent of the necessary number of States, became a part of the Constitution, and now stand the first ten of the Amendments. They were intended to guarantee freedom of religion, speech, person, and property. The positive requests of so many States, and the continued refusal of two States to enter the Union, were strong incentives to their adoption, and the opposition to them came mainly from the extreme Anti-federalists, who considered them delusive and insufficient, and only calculated to create a fatal feeling of security against centralized government.

5. The most important work of this Session was the **Regulation of Commerce** and the settlement of a **Tariff**. During the debate some of the Anti-federalists made an attempt to arrange the duties so as to discriminate against England and in favor of other nations, but the attempt failed in the Senate. A Tariff

Act was passed by both Houses, and approved July 4th. Its preamble stated one of its objects to be "the encouragement and protection of manufactures." This language is notable as stating the main object of the "American," or High Protective Tariff, system, thirty years before it became a party tenet. After directing the Secretary of the Treasury to prepare a plan for the ettlement of the public debt, Congress adjourned September 29th, until the following January. In November, 1789, **North Carolina** finally ratified the Constitution, and entered the Union.

6. Congress met at Philadelphia, January 4th, 1790. **1st Congress, 1st Session.** January 9th Hamilton offered his famous **Report on the Settlement of the Public Debt.** It consisted of three recommendations, *first*, that the foreign debt of the Confederacy should be assumed and paid in full; *second*, that the domestic debt of the Confederacy, which had fallen far below par and had become a synonym for worthlessness, should also be paid at its par value; and *third*, that the debts incurred by the States during the Revolution, and still unpaid, should be assumed and paid in full by the Federal Government.

7. Hamilton's **First** recommendation was adopted unanimously. The **Second** was opposed, even by Madison and many moderate Anti-federalists, on the ground that the domestic debt was held by speculators, who had bought it at a heavy discount, and would thus gain usurious interest on their investment. Ham-

ilton's supporters argued that, if only for that reason, they should be paid in full, that holders of United States securities might learn not to sell them at a discount, and that the national credit might thus be strengthened for all time to come. After long debate the second recommendation was also adopted.

8. Hamilton's **Third** recommendation involved a question of the powers of the Federal Government. It therefore for the first time united all the Anti-federalists in opposition to it. They feared that the rope of sand of the Confederacy was being carried to the opposite extreme; that the "money power" would, by this measure, be permanently attached to the Federal Government; and that the States would be made of no importance. But even this recommendation was adopted, though only by a vote of 31 to 26 in the House. A few days later, however, the Anti-federalists received a reinforcement of seven newly arrived North Carolina members. The third resolution was at once reconsidered, and voted down by a majority of two.

9. Hamilton secured the final adoption of the third resolution by a bargain which excited the deep indignation of the Anti-federalists. A **National Capital** was to be selected. The Federalists agreed to vote that it should be fixed upon the Potomac River, after remaining ten years in Philadelphia, and two Anti-federalist members from the Potomac agreed in return to vote for the third resolution, which was then finally adopted. Hamilton's entire report was thus successful

Its immediate effects were to appreciate the credit of the United States, and to enrich the holders of the Continental debt. Its further effect was to make Hamilton so much disliked by Anti-federalists that, despite his acknowledged talents, his party never ventured to nominate him for any elective office. Congress adjourned August 12th, 1790. During this long Session there was no further decided party contest. In May **Rhode Island** ratified the Constitution, and entered the Union, which now included all the old thirteen colonies.

10. Congress met December 6th, 1790. Its debates were mostly on finance.

**1st Congress, 2d Session.** Hamilton proposed the establishment of a **National Bank,** to act as financial agent of the Government. This involved another question of Federal powers, and renewed party contest. The Federalists claimed that Congress, having the undoubted power to pass all laws necessary for the collection of revenue and taxes, might constitutionally charter a bank for that purpose. The Anti-federalists claimed that such a bank was not *necessary*, though it might be *convenient*, and hence was beyond the power of Congress. This difference of opinion, trivial at first sight, continued to be the subject of bitter party feeling, at intervals, for fifty years. The bill passed both Houses, and the President was importuned to veto it. He demanded the written opinions of his Cabinet. In the struggles of succeeding years upon the same subject, Hamilton's argument in favor of the constitutionality of a National Bank has hardly been improved upon, or added to. It prevailed in the mind of the President over those of Jefferson and Randolph, and he signed the bill.[1] At this Session the unpopular Excise Law, to provide funds for the debts assumed by the Government, passed both House against the opposition of most of the Anti-federalists Congress adjourned March 3d, 1791. March 4th, **Vermont,** formerly called the New Hampshire Grants, whose people had for many years resisted New York's claim of jurisdiction over them, and had claimed to be an independent republic, entered the Union.

11. **IId Congress, 1st Session.** Congress met October 24th, 1791. Jonathan Trumbull, of Connecticut, was chosen Speaker of the House. The number of Federalists was slightly reduced, but the Administration was supported generally by a large majority of both parties. The Anti-federalists opposed an increase of the army and of the Tariff, but both bills became law. An Apportionment Bill was also passed at this Session, which had no party interest. It increased the number of the House of Representatives to 105. Congress adjourned May 8th, 1792. June 1st **Kentucky,** formerly a part of the State of Virginia, entered the Union.

---

[1] The Bank, thus created, continued in existence until 1811, when the opposite party was in power and refused to recharter it. Another National Bank was chartered in 1816, became the object of violent attack by Strict Constructionists, and ceased to exist in 1836. Other attempts were made without success, by Loose Constructionists, to charter a National Bank, and the project slept until 1862. During the Rebellion (1861–1865) the so-called Greenback Currency took the place of a National Bank, with power to make forced loans

12. **Party Organization** may be considered as fairly begun about the close of this Session. The occasional irritation shown in the debates is an evidence that the first ill-defined estimate of the new scheme of government was giving way to positive and settled opinions of its powers, and of the policy which should be followed in managing it. It is probable that a majority of the American people were Anti-federalist in 1789, although the Federalists, by the active assistance of many of their natural opponents, had gained the Executive, the Senate, the House, the Judiciary, and most of the State Legislatures, and were able to defeat the disagreeing factions known collectively as Antifederalists. In 1792 affairs were beginning to settle into a more natural order. The various Anti-federalist factions, by union in resisting the Federalists, had learned to forget minor differences, and had been welded into one party which only lacked a name. That of Anti-federalist was no longer applicable, for its opposition to the Federal Union had entirely ceased.

13. A name was supplied by Jefferson, the recognized leader of the party, after the **French Revolution** had fairly begun its course. That political convulsion had, for some time after 1789, the sympathy of both Federalists and Anti-federalists, for it seemed the direct outgrowth of the American Revolution. But, as its leveling objects became more apparent, the Federalists grew cooler and the Anti-federalists warmer towards it. The latter took great pains, even by dress and manners, to show the keenness of their sympathy

for the Republicans of France, and about this time adopted the name **Democratic-Republican**, which seemed sufficiently comprehensive for a full indication of their principles. This has always been the official party title. It is now abbreviated to Democratic though the name Democrat was at first used by Federalists as one of contempt, and the party called itself Republican, a title which it could hardly claim with propriety, for its tendency has always been toward a democracy, as that of its opponents has been toward a strong republic. The name Republican, therefore, belongs most properly to its present possessors (1879). But it must be remembered that the party which will be called Republican until about 1828 was the party which is now called Democratic.

14. The tendency toward **Party Division** was shown even in the Cabinet. Hamilton and Jefferson were influenced by personal antagonism and suspicion, as well as by political opposition. In this, as in everything else, they were the perfect representatives of their parties. In Cabinet meetings they were, in Jefferson's own words, "pitted against one another like game cocks," to the great grief of the President, who could not see in their wrangling the inevitable operation of political repulsions, which he would not be able to control much longer, either in the Cabinet or in the country.

15. At the request of both Federalists and Republicans Washington consented to serve as President a second time, so that only the Vice-Presidency was left

as an object of party contest. For this office the Federalists supported John Adams, and the Anti-federalists supported George Clinton, of New York. To nave supported Jefferson would have cost the vote of Virinia, whose electors could not have voted for Washington and Jefferson, both from Virginia. The **Presidential Election** took place November 6th, 1792, and resulted in the success of the Federalists.

16. Congress met November 5th, 1792. Its measures had reference mainly to the raising and expenditure of the revenue, in regard to which the Republicans had not yet settled upon any united course of action. The only party contest of the Session was an unsuccessful attempt of the Republicans to pass a vote of censure upon their enemy Hamilton for his management of the Treasury, and for his indignant and somewhat discourteous language in a message to the House. In February, 1793, the electoral votes were counted, and were found to be, for George Washington 132 (each of the electors having given him one vote), for John Adams 77, for George Clinton 50, for Thomas Jefferson 4, and for Aaron Burr 1. **Washington was** therefore declared elected President, and **Adams** Vice-President. March 2d, 1793, Congress adjourned, and March 4th, Washington and Adams were sworn into office.

*IId Congress, 2d Session.*

# CHAPTER III.

## SECOND ADMINISTRATION, 1793-1797.

**George Washington, President.   John Adams, Vice-President.**
**IIId and IVth Congresses.**

1. EARLY in April, 1793, news was received that France had declared war against Great Britain and Holland. It excited the sympathies of the American people for their sister republic, even though that republic was the aggressor. One of the great parties specially affected the leveling principles avowed by the French Republicans, and the opposite party would not have objected to their limited success. There was no open war party as yet, though many considered the treaty (of 1778) still in force, which bound France and the United States to offensive as well as defensive alliance. The country was in a position to drift easily into war as an ally of France; and many of its citizens were certain to criticise severely any act of their own government which seemed unfriendly to the French Republic.

2. Washington always deliberated slowly and calmly

though he was immovable when he had decided. He consulted his Cabinet, and by their unanimous advice determined, notwithstanding the inevitable unpopularity of the act, to regard the former treaty as nullified by the change of government in France, and to issue his **Proclamation of Neutrality** between the French Republic and her enemies. The proclamation roused intense anger. For the first time the extreme Republicans, who might now almost be called the French party, assailed the President personally. He was accused of being an enemy to France and republican institutions, of usurping the functions of Congress in the decision and announcement of peace and war, and of setting at naught a solemn treaty, to whose observance the faith of the country was pledged.

3. The bitterness of the pro-French newspapers was increased by the arrival of **Citizen Genet,** who had been accredited by the French Republic as Minister to the United States. He had reached Charleston, S. C., April 8th, and, misled by the warmth of his reception, he entered on and persisted in a course which would only have been pardonable if he had been still on French soil. He undertook to commission cruisers from American ports, which captured British vessels even in American waters. He created courts for the trial and condemnation of such prizes, and began to raise money and enlist men for the service of France. The British agent complained of these violations of neutrality, and Genet was informed by Jefferson that they must cease. Two of his American recruits were arrested and com

mitted to jail. Against this Genet remonstrated in offensive language, and, making Philadelphia his headquarters, persevered in breaking the law.

4. He was encouraged by the so-called **Democratic Clubs** which had been formed by the more violent Republicans, in imitation of the Jacobin clubs of France. They had adopted the wildest follies of their French prototypes. They had changed their aristocratic title of Mr. to that of Citizen, and their daughters were married under the name of Citess. They were even scandalized by that relic of European aristocracy, the spread eagle upon public papers. To Republicans of this type the character and past services of Washington were no bar to the severest denunciation of his conduct to Genet and the French Republic.

5. Through the Summer of 1793 the insolence of Genet towards the President and Cabinet became still more offensive, and his subordinates imitated their chief. The French consul at Boston, with a body of marines from a French war vessel in the harbor, rescued a libeled vessel from the United States Marshal. An American privateer under French colors left Philadelphia in flat defiance of direct orders from the Federal Government. French officers in Georgia began to organize expeditions against the American possessions of Spain, with which country France was now at war. Finally Chief Justice Jay, and Senator King, of New York, declared over their signatures in a New York newspaper that Genet had in private declared his intention to appeal from the Government to the people

To the astonishment of Genet, who seems not to have been aware of the extent to which free political discussion may harmlessly be carried, this announcement alienated from him all but the most violent of his former supporters. His popularity was gone. The American Government asked his recall, and until this took place in the following winter his only noteworthy action was his declaration that Chief Justice Jay and Senator King had told a falsehood.

6. Congress met December 2d, 1793, with a slight Republican majority in the House, where F. A. Muhlenberg, of Pennsylvania, a Republican, was chosen Speaker. The doubtful vote, however, was still so large that there was no real party majority. The President's Proclamation, and his treatment of Genet, were approved, though no warmly, in the House, where there was increasing **Hostility to England**, provoked by England's systematic neglect of the interests and feelings of the United States.

**IIId Congress, 1st Session.**

7. **England** had never accredited a Minister Resident to the United States, and had refused to carry out those articles of the Treaty of 1783 which bound her to surrender her military posts on United States soil, and to pay for slaves carried away by her armies. It was firmly believed that her agents had interfered to prevent treaties of peace with the savages of the North-West, and had incited them to renewed attacks upon the frontier settlements. An unexpected treaty of peace between Portugal and Algiers, which had let loose the

Algerine pirates for a warfare upon the Atlantic against unprotected American commerce, was attributed to English intervention. The impressment of American seamen, under color of their resemblance to Englishmen, was a growing grievance. All English ships of war had been ordered, on the 8th of June, 1793, to stop vessels bound for France with corn, and compel them to change their course to an English port. This blow at American commerce with France had been supplemented by a further order of November 6th, that all such vessels should be seized and sent to Great Britain for trial by English courts. Her refusal to evacuate the Western posts was grounded on the unjustifiable neglect of the United States to enforce that article of the Treaty of 1783 which provided for the payment of debts due to British subjects. For her further offensive measures no justification was offered, except her sovereign will. She acted apparently under the belief that the United States were the concealed, but soon to be the avowed, ally of her enemy, and thus she contributed in no small degree to swell the current of anti-English feeling.

8. The retaliating orders and decrees of Great Britain and the French Republic had already injured American commerce. In an **Official Report** of December 16th Jefferson advised friendly arrangements for their cessation, if possible, and, in default of these, active retaliation upon the offending nation. As England was more likely to be the offender, the Republicans promptly adopted the suggestion, and, January 4th, 1794, Madi-

son introduced resolutions imposing prohibitory duties upon English goods. They were d.bated, at intervals, for two months, but finally failed.

9. The **Debates** of this Session were mainly upon commercial matters. The Federalists wished to form navy, and to maintain neutrality between England and France, which was all that England's course allowed them to ask. The Republican policy was a mixture of two opposites. It called for a prohibition of trade with England, or, at the least, for discriminating duties against English imports, and yet opposed any naval preparation for the war to which such a policy must have led. Parties were so evenly divided, and the doubtful vote changed sides so frequently that in the middle of April, 1794, no decided result had been reached.

10. An unlooked for step was taken by the President, April 16th. He nominated **Chief Justice Jay** to be Envoy Extraordinary to England, for the purpose of preserving peace by a new treaty. The Senate, where the Federalists had a small majority, confirmed the nomination. The Republicans of the House, on the 18th, endeavored to baulk the mission in advance by a resolution entirely prohibiting trade with England. The Senate rejected the resolution, and Jay sailed for England.

11. **Party Contests** were numerous throughout the Session. The Federalists succeeded in passing a system of indirect taxation to provide for the increased expenses of the Government, the Republicans voting

for direct taxes. A Federalist bill to prevent such practices as Genet's was opposed by the Republicans, and bitterly denounced by the Democratic clubs, but was passed with some modifications. Some of the Republicans again attempted, and again without success, to pass resolutions censuring Hamilton's management of the Treasury. The Republicans had been alarmed by a decision of the Supreme Court that an action brought by a citizen of the United States would lie against a State, just as against any other corporation. At this Session, therefore, an Amendment was adopted, securing States against suit in United States Courts. It was afterwards ratified by the necessary number of States, and became the **XIth Amendment**, which has enabled so many States to repudiate debt with impunity. Congress adjourned June 9th, 1794. Genet's actions had previously been disavowed by a new Revolutionary Government in France, and Fauchet sent in his stead.

12. Before Congress re-assembled the so-called **Whiskey Insurrection** against the enforcement of the Excise Law had been suppressed. It had no political results, except as it strengthened Federalism, by strengthening popular sympathy with the Administration. It was also one cause of the downfall of the Democratic clubs, which Washington had publicly and officially, though perhaps mistakenly, declared to be the instigators of the Insurrection. They thus lost popularity, and the overthrow of Robespierre and the French Jacobin clubs was soon followed by the ignominious death of their American imitations.

13. Congress met November 3d, 1794. In January 1795, Hamilton felt compelled to leave the Cabinet, and resume the practice of law in New York. His last official act was the arrangement of a plan of **Internal Taxation** which was offered to Congress, and furnished material for debate throughout the Session. It was adopted against the opposition of most of the Republicans. Congress adjourned March 3d, 1795.

<small>IIId Congress, 2d Session.</small>

14. Jay had concluded a **Treaty with England,** which did not satisfy him, but was the best that he could procure. It reached America March 7th, and was sent to the Senate in Special Session June 8th. It was ratified by the necessary two-thirds majority, and only awaited the signature of the President to become law. Popular curiosity was stimulated by the secrecy of the debates. When, on the 29th of June, a Senator in violation of his word gave a partial copy of Jay's Treaty for publication, and it was found that by its terms England was still at liberty to impress American seamen, to harass American commerce, and to shut it out from the West India trade, the wrath of the Republicans rose to fever heat, and Federalists could hardly contrive an apology for a surrender with which they also were generally dissatisfied. In all the large cities public meetings condemned the treaty, and called upon the President to withhold his signature.

15. But **The President** felt that a treaty of some kind was necessary, and that no better one could then be obtained. He therefore signed it. Hitherto criti-

cisms on Washington's policy had not been uncommon, but his action in signing Jay's Treaty brought out aspersions upon his private character, which were carried so far that he declared "he would rather be in his grave than in the Presidency." He was charged by the extreme Republicans with usurpation, treason to his country, and hostility to her interests. The continued sufferings of American prisoners in Algiers were ascribed to his criminal indifference. He was accused of having shown incapacity during the Revolution, and of having embezzled the public funds while President. He was threatened with impeachment, with assassination. Even the honored epithet so long given to him was burlesqued, and Washington was for a time known to the Republicans as "The Step-Father of his Country." And yet, within a year, his unyielding common sense was justified by a revival of trade which gained friends for Jay's Treaty, even among its formerly bitter opponents.

16. Congress met December 7th, 1795, with a small Federalist majority in the Senate, and a Republican majority in the House, though even there the Federalists succeeded in choosing Jonathan Dayton, of New Jersey, Speaker. The Senate, in reply to the President's Message, echoed his words, but the Republican majority in the House, in order to censure the President indirectly, voted down the first sentence of their committee's draft of a reply, including an expression of "their confidence in the President, and their approval of his course."

**IVth Congress, 1st Session.**

17. March 1st, 1796, the President sent to Congress a copy of his proclamation, announcing to the people that the treaty with England, having been ratified by the Senate and signed by the President, had become aw In the House this caused dissatisfaction, and, against the wishes of some of the moderate Republicans, a resolution was passed, March 2d, calling upon the President to send to the House all papers relating to Jay's Treaty. The President refused to do so, giving as his reason that the House was not a part of the treaty-making power of the Government. The House retorted by another resolution declaring its right to decide on the necessity of any treaty by which public money was to be expended.

18. From the Federalist side of the House a resolution was then offered, declaring that provision ought to be made by law for carrying the treaty into effect. The **Debate** upon this resolution, in which Fisher Ames, of Massachusetts, led the Federalists, lasted until April 29th. By that time public opinion had pronounced in favor of the treaty too emphatically to be disregarded just before a Presidential election. The Republican majority yielded and the resolution was passed. The beginning and the end of the Session were taken up by debates upon the revenue, in which an increase of duties upon imports was urged by the Federalists, but successfully opposed by the Republicans. Congress adjourned June 1st, 1796. On that day **Tennessee**, formerly a part of North Carolina, became a State of the Union.

19. During the Summer of 1796 preparations were begun, and electors were nominated for the Presidential election in November. Washington's hold was stronger upon the people than upon the politicians, and he was importuned to accept a third term of office. Electors nominated by both parties were called upon to promise that, if elected, their first votes should be given for Washington. His decision to retire to private life could not be altered, but he decided to publish it in a form which should always remain as his answer to the attacks upon him, which had been made, to use nis own words, "in terms so exaggerated and indecent as could scarcely be applied to a Nero, a notorious defaulter, or even to a common pickpocket."

20. **Washington's Farewell Address** to the American people is dated September 17th, 1796. It consists of a modest estimate of his own services to the new Government, a congratulation that the circumstances which gave a temporary value to those services were past, an appeal to the people to preserve intact the unity of the Government, to put down party spirit, and to make religion, education, and public good faith the basis of government, and, lastly, a needed warning against the admission of any foreign influence upon American councils. It can hardly be read without renewing the conviction that George Washington was an unconscious but sincere Federalist, though hardly a fair critic of party spirit, a modest Christian, a devoted lover of country, and a great, unselfish man.

21. The Farewell Address was the preliminary to the first contested **Presidential Election**. The Constitution had fairly shown its merits. Its continued existence was assured, and there was no longer any necessity for keeping the political peace between the two great parties. No formal nominations were made but it was understood that the Republican electors would cast their votes for Thomas Jefferson, of Virginia, and Aaron Burr, of New York, and the Federalist electors for John Adams, of Massachusetts, and Thomas Pinckney, of Maryland. Hamilton's ardent political zeal had made so many enemies that he was not considered a suitable candidate. The Federalists claimed support as the authors of the Government, the friends of neutrality, peace, and prosperity, and the direct inheritors of Washington's policy. The Republicans claimed to be the friends of liberty and the rights of man, the advocates of economy and of the rights of the States, and refused to recognize their opponents as the inheritors of any policy but that of England. The Presidential election took place in November, 1796,[1] and the French Minister undertook to influence it by an extraordinary "Address to the American People," in which he hinted that his Government would cease intercourse with the United States unless the Republicans were successful. Federalist electors were chosen in most of the Northern States, while the Southern States, with the exception of Mary-

---

[1] Until about 1824-1828 electors were generally chosen, not directly by the people, but by the Legislatures of the various States.

land, generally chose Republicans. The result was a slight Federalist majority.

22. **IVth Congress, 2d Session.** Congress met December 5th, 1796, but its proceedings gave little opportunity for party contest. In the House an attempt was made to renew the last year's expression of want of confidence in Washington, but it was defeated. In February, 1797, the electoral votes were counted, and were found to be, for John Adams 71, for Thomas Jefferson 68, for Thomas Pinckney 59, for Aaron Burr 30, and the rest scattering.[1] **John Adams** was therefore declared to be elected President, and **Thomas Jefferson** Vice-President. The Executive was thus Federalist, with a possibility of a Republican succession, in case of the death, disability, or impeachment and removal of the President. It was plain that a mode of election which offered so much temptation to the cupidity of party or the caprice of fortune was faulty, and could not endure. A further experience of its danger, however, was needed to enforce its amendment. Congress adjourned March 3d, 1797. March 4th Adams and Jefferson were sworn into office.

---

[1] Two electors obstinately voted for George Washington.

# CHAPTER IV.

### THIRD ADMINISTRATION, 1797-1801.

John Adams, President.  Thomas Jefferson, Vice-President.
Vth and VIth Congresses.

1. THE beginning of Adams's Administration was marked by a more open manifestation of bad feeling by the **French Republic,** which was ascribed by the Federalists to the anger of the French Directory on account of the Republican defeat, and by the Republicans to the anxiety of two successive Federalist Administrations to be in close dependence upon England. In 1797, Monroe, an ardent Republican, who had been Minister to France, was recalled, and C. C. Pinckney was sent in his place. At Monroe's departure from Paris the French Directory announced, in studied terms of affection for the American people and of contempt for the American Government, their intention to receive no more American Ministers until their grievances were redressed. Prominent among these grievances was Jay's Treaty. At the same time Pinckney was ordered to quit the territory of France at once.

2. Upon receipt of this news the President hastily called an Extra Session of Congress for the 15th of May. Both branches had Federalist majorities, and Jonathan Dayton, of New Jersey, was chosen Speaker of the House The main business of the Session was to listen to ai **Address of the President** in which he announced his intention to send three envoys to France, as a last effort to obtain peace. Many of the Republicans considered the whole trouble to be the result of Federalist intrigues, but a majority of both Houses approved the President's course. Congress adjourned July 10th, 1797, and the envoys soon after departed for France. Through the Summer of 1797 parties remained as before, each accusing the other, perhaps with equal justice, of a willingness to sacrifice the interests of America to those of a foreign country. A foreign traveler about this time said that there seemed to be in America many English, many French, but very few Americans.

> **Vth Congress,**
> **Extra Session.**

3. The envoys to France, after patiently enduring for months a treatment unworthy the embassadors of a free people, including a demand for a bribe to the French Directory, and a loan to the French Republic, as preliminaries to any negotiation, received peremptory orders to quit France, and returned with empty hands. Their mission is frequently called **The X. Y. Z. Mission,** from the initials used by the agents who demanded the bribes. In the mean time French attacks on American commerce, which had hitherto been

cloaked to some extent by a pretense of respect for international law, had now become an open warfare. American shipping papers were a sufficient warrant for the capture and condemnation of the vessels which carried them.

4. Congress met November 13th, 1797. At first the **Vth Congress,** Republican disposition to tolerate **1st Session.** almost any treatment from France was continued, and early in 1798 the House voted down a proposition to arm American vessels. April 8th the Senate voted to publish the X.Y.Z. letters, and the dispatches of the envoys. To England they seemed of such importance that they were sent everywhere in Europe to excite feeling against France. In America one burst of indignation from the Federalists converted many of the Republicans, and silenced the rest. "Millions for defense; not one cent for tribute" became a rallying cry, in and out of Congress.

5. Under the influence of the **War Spirit** a number of acts were passed to place the nation in readiness for hostilities. A provisional army was ordered, of which Washington was commissioned Lieutenant-General. American men-of-war were ordered to seize any French vessels which should commit depredations on American commerce. Intercourse with France was suspended. The treaties with France were declared no longer binding upon the United States, and authority was given to the President to issue letters of marque and reprisal. So far, the acts passed were only the natural evidences of a nation's outraged dignity. But

the Federalists, intoxicated by the possession of unrestrained power, and hurried on by an instinctive passion for strong government, proceeded to force through two acts which were well calculated to convince the popular mind of their disregard for the Constitution. They seem, indeed, to have been in the end the death warrant of the Federal party.

6. June 25th the so-called **Alien Law** was passed. It authorized the President to order any alien whom he should judge to be dangerous to the peace and liberties of America to depart from the United States, and made provision for the fining and imprisonment of such aliens as should refuse to obey the President's order July 14th the so-called **Sedition Law** was passed. It imposed a heavy fine and imprisonment upon such as should combine or conspire together to oppose any measure of Government, and upon such as should utter any false, scandalous, or malicious writing against the Government, Congress, or President of the United States. This act was to remain in force until March 3d, 1801. Congress adjourned July 16th, 1798.

7. These two tremendous statutes were such a stretch of power as had not been ventured upon since the Revolution. Without them, the open attempts of the French Directory to dictate a government and policy to the United States, their discriminating kindness to the Republican member of the mission to France, and the patriotic and successful stand taken by the Federalist Administration, would almost have insured the government to the Federal party for the future It was

evident that the Republicans believed that these two statutes were aimed at them as a party, and were unconstitutional and in violation of the Ist Amendment, which prohibited Congress from passing any law to abridge freedom of speech or of the press. And it should have been evident to the Federalist leaders that, when the war feeling should subside, popular opinion would incline to the Republican view, unless the statutes were repealed as soon as the necessity for them was past.

8. It will be seen that, during the next year, France denied any knowledge of the agents who had demanded bribes, and hastened to conclude a peace. But, though preparations for war were then at an end, the Federalists persisted in enforcing prosecutions under the Alien and Sedition Laws, even in the doubtful States, New York, Pennsylvania, and New Jersey. Though this excited public resentment, it came too late to influence the election for members of the VIth Congress, in which the Federalists, by the help of the war feeling, were completely successful. Seeing no hope of present success in Congress, the Republican leaders determined, if possible, to entrench themselves in the State Legislatures, and, through them, to protest against measures which they were unable to resist. To this end a series of resolutions, drawn up by Jefferson, was adopted by the Legislature of Kentucky, and a similar series, drawn up by Madison, was adopted by the Legislature of Virginia. These are known as the **Kentucky, and the Virginia, Resolutions of 1798**

They are interesting as the first authorized proclamation of the Strict Constructionist party, though allowance must be made for the excited state of political feeling at the time of their passage.

9. The **Virginia Resolutions** declared that the Constitution was a compact by which the States had surrendered only a limited portion of their powers; that whenever the Federal Government undertook to step over the boundary of its delegated authority it was the right and the duty of *the States* to interpose, and maintain the rights which they had reserved to themselves; that the Alien and Sedition Laws were an usurpation by the Federal Government of powers not granted to it, since the abridgment of liberty of speech or of the press had been expressly forbidden by the Constitution; that the State of Virginia solemnly declared those laws to be unconstitutional, and appealed to the other States to join in that declaration and that her Governor should be instructed to transmit copies of these resolutions to the Governors of other States, to be laid before their Legislatures. The response from other States was unfavorable, and Virginia repeated her resolutions the next year, 1799.

10. The **Kentucky Resolutions** were to the same general effect as those of Virginia, but with the additional declaration that *the States* were one party to the compact, and the Federal Government was the other, and that each party must be the judge of infractions of the agreement, and of the mode and measure of redress. The next year the Kentucky Resolutions of

1799 were passed. They declared "nullification" to be "the rightful remedy;" but, as they announced at the same time that the commonwealth "bowed to the laws of the Union," while solemnly protesting against the obnoxious laws, it is apparent that they had in view no such "nullification" as that attempted by South Carolina in 1832.[1] The New England opposition to the Embargo in 1808[2] was a fair example of the first idea of "nullification"—a combination of a State legislative, executive, and judiciary to impede stubbornly, but peaceably, the execution of an unconstitutional law.

11. Congress met December 3d, 1798, with a continued Federalist majority. War against France had not been formally declared, but a species of warfare existed upon the ocean, in which American privateers, armed merchantmen, and even ships of war engaged in conflicts with French vessels. Both parties agreed in voting an increase of the navy, but an increase of the army was earnestly opposed by the Republicans, who believed that this and similar warlike measures were only urged by the Federalists from a desire for party aggrandizement by providing commissions or their party leaders. The President seems to have become at least a partial convert to this view for in February, 1799, without consulting his Cabinet, and in spite of his expressed determination to send no more ministers to France until assured of a friendly reception, he suddenly appointed three envoys to that

Vth Congress, 2d Session.

---

[1] See p. 112.    [2] See pp. 67, 74.

country. Two of the Cabinet protested against this action of the President. Their protest was sustained by leading Federalists throughout the country, and the President began to lose, to some degree, the support of the party which had elected him. Congress adjourned March 3d, 1799.

12. The difficulties of the Federalists were now increased by an evident division between Hamilton, who was the real leader of the party, and Adams, who was its nominal head. No open quarrel had as yet taken place. But when the envoys to France, who had waited until November for assurances of a friendly reception, were ordered to depart by the President, again without consulting his Cabinet, his apparent eagerness for peace and distrust of Hamilton widened the breach between them. The envoys were successful in arranging a treaty with Napoleon Bonaparte, who was then at the head of the French Directory.

13. Congress met December 2d, 1799, with a stronger Federalist majority. Theodore Sedgwick, of Massachusetts, a Federalist, was chosen Speaker of the House. There was little party contest at this Session. The Federalist majority had been chosen during the war fever, immediately after the ignominious return of the envoys to France, and neither represented nor felt the undercurrent of irritation which the continued enforcement of **The Alien and Sedition Laws** was increasing. The Republican minority were kept in check, through their leaders, by Jefferson, who preferred to allow the popular

*VIth Congress,*
*1st Session.*

excitement to work until the Presidential election of 1800. During this Session caucuses of Members of Congress nominated Presidential candidates.[1] The Federalist candidates were John Adams, of Massachusetts, and C. C. Pinckney, of South Carolina, and the Republican candidates were Thomas Jefferson, of Virginia, and Aaron Burr, of New York. Congress adjourned May 14th, 1800.

14. The first important election took place in New York, April 28th, and resulted in the choice of a Republican Legislature, by whom electors were to be chosen. At this first token of **Federalist Defeat** the slumbering animosities of the party broke forth. The President dismissed a part of his Cabinet, consisting of Hamilton's friends, whom he called a "British faction." Hamilton printed a severe attack upon the President, and endeavored to make arrangements for giving Pinckney a majority of Federalist electors, that he might be chosen President, and Adams Vice-President. The **Presidential Election** took place in November 1800. In spite of Federalist divisions the result was doubtful until the vote of South Carolina turned the scale, and gave the Republican electors a majority.

15. Congress met in the new Federal city of Washington, November 17th, 1800

**VIth Congress,**

2d Session. The Session was mainly occupied by **The Undecided Presidential Election**, caused by the defective provisions of the Constitution. In February, 1801, the electoral votes were counted, and

---

[1] Nominating Conventions were not used until 1812.

were found to be, for Jefferson 73, for Burr 73, for Adams 65, for Pinckney 64, and for John Jay 1 There was no name highest on the list. Consequently there was no choice, and an election was to be made by the House of Representatives between the two highest candidates, each State having one vote. It is impossible to say why the Republican leaders, or electors, did not foresee this mischance. The difference of one vote between Adams and Pinckney would seem to show that at least one Federalist elector was more acute, for South Carolina's vote would have seated both the Federalist candidates without trouble.

16. The House was Federalist, but was restricted to a choice between two Republicans. Of the two, many Federalists preferred Burr, partly to keep the Presidency from their most dangerous enemy, Jefferson, and partly to baulk the evident intention of the Republicans. The balloting began February 11th. Eight States voted for Jefferson, six for Burr, and two were without votes because of equal division among their members. There being sixteen States there was even yet **No Election.** Balloting continued with the same result for six days, and the Federalist majority was charged with a design to prolong the balloting in this way until March 4th, the day of inauguration, and then to make Chief Justice Jay provisional President. The charge was denied by the Federalists. Fortunately the trouble came to an end February 17th, when ten States voted for Jefferson, four for Burr, and two blank. **Jefferson** was then declared elected President, and

Burr Vice-President. Congress adjourned March 3d, 1801, and March 4th Jefferson and Burr were sworn into office.

## CHAPTER V.

### FOURTH ADMINISTRATION, 1801-1805.

**Thomas Jefferson, President.**   **Aaron Burr, Vice-President**
**VIIth and VIIIth Congresses.**

1. **Jefferson's Election** completed the first great political revolution in the United States since 1787, except that the Federalists still had control of the Judiciary. The new President's first Inaugural Message announced the future policy of the Republican party to be the careful fostering of the State governments, the restriction of the powers of the Federal Government to their lowest constitutional limit, the immediate payment of the public debt, and the reduction of the army, the navy, the taxes, and the duties on imports, to the lowest available point. The **Republicans** were opposed to any currency but gold and silver, and some of their leaders even desired an Amendment to the Constitution denying to the Federal Government the power of borrowing money, believing that a yearly direct tax for the current expenses of the Government would compel the people to decide more carefully on

questions of peace, war, and finance. Upon most of the articles of Republican belief, the **Federalists** were more willing to give latitude and power to the Federal Government. But the hatred of the parties for each other was a little abated, though the Federalists still called their opponents Democrats and Jacobins, while the Republicans retorted with the name of "Black-Cockade Federalist," in allusion to the party badge worn by them in the time of the war fever of 1798.

2. The **Anticipations of the Federalists** for the future of the country under Republican rule were naturally gloomy. The Federal party probably contained the larger portion of the intellect, wealth, and culture of the country, and, in their honest opinion, the Government was now in bad hands. The President was "an atheist in religion, and a fanatic in politics," and the Vice-President was only more tolerable because less known. The party which supported them was composed of disorganizers, Jacobins, and revolutionists. The President felt it to be his duty to act so moderately as to give Federalist apprehensions no darker color, although he was determined to undo, so far as possible, the centralizing measures of the last Administration. With this view he took the first opportunity after entering office, to issue Executive pardons to those who were imprisoned under the Alien and Sedition Laws.

3. A troublesome problem occupied the summer of 1801. The Republicans were clamorous for **Offices**, and none were vacant They therefore demanded that

Federalist office-holders should be removed to make room for Republican successors. The President followed the course he had previously marked out, removing no person merely for holding Federalist opinions, but removing all office-holders who had used their official power for party purposes, or who had been appointed by President Adams after the result of the last election had become known. The supply of offices thus placed at his disposal satisfied the most pressing demands, and for the future he trusted to the natural decrease in the ranks of the office-holders, of whom, however, he complained that "few died, and none resigned."

4. Congress met December 7th, 1801, with a small Republican majority in both branches. **VIIth Congress, 1st Session.** In the House Nathaniel Macon, of North Carolina, a Republican, was chosen Speaker. Instead of the President's address in person to both Houses of Congress, which had hitherto been the rule, the President sent a written **Message**, as more suited to republican simplicity, and succeeding Presidents have followed the example. In the debates which followed the Message the Republicans advocated and carried reductions in the army, the navy, taxes and duties. Instead of the fourteen years' residence necessary for naturalization under a Federalist law, five years were substituted.

5. The remainder of the Session was occupied by debate on a proposed repeal of a **Judiciary Law** passed at the last Session, by which twenty-four new

Federal Courts had been erected, with the proper complement of officers to each. The Republicans claimed that there had not been business enough to occupy the United States Courts already in existence; that the bill had been hastily drawn up and passed, after the Republican success in the last election had been assured, only in order to provide offices for Federalist leaders, who were about to be driven from power; and that President Adams had been kept busy until midnight of his last day of office in signing commissions for the judges. All this seemed to the Republicans a gross abuse of power, and they were determined to oust the "midnight judges" by repealing the law. The Constitution seemed plainly to prohibit any such repeal, and the existence of the Republican party was based upon a strict construction of the Constitution. Party necessities and vindictiveness, however, soon found available interpretations for the Constitution, and the law was repealed. The Federal party, which had founded and nurtured the Federal Government, was thus driven from its last strong hold in it, and lost forever the control of national politics, though it retained its power in New England for about ten years afterward. Congress adjourned May 3d, 1802.

6. In the Spring of 1802 news came from France which did much to cool the pro-French partizanship of even the most zealous Republicans. France had acquired from Spain the vast territory known as **Louisiana**, stretching from the mouth to the head of the Mississippi, and indefinitely Westward toward the **Pa-**

cific. The United States were thus to be hemmed in by one of the great European belligerents on the North, and by another on the South and West, and the policies and alliances of Europe were to be extended to the Western Continent. The President at once directed the American Minister at Paris to lay the strongest remonstrances before the French Emperor. He was ordered to declare that, while the present possession of Louisiana by a weak nation like Spain would be tolerated, its transfer to a strong, active, colonizing power like France would immediately drive the United States into close alliance with England, and that, in short, the foreign possessor of New Orleans must be the enemy of the United States.

7. Congress met December 6th, 1802. The President's Message stated that $8,000,000 of the public debt had been paid during the year, and called attention to Spain's unfriendly action in closing New Orleans, which she still controlled, against American commerce. Resolutions condemning Spain's conduct were introduced and passed by the Republicans. A constitutional Amendment changing the mode of the Presidential election was debated, but did not obtain the necessary two-thirds vote. Some of the Republicans made an unsuccessful attempt to abolish the Mint, as a useless piece of expense, and the Federalists were equally unsuccessful in attempting to fasten a charge of mismanagement upon the Treasury. The rest of the Session was spent in considering the Yazoo Frauds

*VIIth Congress, 2d Session.*

which had no party interest. Congress adjourned March 3d, 1803.

8. **Ohio** had become a State of the Union November 29th, 1802. It was formed from the North-West Territory, which had been organized by an ordinance of July 13th, 1787. Article VI of this ordinance reads: "There shall be neither slavery nor involuntary servitude in the said Territory, otherwise than in the punishment of crimes whereof the party shall have been duly convicted." The ordinance of 1787 is noteworthy as an exercise by the Congress of the Confederacy of the right to exclude Slavery from the Territories.[1]

9. James Monroe had been sent to France to buy Florida and the island of Orleans. France was preparing for renewed war with Great Britain and was in need of money. Monroe therefore transcended his instructions, and made a bargain for all Louisiana for $15,000,000. The President at once agreed to it though he believed that the Constitution gave the Federal Government no power to purchase foreign territory and make it a part of the Union. But he likened his action to that of a guardian who makes an unauthorized purchase for the benefit of his ward, trusting that the latter will afterward ratify it. In this instance the ratification was prepared as an Amendment to the Constitution, but was never offered, the President's

---

[1] It will be found that the language of this ordinance was copied in the efforts made in 1819 (Missouri), 1846 (Wilmot Proviso), and 1865 (XIIIth Amendment), to assert and maintain for the Federal Congress under the Constitution this power of regulating and abolishing Slavery in the Territories of the United States, and finally, in the States, as the result of civil war.

action having been in effect ratified by general acquiescence in it, and imitated without question in several instances afterward.

10. Congress met October 17th, 1803, having been called to an early session by the President that there might be more time for discussing the **French Treaty**. Both branches had Republican majorities, and in the House Nathaniel Macon was again chosen Speaker. The Treaty was ratified, and appropriations made for its execution, after a debate which was almost a repetition of that on Jay's Treaty in 1795, each party, however citing the arguments and resolutions then offered by the opposite party. During this Session the manner of the Presidential election was amended to the form which it has at present. Having been ratified by the necessary number of States, this became the **XIIth Amendment**. Articles of impeachment were voted by the House against a Federalist Judge, Chase, of Maryland, for arbitrary and oppressive conduct in trying cases under the Alien and Sedition Laws. Congress adjourned March 27th, 1804.

**VIIIth Congress, 1st Session.**

11. The Republicans offered the President and George Clinton, of New York, as their Presidential candidates. Burr had come too near the Presidency in 1801 to be made prominent again with Jefferson's consent. He was therefore dropped, and Clinton took his place. The Federalists offered as their candidates Charles C. Pinckney, of South Carolina, and Rufus King, of New York. The **Presidential Election**

in November resulted in the overwhelming defeat of the Federalists, who carried only Connecticut and Delaware, with two electors in Maryland.

12. Congress met November 5th, 1804. The Trial of Judge Chase by the Senate, on articles of impeachment prepared by the House at its last Session. Unfortunately the trial became a party struggle. The Federalists espoused the cause of Judge Chase, and the Republicans were determined to convict him. Vice-President Burr, who presided at the trial, had shot Hamilton in a duel near New York in July, 1804, and thus deprived the Federalists of their ablest leader. But his impartiality and contempt for party demands during the Chase trial went far to induce them to condone his offense. A sufficient number of Senators did not vote to condemn Judge Chase on any one charge, and he was found not guilty on all. The angry disappointment of the Republicans led them to introduce several Amendments to make impeachment and conviction more easy and certain, but none were adopted. In February, 1805, the electoral votes were counted, and were found to be, 162 for Jefferson and Clinton and 14 for Pinckney and King. **Jefferson and Clinton** were therefore declared elected. March 3d, 1805, Congress adjourned, and March 4th Jefferson and Clinton were sworn into office.

*Session VIIIth Congress, 2d Session.*

# CHAPTER VI.

### FIFTH ADMINISTRATION, 1805–1809.

**Thomas Jefferson, President.   George Clinton, Vice-President.**
**IXth and Xth Congresses.**

**IXth Congress, 1st Session.** 1. CONGRESS met December 2d, 1805, with an overwhelming Republican majority in both branches. Nathaniel Macon was again chosen Speaker in the House. Federalism still retained control of New England, with the exception of Vermont. In the other States it seemed to be dead or dying. But New England's influence was so much greater than its proportionate size that the party which controlled it was certain to be at least a strong minority in national politics.

2. The Napoleonic wars still continued, and Great Britain and France were using every expedient to cripple each other, without regard to the rights of neutral nations. While the President was anxious to defend American commerce, he was averse to increasing the expenses of his Administration by building a navy. He therefore recommended, and Congress adopted, a

plan for the building of a number of small gun-boats, as more economical than ships of war. This "**Gunboat System**" was always hateful to the navy, and was a constant object of Federalist ridicule and attack.

3. The President again called the attention of Congress to the unfriendly actions of the Spanish authorities at New Orleans. His Message on this subject was referred to a committee of which **Randolph**, of Virginia, was chairman. Randolph had been one of the Republican leaders while the party was in opposition, but his irritable spirit disqualified him for heading an Administration party. He could attack, but could not defend. He had taken offense at the President's refusal to make him Minister to England, and immediately took sides with the Federalists, followed by a number of his friends, though not sufficient to give the Federalists a majority. Randolph's committee reported resolutions which the Republicans voted down, on the ground that they were calculated to provoke a needless collision with Spain. A substitute was then passed authorizing the President to purchase the Floridas from Spain.[1] This was afterward modified by a resolution that it was advisable to exchange a part of Louisiana for East and West Florida. The Randolph faction popularly called "**Quids**," gave fresh life to the Federalists in Congress, and made them an active and useful opposition party.

4. Through the first three months of 1806 various resolutions were offered in Congress, looking toward **Retaliation upon England**. They culminated in

---

[1] This was not effected, however, until 1819.

the adoption of an Act to prohibit the importation of certain English goods after November 15th. The vote upon this bill (93 to 32 in the House, and 19 to 9 in the Senate) is a fair statement of the Administration majority at this Session. Another unsuccessful attempt was made to facilitate the removal of Federal Judges. The increase of loose constructionist ideas among the Republicans was marked by the passage of a bill for the construction of a **National Road** from Maryland to Ohio.[1] Congress adjourned April 21st, 1806.

5. The summer of 1806 was spent by the *quids* in efforts to bring Monroe back from his mission to England, to be used as a Presidential candidate against Madison, whom the President was supposed to favor The late Vice-President, **Burr,** came up again to public notice, by a mysterious expedition down the Mississippi, by which he hoped to retrieve his fallen fortunes. It was not known whether its object was colonization, an attack upon the Spanish possessions, or the founding of an independent western empire. The President, by proclamation, cautioned all citizens not to engage in the enterprise, and gave orders for Burr's arrest.

6. Congress met December 1st, 1806. The **President's Message** called attention to the growing excess of receipts over expenditures, and suggested Amendments to the Constitution giving Congress the doubted power to ex-

**IXth Congress, 2d Session.**

---

[1] This was the first appearance of the question of making Internal Improvements at Federal Expense, which afterwards divided parties from 1830 until 1856.

pend the surplus on roads, canals, and education. No action was taken upon them. The Act prohibiting importations from England, passed at the last Session was suspended until July 1st, 1807, and the President was given discretionary power to suspend it until December.

7. January 22d, 1807, the President sent to Congress the dispatches which showed the progress of **Burr's Expedition** up to that time. The Senate, in great alarm, passed unanimously a bill to suspend the writ of habeas corpus for three months, a measure repugnant to all the principles of the dominant party Three days afterward the House rejected the bill, by a vote nearly unanimous. Congress adjourned March 3d, 1807. Burr's expedition had by this time disbanded, and its leader was on his way to Virginia, to be tried for treason, his enterprise having been begun within the limits of that State.

8. In December, 1806, a **Treaty with England** had been arranged, which was almost identical with Jay's treaty of 1795. As it left England at liberty to impress American seamen, and to search American ships, the President rejected it, without laying it before the Senate, and tried further negotiation, but without success. His action was supported by the Republicans, and attacked by the Federalists, who were the commercial part of the community, and were anxious for almost any treaty with England. The rejection of this treaty embittered English feeling against the United States, and was probably a leading cause of the re

newed English aggressions, the Embargo, and the War of 1812.

9. **Burr's Examination** began in May, 1807, before the Grand Jury in Richmond, Va. It took a party aspect almost from the beginning. The Federalists considered Burr's arrest an Executive usurpation of power. The President was determined that the result of the trial should justify his action, and became notorious for his interference in the management of the case. His letters to the District Attorney were frequent, and his anxiety for Burr's conviction roused the Federalists to greater exertions for Burr's acquittal. The counsel for defense even caused a writ to be served upon the President, commanding his personal attendance as a witness. The President refused to obey, on the ground of public inconvenience, and the matter was not pressed. The Grand Jury found an indictment against Burr. His trial came on in August, before Chief Justice Marshall, and resulted in his acquittal for want of jurisdiction. The administration was thus defeated, and abandoned any further earnest prosecution of Aaron Burr.

10. In June, 1807, the British frigate **Leopard**, off Hampton Roads, had taken by force four seamen from the United States frigate **Chesapeake**, after a shamefully feeble resistance. Both political parties joined heartily in the indignation excited by this outrage, and war with England would have been everywhere popular, for the day was past when parties were ready to go all lengths in support of either France or England. The President was anxious for peace, and left the mat-

ter to be settled, some years afterward, by negotiation
It would be out of place to discuss here the alternating
attacks on neutral rights by the great European belligerents, before and after this date, the proclamation by
England of a paper blockade of the whole French
coast, the counter proclamation by France of a paper
blockade of the British islands, the Orders in Council
to the English navy to search neutral vessels for French
goods, and the counter orders to the French navy to
capture every vessel which should submit to such
search.[1] England's power being the greater on the
ocean, her aggressions bore most heavily on the United
States, whose commerce was rapidly being destroyed.

11. The President, by proclamation, had warned all British armed vessels not to enter American ports, and had called an early session of Congress. It met October 26th, 1807, with a Republican majority in both branches. In the House a Republican, Joseph B. Varnum, of Massachusetts, was chosen Speaker. The President recommended a bill by which American vessels should be prohibited from leaving foreign ports, and foreign vessels from taking cargoes from the United States, and all coasting vessels should be required to give bonds to land their cargoes in the United States This was the celebrated **Embargo Bill**, which destroyed, for the time, all American commerce, intensified party feeling, and even threatened the exist-

**Xth Congress, 1st Session.**

---

[1] Jefferson, in a private letter, said that "England seemed to have become a den of pirates, and France a den of thieves."

ence of the Union. It was passed by strict party votes, being opposed vehemently by the Federalists and *quids*, cn the ground that it would injure the United States rather than England, and would complete the commercial ruin which foreign attacks had begun. Having given the President the power of suspending the Embargo Act whenever it should seem advisable to him to do so, Congress adjourned April 25th, 1808.

12. **Presidential Nominations** were made at this Session by Congressional caucuses. The Republicans nominated James Madison, of Virginia, for President, and George Clinton, of New York, for Vice-President. Madison's chief competitors for the nomination were James Monroe, who was supported by the *quids* of the Virginia Assembly, and George Clinton, who was supported by a part of the New York Republicans. The Federalists nominated C. C. Pinckney, of South Carolina, for President, and Rufus King, of New York, for Vice-President. The President had been requested by the Legislatures of most of the Republican States to accept a third term, but declined.

13. During the summer of 1808 the Embargo began to bear so heavily on the commercial interests of New England and the Middle States that their complaints drowned other subjects of discussion, and took away much of the excitement of a Presidential election. The remaining strength of the Federalists was concentrated in these States, so that party bitterness aggravated financial distress. It was said that the Repub-

lican States had devised the Embargo as a substitute for war, because its ill effects would fall mainly upon the Federalist States. There was every indication that New England would obey it with reluctance. The choice, however, lay between war, an embargo, or submission. For the latter there were very few advocates The war party was divided, some of its members wishing for war against England, others for war against France, and still others for war against both. The great majority of the people still favored the Embargo, and the **Presidential Election** in November resulted largely in favor of the Republicans. New England stood almost alone in choosing Federalist electors.

14. Congress met November 7th, 1808. Its proceedings were confined to resolutions and protests against French and English aggressions, and the rejection of Federalist resolutions to repeal the Embargo, until February, 1809. In that month **John Quincy Adams**, who had resigned the Massachusetts Senatorship because his support of the Embargo had been disapproved by his State Legislature, informed the President that the Embargo could no longer be enforced in New England, that the Federalist leaders had made all arrangements to break off from federal relations with the rest of the Union unless the Act was repealed, and that an agent from the Canadas was then in New England to offer the assistance of the English Government to the scheme.[1]

**Xth Congress, 2d Session.**

15. Adams's warning impressed the President and the

---

[1] Adams's accuracy has been denied, and it has even been asserted that his

Republican leaders so much that they at once secured the passage of a modification of the Embargo, known as the **Non-Intercourse Act.** By this the Embargo was repealed, after March 4th, as to commerce with all nations excepting England and France. It was hoped that this would quiet the excitement in New England, without yielding the principle of the Embargo

16. In February the electoral votes were counted, and were found to be, for President, 122 for James Madison, 6 for George Clinton, and 47 for C. C. Pinckney, and for Vice-President, 113 for George Clinton, 47 for Rufus King, and 15 scattering. **Madison and Clinton** were therefore declared elected. March 3d, 1809, Congress adjourned, and March 4th Madison and Clinton were sworn into office.

---

appointment, soon after, as Minister to Russia was the reward of his wilful falsification.

# CHAPTER VII.

## SIXTH ADMINISTRATION, 1809-1813.

James Madison, President.   George Clinton, Vice-President
XIth and XIIth Congresses.

1. THE **Difficulties with England** were compli-
XIth Congress, cated, at the beginning of Madi-
Extra Session. son's term of office by an unfortunate mistake of the British Minister, Mr. Erskine,
caused by his desire for peace. Shortly after the
inauguration he informed the President that he was
authorized by his Government to withdraw the objectionable orders to the English navy. The President
therefore, by proclamation, summoned a Special Session of Congress to meet May 22d, 1809, and suspended the Non-Intercourse Act, as applied to England, after June 10th. This he was authorized to
do by the terms of the Act. Congress met on the day
appointed, with a Republican majority in both branches.
In the House Speaker Varnum was re-elected. England had in the mean time disavowed her Minister's
offer, and recalled him, and a new proclamation by the

President restored the Non-Intercourse Act as before. The Federalists represented the whole misunderstanding as a Republican trick to influence the elections. There being no business to occupy Congress, it adjourned June 28th.

2. **XIth Congress, 1st Session.** Congress met November 27th, 1809. The Republican majority was so large that every Administration measure was promptly carried, and there was little party conflict. A continuance of the Non-Intercourse Act was voted. Mr. Erskine's successor had contradicted the Secretary of State so frequently and so offensively that Congress, by a strict party vote, passed a resolution declaring his language to be insolent, and requesting the President to recognize him no longer. Congress adjourned May 1st, 1810.

3. **XIth Congress, 2d Session.** Congress met December 3d, 1810. France had managed so adroitly as to leave it in doubt whether her objectionable decrees had been withdrawn or not. The Republicans chose to consider them withdrawn, and repealed the Non-Intercourse Act, as applied to **France.** The President endeavored to induce England to withdraw her Orders in Council, but this was refused on the ground that there was no evidence of any repeal by France. The Non-Intercourse Act was therefore continued against **England.**

4. An effort was made at this Session to re-charter the **National Bank,** which had been chartered in 1791 for twenty years. Opposition to such a bank

was a necessary article of belief among Strict Construc
tionists. But the corporation had so many Republican friends in Congress that a bill to recharter it was favorably reported by the committees of both branches, and after long debate was only defeated by a majority of one vote in the House, and by the casting vote of the Vice-President in the Senate. Thereupon the Bank wound up its business, and ceased to act. Congress adjourned March 3d, 1811.

5. Congress met November 4th, 1811. The Republican majority was still overwhelmingly large, but it contained several rising and energetic members, who afterward became party leaders, and who were now successfully urging upon the party a **Change of Policy.** Hitherto Jefferson and Madison had made it a peace party, and had carefully avoided direct conflict with France or England. The capture of over 900 American merchant vessels since 1803 had been no more effectual than such isolated outrages as the Chesapeake case in rousing the Administration to the idea of forcible resistance. Under the new leaders the Republicans became a war party. **Henry Clay,** of Kentucky, was chosen Speaker of the House. **William H. Crawford,** of Georgia, in the Senate, and **John C. Calhoun,** of South Carolina, in the House, became the recognized Congressional leaders of the party. The economical and retrenching policy of Jefferson was abandoned, and preparations were begun for hostilities, against the opposition of the Federalists, and the timid or peace lov

*The Re-*
**XIIth Congress,**
**1st Session.**

ing Republicans. Bills were passed to enlist men, to organize the militia, and to equip and enlarge the navy.

6. **The President** was given to understand that his nomination for a second term of office depended upon his adoption of the war policy and that his refusal to do so would cause the nomination of De Witt Clinton, of New York, in his stead. Thus pressed the President yielded, and was consequently renominated by the usual caucus of Republican members of Congress, with Elbridge Gerry, of Massachusetts, for Vice-President. Clinton refused to be bound by this bargain, and, having been nominated by a Republican caucus of the New York Legislature, persisted in his candidacy. To profit by this promising division among the Republicans, a caucus of leading Federalists, held in New York City, decided to support Clinton, with Jared Ingersoll, of Pennsylvania, for Vice-President.

7. In March, 1812, the President took the first step in fulfillment of his bargain by sending to Congress, with a special Message, certain documents, which he had purchased from one **John Henry** for $50,000. Henry claimed to have been the agent sent from Canada in 1809 to detach the New England Federalists from their allegiance to the Union, and his documents purported to show the complicity of the British Government. The British Minister solemnly denied all knowledge of, or belief in, any such agent, but Congress, by resolution, proclaimed Henry's documents authentic, and denounced England's perfidious attack on the unity of a friendly nation. The principal ef

fect of this episode was to outrage and exasperate the Federalists of New England.

8. As a preliminary to war an **Embargo** was laid upon American shipping for 90 days. The British Minister finally declared, May 30th, that his Government would not recede from its policy toward neutrals. Dispatches from the American agent in London informed the President that the same declaration had been made by the English Ministry in Parliament. The President therefore sent a Message to Congress, June 1st, reviewing the past and present difficulties with Great Britain. It was referred to a committee, whose report was a summary of American grievances against England, the impressment of American seamen, the Orders in Council, the system of paper blockades, and the refusal to settle American claims for damages. It concluded by recommending a declaration of war.

9. An Act was consequently passed, and signed by the President, June 18th, declaring that a **State of War** existed between the United Kingdom of Great Britain and Ireland and its dependencies, and the United States of America. Of the 98 members who voted for the war 76 were from the South and West. On the following day the President's proclamation announced that the war had begun. We have nothing to do with its events, except as they influenced politics in the United States. It was soon learned that the Orders in Council had been revoked in London five days after the declaration of war, but the revocation came too late. Even if it had been made in 'ime, the

war party would probably have insisted upon the abandonment by England of the right of search and impressment, and would have declared war on that issue Congress adjourned July 6th, 1812. April 30th **Louisiana** had become a state of the Union.

10. The **Presidential Election** in November resulted in the success of a large majority of Republican electors, and of members of the XIIIth Congress pledged to support the Administration and the war. But the **Opposition to the War** was manifested by every legal method from its very beginning. Immediately after the declaration the Federalist members of Congress had published their protest against it in an address to their constituents. Under the Act passed by Congress to embody the militia, requisitions were made by the President upon the Governors of the different States for their respective quotas. The Governors of Massachusetts and Connecticut refused to allow their militia to leave their States, on the ground that the Federal Government could not constitutionally call out the militia until an invasion had taken place, or the laws of the United States had been resisted. In this, as in many other instances throughout the war, the possession of power by the Republicans inclined them toward a loose construction of the Constitution, and the Federalists toward a strict construction of it.

11. Congress met November 2d, 1812. The large Republican majority prevented any party contest. The Randolph faction, or **Quids**, had ceased to have a separate

**XIIth Congress, 2d Session.**

existence after its failure to nominate Monroe. Most of its members were now supporters of the Administration. The remainder, with the Federalists and those Republicans who opposed the war, had formed a "**Peace Party.**" But their defection was more than compensated by the number of Federalists whom it drove into political union with the war party. In Congress both parties united in rewarding, encouraging, and increasing the **Navy,** whose brilliant exploits had intoxicated the whole nation with the unexpected consciousness that it alone, of all the nations of the earth, could match and master England upon her own element, the ocean. This Session was occupied mainly in measures necessary for the active prosecution of the war, which were all passed by party votes. In February the electoral votes were counted and were found to be, for President, 128 for Madison, and 89 for Clinton, and, for Vice-President, 131 for Gerry, and 86 for Ingersoll. **Madison** and **Gerry** were therefore declared elected. March 3d, 1813, Congress adjourned, and March 4th Madison and Gerry were sworn into office.

# CHAPTER VIII.

## SEVENTH ADMINISTRATION, 1813-1817.

**James Madison, President.**  **Elbridge Gerry, Vice-President**
**XIIIth and XIVth Congresses.**

1. **XIIIth Congress, Extra Session.** Congress met May 24th, 1813, having been summoned by the President to a Special Session to consider the difficulties encountered in raising money for the War. The President's Message also mentioned the proffered mediation of the Czar of Russia, which England afterward declined. In the House Henry Clay, of Kentucky, was chosen Speaker, and the vote (89 to 54) represents the Administration majority. The Republican majority in the Senate was weakened by a faction opposed to the Administration. The business of this Session was mainly routine. Congress adjourned August 2d.

2. The **Dislike to the War** and its management became more apparent as it went on. The Connecticut Legislature had declared it to be the solemn and deliberate opinion of the people of that State that the

war was unnecessary. So notorious was the general feeling of the Eastern States that England had endeavored to mark a political division between New England and the rest of the Union by exempting Massachusetts (which included the present State of Maine) Rhode Island, and New Hampshire, from the blockad of the Atlantic Coast.

3. Congress met December 6th, 1813. This Session XIIIth Congress, was also occupied chiefly with 1st Session. routine business, and in efforts to improve the condition of the finances. Illicit trade from the New England coast to the English ships had become so common that a **New Embargo Act** was passed, applying to all vessels, large or small. Congress adjourned April 18th, 1814. In August occurred the sack and burning of Washington by an English expedition, an affair almost equally disgraceful to both nations.[1]

4. Congress met September 19th, 1814. **Negotia-** XIIIth Congress, **tions for Peace** had been be- 2d Session. gun in August. Napoleon was, for the time, overthrown, and the American Government was anxious for almost any honorable peace, in preference to continuing the war with England. The Orders in Council had been revoked long before, and the American Commissioners were instructed not to insist upon the other object of the war, the abandonment of the rights of search and impressment. The English demands rose as those of the United States fell. En-

---

[1] The President barely escaped capture.

gland now insisted that an independent Indian nation should be organized between Canada and the United States, and that the United States should maintain no fleet or military posts on the Great Lakes.

5. The publication of these conditions in October gain roused the war feeling of the Republicans, and some of their leaders began to meditate measures which the strict constructionist principles of the party could not justify. The Secretary of War proposed the increase of the army by a draft, or conscription. The Secretary of the Navy proposed to introduce the Enlish system of impressment of seamen. To Republicans generally such measures seemed unconstitutional, and they were rejected, though strongly urged by the Administration. Fresh discontent was excited by a bill offered in the Senate, allowing officers of the army to enlist minors over 18 years old without consent of their parents or guardians. The Connecticut Legislature ordered the Governor to resist the execution of these and similar measures, if they should become laws.

6. The commercial distress in New England, the possession by the enemy of a large part of the District of Maine, the fear of their advance along the coast, and the apparent neglect of the Federal Government to provide any adequate means of resistance, had led the Legislature of Massachusetts, in October, to invite the other New England States to send delegates to Hartford, Connecticut, "to confer upon the subject of their public grievances." Delegates from Massachusetts, Rhode Island and Connecticut, and from parts of Ver

mont and New Hampshire, met at Hartford in December and remained in session for three weeks. In their **Report** to their State Legislatures they reviewed the state of the country, the origin and management of the war, and the strong measures lately proposed in Congress, and recommended several Amendments to the Constitution, chiefly with intent to restrict the powers of Congress over commerce, and to prevent naturalized citizens from holding office. In default of the adoption of these Amendments, another convention was advised, "in order to decide on the course which a crisis so momentous might seem to demand."

7. This was the famous **Hartford Convention**. The peace which closely followed its adjournment removed all necessity or even desire for another session of it. Its objects seem to have been legitimate. But the unfortunate secrecy of its proceedings, and its somewhat ambiguous language, roused a popular suspicion, sufficient for the political ruin of its members, that a dissolution of the Union had been proposed, perhaps resolved upon, in its meetings. Some years afterward those concerned in it were compelled in self-defense to publish its journal, in order to show that no treasonable design was officially proposed. It was then, however, too late, for the popular opinion had become fixed. Neither the Federal party which originated, nor the Federalist politicians who composed the assembly were ever freed from the stigma left by the mysterious Hartford Convention.

8. In February, 1815, the welcome and unexpected

news of **Peace** reached Congress. It was welcome to the Administration, whose inexperience in the conduct of the war had involved it in great financial straits, to the Federalists, who considered the war iniquitous, and even to the war party, who had begun to anticipate a single contest with England. Therefore the peace, which actually secured not one of the objects for which war had been declared, occasioned rejoicings which would have been more appropriate for a more successful termination of the war. The rest of this Session was necessarily spent in the active reduction of government to a peace establishment, and in the reduction of expenses, with the exception of the navy. The Acts which had been necessary in preparing for or carrying on the war were repealed. Congress adjourned March 3d, 1815.

9. The close of the war marks the final **Extinction of the Federal Party.** The few remaining Federalists from this time began to desist from any united party action. The whole people composed one party whose principles were neither those of the original Federal, nor those of the original Republican, party, but a combination of both. The cardinal principle of the Federal party, the preservation and perpetuity of the Federal Government, had been quietly accepted and adopted by the Republicans, while the Republican principle of limiting the Federal Government's powers and duties had been adopted by the Federalists when the Federal Government had fallen into Republican hands. But, though the principles of the Federalists

had made an abiding impression upon the form of government, their party opposition to the war had made the name so unsavory that it soon began to fall into disuse.

10. Congress met December 4th, 1815, with a large Republican majority in both branches. In the House Henry Clay was again chosen Speaker. This Session was occupied chiefly by the regulation of **Internal Affairs,** which occasioned but little party contest. Taxes were reduced, and a slight increase was made in the Tariff. Some indications appeared, during the debate, of a growing feeling among Republicans that the Tariff ought to be so arranged as to give protection to those manufactures which had sprung up in America during the war, but were now being endangered by the importation of cheaper goods of English make. The matter went no further than debate at this Session.

<small>XIVth Congress, 1st Session.</small>

11. The spread of loose constructionist ideas among the Republicans was marked in April, 1816, by the passage of a bill for the charter of a **National Bank,** to expire in 1836. It was modeled upon the one which the Republicans had opposed in 1791 and 1811. Hamilton's argument in favor of such a bank was republished by Republican newspapers with a warmth of approval which showed how far the party had forgotten its strict constructionist principles. Congress adjourned April 30th, 1816.

11. **Presidential Candidates** were nominated by the usual Congressional caucuses. Among the Repub

licans the Virginia influence, which had named the President for 24 of the 28 years since 1789, was again successful in nominating James Monroe, his principal competitor being Wm. H. Crawford, of Georgia. Daniel D. Tompkins, of New York, was nominated for the Vice-Presidency. For President the Federalists supported Rufus King, of New York, but united on no one for the Vice-Presidency. The **Presidential Election** in November resulted in complete Republican success. Only three States, Massachusetts, Connecticut, and Delaware, chose Federalist electors.

13. Congress met December 2d, 1816. December 11th, Indiana became a State of the Union. This Session was almost without party contest. In February, 1817, the electoral votes were counted and were found to be, for President, 183 for Monroe, and 34 for King, and, for Vice-President, 183 for Tompkins, and 34 for various other persons. **Monroe** and **Tompkins** were therefore declared elected. March 3d, 1817, Congress adjourned, and March 4th Monroe and Tompkins were sworn into office.

**XIVth Congress, 2d Session.**

# CHAPTER IX.

### EIGHTH ADMINISTRATION, 1817--1821.

James Monroe, President.   Daniel D. Tompkins, Vice-President.
XVth and XVIth Congresses.

1. **The President** appointed a Republican Cabinet.  He had been urged to ignore parties in his appointments, but in his opinion the time had not yet come to do so.  May 31st he began an extended tour through the Northern States, being the first President to imitate Washington's example in this respect.  The welcome everywhere given him probably helped to blot out the last remnant of Federalist opposition.

2. Congress met December 1st, 1817.  The professed Federalists were very few.

**XVth Congress, 1st Session.**  In the House Speaker Clay was re-elected almost unanimously.  December 10th Mississippi became a State of the Union.[1]  The first Act of this Session abolished the internal taxes which had

---

[1] Appendices C and F will show how carefully a new Free State was at once balanced by the creation of a new Slave State, in order to control the Senate.

been imposed during the war. In his Message the President had taken occasion to recommend a **Protective Tariff.** The question was compromised, nearly unanimously, by the passage of a bill continuing for seven years the Tariff of 1816 on cottons and woolens, which was slightly protective. A proposition was made to use the dividends of the United States from the National Bank, instead of appropriations. It was postponed because of the opposition of Strict Constructionists. A resolution, supported by Clay, to recognize the South American Republics, formed by Spain's revolted colonies, was rejected. Congress adjourned April 20th, 1818.

3. It is plain that the all-powerful Republican party already contained the **Nucleus of a New Party,** and a leader for it in the person of Henry Clay. He had headed, or advocated, every attempt to increase the army and navy, to make the Tariff protective, to begin a system of general public improvements at national expense, or to make the Federal Government prominent in foreign affairs, as the guardian of the infant Republics of South America. All of these measures seemed to Strict Constructionists either unconstitutional or unwise. Some of Clay's followers were only temporarily attracted by his personal influence, but the great majority were Loose Constructionists, Federalists in reality, though they would have disliked the name.

4. The summer of 1818 was marked by Indian difficulties in Florida, which deserve mention because their

investigation took up much of the time of the next Session of Congress. In quelling disturbances among the Georgia Indians **Andrew Jackson** had been systematically thwarted by the Spanish authorities of Florida. He therefore entered their territory, seized heir principal towns, and captured and put to death, " as outlaws and pirates," Arbuthnot and Ambrister, two British subjects, who had led the Seminole Indians.

5. Congress met November 16th, 1818. December 3d Illinois became a State of the Union. In the House the Committee on Military Affairs offered two reports on **The Seminole War.** The majority report proposed a censure upon Jackson for his execution of Arbuthnot and Ambrister, declaring it to be unwise, unnecessary, and unjustifiable by the laws of war or of nations. The minority report approved his action. The majority report was rejected by the House and postponed by the Senate. The contest was then transferred to the newspapers, where it raged violently.

**XVth Congress, 2d Session.**

6. February 22d, 1819, a treaty was concluded by which Spain sold the **Floridas** to the United States for $5,000,000, and the United States abandoned all claim to the territory West of the Sabine River (afterwards known as Texas), which had formed part of Louisiana as purchased from France.[1] A territory worth ten Floridas was thus surrendered to Spain, and became a part of the Republic of Mexico two years later.

---

[1] Within thirty years the determination of the South to regain this abandoned territory forced the United States into war with Mexico.

7. At this Session the people of the **Territory of Missouri** (a part of the Louisiana Purchase) applied for permission to form a State government. In the House an amendment was offered to the bill, forbidding Slavery or involuntary servitude in Missouri, except as a punishment for crime.[1] Party lines were at once dropped. The members from the Free States voted for, and the members from Slave States against, the amendment. It passed the House, was rejected by the Senate, and the bill was lost. Congress adjourned March 3d, 1819.

8. The application of Missouri thus suddenly brought up the **Slavery Question**,[2] which was to be argued and compromised for forty years, and then settled by civil war. Negro Slavery, in the early colonial days, had been common in all the colonies, excepting Massachusetts, and had even been decided legal by the highest English court of law. In the North it had since been abolished in the States lying north of the dividing line run by the old surveyors, Mason and Dixon, between Maryland and Pennsylvania. In the South it worked mildly, and was considered a necessary and hereditary evil. But the invention of Whitney's cotton gin in 1793 had made slave labor profitable, and had made Slavery an institution to be defended and extended by the Southern States. While the Union was confined to the fringe of States along the Atlantic coast

---

[1] This was copied, in part, from that of the ordinance of 1787.
[2] Its appearance was so sudden that Ex-President Jefferson said it startled him "like a fire-bell in the night."

the Slavery question was not troublesome. And it was at first possible to unite the representatives of both sections in the admission of new States, by using the Ohio as a dividing line between the States in which Slavery should be forbidden, and those in which it should be allowed. But when the tides of emigration had crossed the Mississippi and had begun to fill the Louisiana Purchase, conflict was inevitable, for the dividing line was lost. In the House the members from the Free States were a majority. In the Senate the sections had been carefully equalized, but a few Northern Senators generally voted with the South, thus giving it a majority in that body.

9. **XVIth Congress, 1st Session.** Congress met December 6th, 1819. The state of parties was unchanged. In the House Speaker Clay was re-elected almost unanimously. December 14th **Alabama** became a State of the Union. At this Session a **Protective Tariff** was passed by the House, but rejected by the Senate. The result, though it disappointed the Eastern manufacturers, who had confidently expected relief from Congress, shows a still further advance of loose constructionist principles in the dominant party. Strict Constructionists believed that the Constitution gave Congress power to lay duties only with a design to provide for the expenses of the Government and for the payment of the debt, and that the arrangement of duties for the benefit of any branch of manufactures was usurpation of a power not

granted or implied.[1]  Loose Constructionists believed that the power to regulate commerce and provide for the common defense implied the power to lay a Protective Tariff, and that any consequent benefit to manufacturers would be more than offset by the creation of a domestic market for agricultural products.

10. At this Session **Missouri** again applied for permission to form a State government, and **Maine** (formerly a part of Massachusetts) made a first application for the same permission. The House passed the Maine bill without opposition, but, by a sectional vote, again prohibited Slavery in Missouri. In the Senate, also by a sectional vote, the Maine bill and a Missouri bill permitting Slavery were united and then passed. This was for the purpose of compelling both bills to stand or fall together, and of throwing upon the House the responsibility for their acceptance or rejection. The House rejected the combined bills, as passed by the Senate, and adhered to its first action.

11. The difficulty was settled by the famous **Missouri Compromise of 1820**, which was adopted by the active exertions of Clay and the moderate members from both sections. By this measure each section yielded a part of its demands, the Senate by permitting Maine and Missouri to be voted upon separately, and the House by permitting Slavery in Missouri. Both branches then united in forever prohibiting Slavery in

---

[1] But there have been very few advocates of absolutely *Free* Trade removal of *all* duties on imports), and the entire payment of Government expenses by internal taxation. The party distinction given in the text seems to have generally governed our political history.

all other territory north of the line of 36° 30'.[1] Maine was then admitted as a State of the Union, and the bill authorizing a State government to be formed in Missouri was passed. Congress adjourned May 15th, 1820.

12. No Presidential candidates were nominated this year, there being no opposition to the re-election of President Monroe and Vice-President Tompkins. All the electors chosen in the **Presidential Election** in November were Republican, but one of them refused to vote for Monroe, so that his election was not unanimous.

13. Congress met November 13th, 1820. Speaker Clay resigned his position on account of private affairs. After three days' balloting for a successor John W. Taylor, of New York, a Loose Constructionist, in favor of a Protective Tariff and an internal improvement system, and opposed to extension of Slavery, was chosen. His election shows the progress of the division in the Republican party. It gave great offense to the Southern members, and they for a time debated a dissolution of the Union, a remedy which has been proposed at various times by almost every section for every variety of grievance

**XVIth Congress, 2d Session.**

14. **Missouri**, having formed a State government,

---

[1] Thirty-five Southern members, who believed that Congress had no power to prohibit Slavery in the Territories, voted against the Missouri Compromise. Randolph called it "a dirty bargain," and gave those who voted for it the name of "doughfaces." This title was always afterward applied to Northern men "of Southern principles."

applied for admission. It was rejected in the House by a sectional vote, on account of a clause in its constitution, prohibiting the entrance of free negroes into the State.[1] It was not until March 2d, 1821, that this difficulty was settled, again by Clay's exertions. Missouri was then admitted, on condition that the State should never pass an act to interfere with the constitutional privileges of the citizens of other States. But the Legislature only accepted the condition in June, 1821.

15. In February, 1821, the **Electoral Votes** were counted. It was known that Missouri, which claimed to be already a State, and protested against the right of Congress to reject her application, had chosen electors. It was also known that Southern members would make a vigorous effort to have these votes counted. After a stormy session on the day of counting, lasting in the House for several hours after the time appointed for joint meeting with the Senate, another compromise was affected. The President of the Senate was directed, in case any objection should be made to the vote of Missouri, to announce that "if the votes of Missouri were counted, the number of votes for A. B. for President would be so many, and if the votes of Missouri were not counted the number of votes for A. B. for President would be so many, and that in either case A. B. was elected." There being no opposition to the Republican candidates, the result of course was foreknown.

---

[1] In some of the Northern States free negroes were citizens.

16. Considerable delay and confusion was caused in joint meeting by an unsuccessful attempt of some of the Southern members to renew the contest, but the vote was finally announced as previously agreed. There were 235 votes, including that of Missouri, and 232 without it. Not counting the vote of Missouri there were, for President, 228 votes for James Monroe, and 1 for John Quincy Adams, and, for Vice-President, 215 votes for Daniel D. Tompkins, and 14 for various other persons.[1] **Monroe** and **Tompkins** were therefore declared elected. March 3d, 1821, Congress adjourned, and on Monday, March 5th, Monroe and Tompkins were sworn into office.

---

[1] Three electors had died before having an opportunity to vote.

## CHAPTER X.

### NINTH ADMINISTRATION, 1821-1825.

James Monroe, President.     Daniel D. Tompkins, Vice-President
XVIIth and XVIIIth Congresses.

1. MONROE'S election had been so nearly unanimous, and party divisions had nominally so far disappeared, that this Administration is commonly called **The Era of Good Feeling.** In reality there was as much bad feeling between the Strict Constructionists and the Loose Constructionists of the Republican party as could have existed between two opposing parties. The want of regularly organized parties had only the effect of making the next Presidential election a personal instead of a party contest, the worst form which a political struggle can take.

2. Congress met December 3d, 1821. In the House **XVIIth Congress,** P. P. Barbour, of Virginia, a 1st Session. Strict Constructionist, was chosen Speaker. The Loose Constructionists, however, succeeded in passing a bill for the preservation of the **Cumberland Road,** but it was vetoed by the Presi

dent, on the ground that "Congress do not possess the power, under the Constitution, to pass such a law." But his Message gave his opinion that an Amendment to the Constitution should be adopted, giving the Federal Government power to make improvements for great national purposes. The Strict Constructionists succeeded in defeating further propositions to make surveys for a national canal system, and to make the Tariff more protective. Congress adjourned May 8th, 1822.

3. **XVIIth Congress, 2d Session.** Congress met December 2d, 1822. There was little party contest at this Session. The Strict Constructionists defeated bills for an increase of the Tariff, and a renewed attempt to create a national canal system. All other bills necessary for the support of the Government were passed, generally by large majorities. Congress adjourned March 3d, 1823.

4. **XVIIIth Congress, 1st Session.** Congress met December 1st, 1823. Henry Clay, of Kentucky, who was now the leader of the Loose Constructionists in Congress, was chosen Speaker in the House. In his Message President Monroe mentioned the war then waged by Spain against her revolted colonies, and declared that the United States would neither interfere in any European war, nor tolerate any attempt by any European power to acquire a controlling influence in this hemisphere. This has since been called the **Monroe Doctrine**, and has passed into a settled rule of foreign policy for all American political parties

5. The President's Message showed that his views had slightly changed, for he incidentally recommended Protection and Internal Improvements. The Loose Constructionists were in a majority in this Congress, and after a debate of more than two months the **Tariff of 1824** was adopted by very small majorities. It was an advance on all preceding Tariffs in its consistent design to exclude foreign competing goods from American markets. It was passed by the Northern members, except those from the North-East, against the almost unanimous vote of the Southern members, who considered it sectional, unconstitutional, and unjust. The Loose Constructionists were also successful in passing a bill for surveys for a **National Canal System.** Congress adjourned May 27th, 1824.

6. An effort was made at this Session by the friends of William H. Crawford, of Georgia, to revive the **Caucus System** of nomination for the Presidency. Very few members of Congress obeyed their call for a caucus, and Crawford's nomination by this body really injured his chances of success. As there were no recognized parties, the Presidential election degenerated into a personal contest, in which the leading candidates were Henry Clay, of Kentucky, Speaker of the House, John Quincy Adams, of Massachusetts, Secretary of State, William H. Crawford, of Georgia, Secretary of the Treasury, and Andrew Jackson, a private citizen of Tennessee.[1] Clay and Adams were Loose Constructionists. Crawford and Jackson were Strict Constructionists, but Jackson was objectionable to the Crawford

---

[1] Hence it is known as "the scrub race for the Presidency."

faction, on account of his leaning toward a Protective Tariff. John C. Calhoun, of South Carolina, Secretary of War, was generally supported for the Vice-Presidency by the friends of all the other candidates. The **Presidential Election** in November gave no candidate a majority of all the electors chosen, and therefore left the President to be chosen by the House of Representatives.

7. Congress met December 6th, 1824. The yet undecided Presidential election was almost the only party contest of the Session. In February, 1825, the electoral votes were counted and were found to be, for President, 99 for Andrew Jackson, 84 for John Quincy Adams, 41 for William H. Crawford, and 37 for Henry Clay, and, for Vice-President, 182 for John C. Calhoun, and 78 for various other persons. **Calhoun** was therefore declared elected Vice-President, and the House proceeded to choose a President from the three highest candidates, each State having one vote. As Clay stood fourth on the list he was not eligible, and it was natural that he and his friends should unite on John Quincy Adams, the other Loose Constructionist candidate Through this coalition 13 States voted for Adams, 7 for Jackson, and 4 for Crawford. **Adams** was therefore declared elected President. The feeling excited by this result still further increased the division between the Strict Constructionists and the Loose Constructionists, who were soon to be openly opposing parties. March 3d, 1825, Congress adjourned, and March 4th Adams and Calhoun were sworn into office

*XVIIIth Congress,*
*2d Session.*

# CHAPTER XI.

## TENTH ADMINISTRATION, 1825-1829.

*John Quincy Adams, President.     John C. Calhoun, Vice-President
XIXth and XXth Congresses.*

1. FROM the very beginning of this Administration both factions of the Strict Constructionists united in an opposition to the President, which became stronger through his whole term of office, until it overcame him. His ill-advised **Nomination of Clay** to a post in his Cabinet gave color to the charge of a corrupt bargain between him and Clay, by which Adams was to receive the Clay vote in the House, and Clay was to be rewarded by the position of Secretary of State, which was then usually considered a stepping stone to the Presidency. Clay angrily denied any such bargain, and the renewal of charges and denials, each with its appropriate arguments, gave abundant material for debate.

2. The Clay and Adams factions soon united and took the distinctive party name of **National Republicans.** Some years afterward this name was changed

to that of Whigs. They maintained the loose construc tionist principles of the Federalists, and, in addition, desired a Protective Tariff and a system of public improvements at national expense. This policy was suggested by the President's Inaugural, and repeated in his first Message.

3. In October, 1825, the Tennessee Legislature nominated Jackson for the Presidency in 1828, and Jackson accepted the nomination. Crawford's continued ill-health compelled his adherents to look elsewhere for a candidate, and they gradually united upon Jackson. At first the resulting coalition was known as "**Jackson Men**," but, as they began to take the character of a national party, they assumed the name of **Democrats**, by which they have since been known. They maintained the strict constructionist principles of the Republican party, though the Crawford faction in the South went further, and held the extreme ground of the Kentucky Resolutions of 1799.[1] This had already borne fruit in the case of the State of Georgia and the Cherokee Indians, in which a collision had almost taken place between the State and the Federal Government.

4. Congress met December 5th, 1825. In the House John W. Taylor, of New York, a Loose Constructionist, was chosen Speaker. His small majority (99–94) represents the Administration majority in the House. In the Senate its majority was larger, but in both branches of Congress the "Jackson men" and the Crawford fac-

**XIXth Congress,**
    1st Session.

---

[1] See page 47.

tion united in a determined **Opposition**. One-third of the Session was taken up by the discussion of proposed changes in the manner of electing the President. It drifted off into an angry debate on the ' Clay and Adams bargain," and came to no result. The Opposition also made a fruitless effort to limit the President's appointing power.

5. Most of the measures proposed by the President at this Session, or known to be favored by him, were passed with difficulty or failed altogether. In the Senate Vice-President Calhoun, who was disposed to act with the "Jackson men," had given them the majority on the committees. In the latter part of this Session, therefore, the Senate took the then unusual step of depriving its presiding officer of the power of appointing committees. Much time was spent in debating the President's appointment of delegates to the Congress of American Republics at Panama. It was at length approved, and forgotten almost immediately. Appropriations for internal improvements were increased. Congress adjourned May 22d, 1826. The summer of 1826 was spent by the opposing factions in endeavors to recruit or cement their organizations.

6. Congress met December 4th, 1826. The ob-
**XIXth Congress,** structive spirit of the **Opposi-**
   **2d Session.** tion was so determined that few measures of national importance were passed at this Session. The Administration's supporters in the House succeeded in passing a bill for an increase of the Tariff, but the Vice-President's casting vote de

feated it in the Senate. The Opposition introduced bills, which were defeated, to divide a part of the revenue among the States, and to repay fines levied under the Sedition Act of 1798. Congress adjourned March 3d, 1827.

7. This was the only Session of Congress in which the Adams Administration had even a nominal majority. The election for members of the **XXth Congress** had resulted in the success of the Adams candidates, or National Republicans, in New England, New Jersey, Delaware, Ohio, Indiana, and Louisiana. In New York, Pennsylvania, and Illinois, and in every Southern State, with the exception of Louisiana, the Jackson candidates, or Democrats, were successful, and thus obtained control of the House.

8. From this time the idea of a connected system of roads and canals, to be built and maintained by the Federal Government, was abandoned, and its advocates confined themselves to voting for isolated public improvements in various parts of the country. But the demand for a higher Tariff than that of 1824 was brought still more strongly into politics by a **National Convention of Protectionists**, at Harrisburgh, Pa., July 30th, 1827. Many of the Democratic members elect to the XXth Congress from the North supported the National Republicans in their demand for Protection. The Strict Constructionists from the South were in favor of a Tariff for revenue only. The division upon this point was therefore becoming one of sections, rather than of parties.

9. Congress met December 3d, 1827. In the House
**XXth Congress,** Andrew Stevenson, of Virginia, a
**1st Session.** Democrat, was chosen Speaker.
This gave the Opposition the organization of the
House and the appointment of its committees. In the
Senate the hitherto doubtful members at once joined
the Democrats, and the Opposition became a majorit
there also. The **Debates** at this Session were almost
entirely political. A proposition to order a painting
of Jackson's successful battle of New Orleans, and a
counter proposition to investigate his execution of six
insubordinate militiamen, were solemnly debated for a
month. The increased expenditure of the Government was also the subject of long debate without result.

10. The most important event of this Session was
the success of the Protectionists in passing the **Tariff
of 1828,** after a debate of six weeks. It was so protective as to be satisfactory to manufacturers and very
objectionable to the Southern States, where it was considered a legalized robbery. From this time the Nullification doctrine of the Kentucky Resolutions of 1799
gained strength rapidly in the South. Congress adjourned May 26th. 1828.

11. The Democratic candidates for the Presidential
election in 1828 were Andrew Jackson, of Tennessee,
and John C. Calhoun, of South Carolina. The National Republican candidates were John Quincy
Adams, of Massachusetts, and Richard Rush, of Pennsylvania.[1] The candidates on both sides were nomi-

---

[1] It will be noticed that the candidates of both parties were 'sectional'

nated by common consent, or by State Legislatures The system of Congressional caucuses had been abandoned, and that of National Conventions had not yet been adopted. The **Presidential Election** in November resulted in the complete success of the Democratic electors.

12. Congress met December 1st, 1828. In his **XXth Congress,** Message the President for the **2d Session.** first time earnestly advocated Protection. This Session was uneventful, as is usually the case after an exciting Presidential election. The Democratic majority were not disposed to obstruct the Administration while engaged in putting its affairs in order for its successor. After long debate upon their constitutionality, unusually large appropriations were voted for **Internal Improvements,** and approved by the President. In February, 1829, the electoral votes were counted, and were found to be, for President, 178 for Jackson, and 83 for Adams, and, for Vice-President, 171 for Calhoun, 7 for William Smith, of South Carolina, and 83 for Rush. **Jackson** and **Calhoun** were therefore declared elected. March 3d, 1829, Congress adjourned, and March 4th **Jackson and Calhoun** were sworn into office.

# CHAPTER XII.

## ELEVENTH ADMINISTRATION, 1829-1833.

Andrew Jackson, President.     John C. Calhoun, Vice-President
XXIst and XXIId Congresses.

*Popular vote for President in* 1828 *:*[1] *Jackson (Dem.)* 647,231, *Adams (Nat. Rep.)* 509,097.

1. **Jackson's First Administration** was stormy in both foreign and domestic relations. Serious disagreements with England as to commerce with her colonies and the boundary between Maine and British America, and with France as to the payment of the long standing indemnity for French spoliations, repeatedly threatened war, but were all peaceably settled. At home the Administration was engaged in constant struggle with its opponents, the National Republicans, the Anti-Masons, and the United States Bank, and was abandoned by a part of its own party, the Loose Constructionists, who advocated Protection and Internal Improvements, and the Nullificationists. The

---

[1] Hitherto electors had been generally chosen by the State Legislatures. After 1824 they were chosen generally by popular vote. South Carolina continued to choose electors by State Legislature until 1868.

President's final success came from the impossibility of a hearty union of his opponents, though many doubtful voters were attracted to him by his military achievements, by the undoubted sincerity of his intentions, and by natural sympathy for one man contending against odds.

2. The **National Republicans** were in a minority in 1829, but were continually reinforced by loose constructionist Democrats. They never became a majority party, but, by combining with the other elements of opposition, were frequently able to thwart the President's plans, and even to censure his actions. Their leader was Henry Clay, now Senator from Kentucky. His popularity with his party was already great, though not so unbounded as afterward, when the Whig party almost became Clay's personal party.

3. In 1826 William Morgan, of Batavia, New York, who had advertised a book exposing the secrets of Free Masonry, was kidnapped and never seen again. The crime was charged upon the society, and investigation, as it was alleged, was impeded by leading Free Masons. A party soon grew up in Western New York, pledged to oppose the election of any Free Mason to public office. The **Anti-Masonic Party** acquired influence in other States, and began to claim rank as a national political party. On most points its principles were those of the National Republicans. But Clay, as well as Jackson, was a Free Mason, and consequently to be opposed by this party.[1]

---

[1] In 1832 it even nominated a Presidential ticket of its own, but, having no national principle of controlling importance, it soon after declined.

4. Financial mismanagement, and the distress growing out of the War of 1812, had compelled Republicans in 1816 to abandon their strict constructionist principles and charter a **National Bank** for twenty years. It was empowered to hold $55,000,000 in property, to issue $35,000,000 in notes receivable by the United States as cash for all debts, had the use without interest of the United States revenues deposited with it, and was not amenable to State Laws. It had friends and dependents in all parts of the Union, some seated in Congress, and many prominent in both parties. Its power seemed to Jackson anti-democratic, and his first Message opened upon it a war which soon drove it into politics, and ultimately destroyed it.

5. Among Jackson's warmest supporters were many who were sufficiently loose constructionist in opinion to support **Protection** and **Internal Improvements.** Jackson himself had formerly been no opponent of either, and on that account had been objectionable to the Crawford faction. His increasing dislike to both became apparent soon after the meeting of Congress in 1829, and alienated many of his supporters. But these very generally returned to his support when he had yielded to necessity, and, at least i appearance, ceased his opposition to their favorit measures.

6. The extreme Democracy of the South had only accepted Jackson because of the loss of their former leader, Crawford. As the progress of Jackson's Administration showed that he could not be relied upon

as a representative of their determined hostility to Protection, they learned to regard Vice-President Calhoun as their leader. They had already acted upon the doctrines of the Kentucky and Virginia Resolutions of 1798,[1] and the States of Georgia and South Carolina, through their Legislatures, had protested against the Tariff of 1828 as unjust and unconstitutional. Finding that this protest had no effect upon other States or upon Congress, they advanced, during Jackson's first Administration, to the ground taken by the Kentucky Resolutions of 1799,[2] affirming the right of *any State* to declare null and void any Act of Congress which, the State being judge, appeared unconstitutional. This was the doctrine of **Nullification**, which grew to Secession in 1860.[3]

7. After the first great party overthrow in the United States, the new President, Jefferson, though he found many Federalists in office, had been able to trust to time and the assured future supremacy of his party to bring about a change of occupants of public offices. Successive Presidents of the same political belief saw no necessity of changes. But Jackson, following a President who had almost created a hostile party, and being opposed by so many open and concealed enemies, decided to fill every vacancy with a partizan of the Administration, and, further, to create vacancies, whenever it should seem of party advantage, by exer-

---

[1] See page 46.  [2] See page 47.
[3] Its announcement in 1832 drew from Madison a protest against the use of Jefferson's name "as a pedestal for this colossal heresy."

cising the almost unused privilege of **Removal from Office.** This made necessary, during the summer of 1829, the application of the comparatively novel theory of "rotation in office,"[1] by which nearly 500 postmasters were removed during Jackson's first year of office The practice thus begun in self-defense has since been adopted by all parties in all elections, great and small, national and local.

8. **XXIst Congress, 1st Session.** Congress met December 7th, 1829, with a Democratic majority in both branches. In the House Andrew Stevenson was again chosen Speaker. But his overwhelming majority (152–39) did not long cohere. The **President's Message** avoided the Tariff question, and advised the election of President and Vice-President directly by the people, an inquiry into the constitutionality and advisability of renewing the Bank's charter in 1836, and the distribution of surplus revenue among the States in preference to using it for Internal Improvements. Such recommendations were enough to alienate many supporters of the Administration at once, and the committees to which they were referred reported in flat opposition to the President's views.

9. In the Senate a resolution was introduced by Foot, of Connecticut, directing an inquiry into the expediency of limiting public land sales in future. The debate upon this apparently harmless resolution lasted intermittently for five months, and drifted off to a great

---

[1] Stated by Marcy, of New York, in the Senate, as the axiom that "the spoils of the enemy belong to the victor."

variety of subjects, such as Slavery, Western and Southern grievances, New England Federalism, the relative powers of the State and Federal Governments, and Nullification. During its progress, in February, 1830, the doctrine of Nullification was formally announced by Hayne, of South Carolina, in reply to Webster, of Massachusetts, but limited, as yet, to peaceable resistance. The eloquence, learning, and party zeal of the **" Great Debate in the Senate,"** as it has always been called, make it almost a political history of the United States up to its date.

10. The case of the **Cherokee Indians** in Georgia was introduced at this Session. Under treaties with the United States these Indians held lands desired by the State. Acts were passed by the Legislature to open up the Indian country to white settlers, against the protest of the Indians. To settle the trouble an Act was passed at this Session to pay the Indians for their lands and to remove them beyond the Mississippi. It was opposed with much feeling by the National Republicans, and failed to accomplish its purpose, for the Indians refused to sell their lands.

11. A bill was passed at this Session authorizing a Government subscription to the stock of the **Maysville Turnpike Road** in Kentucky. The President, believing that Congress had no power to pass such a aw, vetoed it. Two days before the adjournment of Congress two bills of a similar nature to that of the Maysville Turnpike bill were passed. The President could legally retain them for ten days before signing

them. He did so, and in the interval came the day previously fixed for the adjournment of Congress, while the bills remained, as it were, in the President's pocket, without force of law. This new method of veto, angrily called a **Pocket Veto**, was employed by the President on several occasions afterward. Congress adjourned May 31st, 1830.

12. April 13th, 1830, the leading Democrats at Washington gave a dinner to celebrate **Jefferson's Birthday.** At the close of the regular toasts, which had been so drawn as to suggest Nullification, the President rebuked the whole proceeding by giving a volunteer toast, "Our Federal Union: it *must* be preserved." The Vice-President retorted with another to "Liberty, dearer than the Union." These counter defiances called the attention of the whole country to the progress of Nullification among Democratic leaders, and indirectly gave the Nullificationists warning to regard the President as an obstacle to their designs. Calhoun, for whom Jackson had previously had a high regard, and from whose friends he had in great part formed his Cabinet, recognized the President's growing suspicion and dislike of him, and spent the summer of 1830 in obtaining materials, by letter and otherwise, for a pamphlet criticism of Jackson's course in the Seminole War of 1818.

13. Congress met December 6th, 1830. The President's Message again attacked the Bank, and argued against the power of Congress to vote public money for any

XXIst Congress, 2d Session.

internal improvement which was local in its nature, and not beneficial to the country at large. The temper of Congress was not that of the President. A **Harbor Improvement Bill** was at once introduced and passed by majorities so large that the President yielded and signed it. He also signed other bills of a similar nature, making large appropriations for the improvement of roads and rivers, and for a light-house system. Much of this Session was taken up by the impeachment and trial of Judge Peck, of Missouri, which had no political bearing. Congress adjourned March 3d, 1831.

14. The long promised attack upon the President by Vice-President Calhoun appeared in March, 1831, and was followed by the **Breaking up of the Cabinet.** Its Calhoun element had for a long time lost the confidence of the President, who apparently trusted more to the advice of Van Buren, Secretary of State, and some private friends, commonly called the Kitchen Cabinet. Van Buren, to whose machinations Calhoun attributed the bad feeling between himself and the President, at once resigned, and the other members of the Cabinet, by request, followed his example.[1]

15. Congress met December 5th, 1831. The Senate, though doubtful at first, proved to have an Opposition majority. In the house Speaker Stevenson, the Administration candidate, was re-elected by one vote (98–97). The President's Message attacked the **Bank**

**XXIId Congress, 1st Session.**

---

[1] It was commonly believed, however, that the breaking up of the Cabinet was precipitated by trouble between the families of its members.

for the third time, and, although its charter still had five years to run, it felt compelled to begin the conflict. It therefore made application for a renewal of its charter. The President's supporters in the House asked for an investigation of the affairs of the Bank. The committee appointed for this purpose made two reports, the majority approving, and the minority condemning, the Bank's management. After long debate the bill to renew the charter passed both Houses, and was vetoed by the President, July 10th, 1832. An effort to pass it over the veto lacked a two-thirds majority, and failed. The veto made many new friends and many new enemies for the President, but only increased the bitterness of the struggle between him and the Bank.

16. In January, 1832, the **Nomination of Martin Van Buren**, of New York, late Secretary of State, to be Minister to England, came up in the Senate for confirmation. His nomination was rejected, although he was already in England. The vote was so arranged as to make a tie (23-23), thus giving Vice-President Calhoun the "vengeance" of a casting vote on the rejection. The spiteful feeling shown by some of the Opposition probably made the rejection rather a benefit to Van Buren.

17. At this Session a bill was passed and signed by the President, appropriating $1,200,000 for **Internal Improvements.** Another bill of a similar nature was also passed, but was killed by a "pocket veto." The **Tariff of 1832** was passed and signed by the

President. It was intended and expected to pacify the continued discontent in the South, particularly in South Carolina. This it failed to accomplish, for, though it reduced the duties of 1828, it still recognized the *principle* of Protection. Congress adjourned July 14th, 1832.

18. Presidential nominations were made this year for the first time by all the parties in **National Conventions.** All three Conventions were held at Baltimore. That of the Anti-Masons was held first, in September, 1831, in the hope of compelling the National Republicans to abandon Clay, and adopt the Anti Masonic candidates. Judge McLean, of Ohio, having declined a nomination, William Wirt, of Virginia, and Amos Ellmaker, of Pennsylvania, were nominated. In December, 1831, the National Republican Convention nominated Henry Clay, of Kentucky, and John Sergeant, of Pennsylvania. The platform pronounced in favor of Internal Improvements, Protection, and the Bank, and against the Administration and its course in the Cherokee case. Jackson had already (in February, 1830) been renominated for the Presidency by his friends in the New York Legislature. In March, 1832, the Democratic National Convention confirmed this renomination, and nominated Martin Van Buren, of New York, for the Vice-Presidency. For his success in gaining the nomination Van Buren was indebted to Calhoun's "vengeance."

19. In the **Presidential Election** in November South Carolina held sullenly off from both parties and

chose electors pledged to candidates of her own, John Floyd, of Virginia, and Henry Lee, of Massachusetts. Anti-Masonic electors were chosen by Vermont alone. All the other States, with the exception of six, chose Democratic electors. But Jackson's popular majority was smaller than at his first election, and the Opposition, if it had been possible to unite it, might have defeated him.

20. Southern politicians had perhaps only aimed at obtaining the repeal of the Tariff of 1828 by *threats* of Nullification and Secession. But when the modified Tariff of 1832 showed that Protection in some form was to be the settled policy of the Government, they had lost control of their constituents, and were compelled to follow the current. In the case of the Cherokee Indians, the State of Georgia had already nullified an Act of Congress, and refused obedience to the United States Supreme Court. Emboldened by this example, and by the belief that the passage of Federal troops across Virginia and North Carolina would be forcibly resisted by those States, a State Convention, held at Columbia, S. C., November 19th, 1832, formally declared the Tariffs of 1828 and 1832 to be "null, void, and no law, nor binding upon South Carolina, her officers and citizens," made any appeal to the United States Supreme Court a punishable offense, prescribed an oath of obedience to this ordinance to be taken by all jurors and State officers, and concluded with a warning to the other States that any attempt at force would be followed by the secession of South

Carolina from the Union.  The **Ordinance of Nullification** was to take effect February 1st, 1833.  In November the State Legislature met and proceeded to make the State ready for war, and to pass various Acts re-assuming those powers which had been expressly bandoned under the Constitution.

21.  December 16th, 1832, the President issued his **Proclamation** to the people of South Carolina.  It reviewed the history of Nullification, showed its treason, danger, and folly, and declared his unflinching purpose of carrying out the laws in the face of any resistance whatever.  He followed up his words by occupying Charleston Harbor with a naval force, and providing guards for the protection of officials engaged in collecting the revenue under the Tariff of 1832.

22.  Congress met December 3d, 1832.  Soon afterward Calhoun resigned the Vice-Presidency, and became Senator from South Carolina.  Early in 1833 he took an opportunity to declare that his State had never intended forcible resistance to the Federal Government, and a meeting of leading Nullifiers in Charleston decided to yield to the collection of the revenue until after the adjournment of Congress.  At this Session a **Bill for Enforcing the Tariff**[1] was passed and signed by the President.  It provoked much angry declamation in South Carolina, but no secession.  After long discussion of various proposed modifications of the Tariff,

**XXIId Congress, 2d Session.**

---

[1] Commonly called, in South Carolina, the "Bloody Bill." Its opponents in the Senate refused to vote, with the exception of John Tyler, of Virginia.

Clay's **Compromise Tariff of 1833** was passed, and signed by the President. It provided for the gradual reduction of the Tariff until 1842, after which year the duties on all goods were to be 20 per cent. The Nullificationists claimed this as a complete triumph, and the Anti-Tariff excitement in South Carolina ended at once.

23. Not even Nullification could compel the President to desist for a time from his warfare upon the **United States Bank.** In his Message at this Session he astonished Congress and the country by expressing doubts of the solvency of the Bank. He recommended a cessation of the deposits of United States revenue in it, and a sale of the stock belonging to the United States. Both these propositions were easily defeated by the Congressional friends of the Bank. Clay's bill for the loan to the States of the proceeds of the sales of public lands was passed, but was disposed of by a " pocket veto."

24. In February, 1833, the electoral votes were counted, and were found to be, for President, 219 for Jackson, 49 for Clay, 11 for Floyd, and 7 for Wirt, and, for Vice-President, 189 for Van Buren, 30 for William Wilkins, of Pennsylvania, 49 for Sergeant, 11 for Lee, and 7 for Ellmaker. **Jackson** and **Van Buren** were therefore declared elected. March 2d, 1833, Congress adjourned, and March 4th Jackson and Van Buren were sworn into office.

# CHAPTER XIII.

## TWELFTH ADMINISTRATION, 1833-1837.

**Andrew Jackson, President.**   Martin Van Buren, Vice-President.
XXIIId and XXIVth Congresses.

*Popular vote for President in* 1832 : *Jackson (Dem.)* 687,502, *Clay (Nat. Rep.)* 530,189.

1. THE Act of 1816, which created the Bank of the United States, required that the public moneys should be deposited in it, subject to removal at any time on the order of the Secretary of the Treasury, with the proviso that the Secretary should afterwards give Congress his reasons for such removal. At the last Session the President had recommended Congress to order the removal of the deposits from the Bank, and Congress, by large majorities, had refused to do so. The President, taking his re-election as a popular approval of his war upon the Bank, now determined to assume the responsibility of removal himself.

2. With this view he removed (in the Spring of 1833) the Secretary of the Treasury, who would not consent to remove the deposits, and appointed William J

Duane, of Pennsylvania, in his place. He proved to be no more compliant than his predecessor. After many attempts to persuade him, the President announced to the Cabinet his final decision that the deposits must be removed. The **Reasons** given were that the law gave the Secretary, not Congress, control of the deposits, that it was improper to leave them longer in a bank whose charter would so soon expire, that the Bank's funds had been largely used for political purposes, that its inability to pay all its depositors had been shown by its efforts to procure an extension of time from its creditors in Europe, and that its four Government directors had been systematically kept from knowledge of its management. Secretary Duane refused either to remove the deposits or to resign his office, and pronounced the proposed removal unnecessary, unwise, vindictive, arbitrary, and unjust. He was at once removed from office, and Roger B. Taney, of Maryland, appointed in his place.

3. The necessary **Orders for Removal** were given by Secretary Taney. It was not strictly a removal, for all previous deposits were left in the Bank, to be drawn upon until exhausted. It was rather a cessation. The deposits were afterwards made in various State banks,[1] and the Bank of the United States was compelled to call in its loans. The commercial distress which followed in consequence probably strengthened the President in the end by giving a convincing proof of the Bank's power as an antagonist to the Government.

---

[1] Commonly called the "pet banks."

4. **XXIIId Congress, 1st Session.** Congress met December 2d, 1833. In the Senate the still existing alliance between the National Republicans and the Calhoun States Rights Democracy formed a majority against the Administration and in favor of the Bank. In the House the strong Administration majority was shown by the re-election of Speaker Stevenson, Democrat, (142–61). The President's Message and the report of the Secretary of the Treasury defended the removal of the deposits. In the Senate Clay at once introduced condemnatory resolutions, which were debated for three months and then passed. The first declared the reasons given for the removal to be unsatisfactory and insufficient. The second was modified during the debate into a declaration that the President by removing the deposits "had assumed upon himself authority and power not conferred by the Constitution and laws, but in derogation of both." To the Senate's **Resolution of Censure** the President replied by a protest, on the ground that it accused him of perjury in violating his oath of office, and was thus an indirect and illegal method of impeachment, a condemnation against which he had no opportunity to defend himself. The Senate refused to receive the protest or place it upon record.

5. In the House the President's Message was followed by the appointment of a committee to investigate the affairs of the Bank. The majority report complained that the powers of the committee had been so restricted by the Bank that a full investigation had

been impossible. The minority report approved the Bank and its management. In April the House passed resolutions that the Bank ought not to be re-chartered, and that the deposits ought not to be restored. In June the Senate resolution, condemning the reasons for the removal of the deposits, came to the House for concurrence, and was tabled. The long struggle was thus practically ended by the **Success of the President.** The Bank of the United States was soon afterward chartered by the State of Pennsylvania, but no longer had the funds of the United States at its disposal.[1]

6. **Rejections of the President's Nominations** by the Senate were frequent at this Session. The four Government Directors of the Bank, who had joined the President in attacking it, were renominated by him, and rejected. The rejected names were again sent to the Senate, and again rejected. No more nominations for Government Directors were made at this Session. Secretary Taney's nomination was not sent to the Senate until June, 1834, and was then rejected. Speaker Stevenson's nomination to be Minister to England was also rejected. An unsuccessful attempt was made to limit the President's appointing power, and his appointments to office for political reasons were severely condemned by the Senate. A committee of

---

[1] These were at first deposited in various State banks. In the Session of 1834–35 the "Sub-Treasury plan" was suggested by the Opposition, and voted down by the Democrats. Later, it was adopted by the Democrats, and made law against the Whig efforts to revive a National Bank. It has since remained in force.

the House investigated the **Post Office Department** at this Session, and reported that it had been managed without frugality, system, intelligence, or adequate public utility. As the investigating committee was composed of supporters of the Administration, their eport was decisive. A bill for reforming the Post Office Department was introduced and passed. Congress adjourned June 30th, 1834.

7. Congress met December 1st, 1834. There was little party contest at this Session. Further appropriations were made for **Internal Improvements.** Regulations were made to govern the deposit of public moneys in State banks. This system of deposit, called the **State Bank System,** still received the support of the Democrats. The Opposition proposed at this Session the system afterwards known as the "Sub-Treasury plan," by which agents of the United States Treasury were to be appointed, wherever necessary, to receive and disburse United States revenue, giving suitable bonds for the performance of their duties. The Sub-Treasury plan was voted down. Congress adjourned March 3d, 1835.

**XXIIId Congress, 2d Session.**

8. The President wished Vice-President Van Buren to be his successor. He therefore recommended that the Democratic nomination should be made in National Convention. This was opposed by the friends of the other Democratic candidate, Hugh L. White, of Tennessee, who had been nominated by the Alabama Legislature The convention, which met at Baltimore

in May, 1835, was attended only by Van Buren delegates. It nominated Martin Van Buren, of New York, and Richard M. Johnson, of Kentucky, and adopted no platform. The friends of White supported John Tyler, of Virginia, for Vice-President. The National Republicans had by this time generally adopted the name of **Whigs**.[1] They generally supported the candidates nominated by the Whig and Anti-Masonic State Conventions of Pennsylvania, William H. Harrison, of Ohio, and Francis Granger, of New York. John McLean, of Ohio, and Daniel Webster, of Massachusetts, were also nominated for the Presidency by the Legislature of those States. All these nominations, however were made over a year before the Presidential election took place.

9. Congress met December 7th, 1835. In the Senate the Opposition, composed of Whigs, Nullification Democrats, and Anti-Masons, were at first a majority, but the Administration gained a majority toward the end of the Session. In the House there was a strong Administration majority, divided into Van Buren and White factions. James K. Polk, of Tennessee, a Democrat, was chosen Speaker. The President's Messag announced that the National Debt would soon be pai off. The expected **Surplus of Revenue** caused long debate in Congress. In June, 1836, an Act was

**XXIVth Congress,**
**1st Session.**

---

[1] The name seems to have been first used by them in New York in the Winter of 1834-35. The name "Loco-foco" was at the same time given to the Democrats by the Whigs.

passed providing that, after January 1st, 1837, all surplus revenue exceeding $5,000,000 should be divided among the States as a *loan*, only to be recalled by direction of Congress.[1] The President signed the bill. June 15th, 1836, **Arkansas** became a State, after some opposition to its application as irregular. Congress adjourned July 4th, 1836.

10. After the fall of the United States Bank a number of State banks had been formed, often without adequate capital, to supply the expected need of paper money. Their notes were used in large quantities for the purchase of public lands from the United States, and the Treasury was thus accumulating paper currency of doubtful worth. Soon after the adjournment of Congress the Secretary of the Treasury, by direction of the President, issued the so-called **Specie Circular**, ordering United States agents to receive in future only gold and silver in payment for lands. This caused a demand for specie which could only be met by the banks in which the revenue was deposited. Other banks fell into difficulties which culminated in the "Panic of 1837."

11. The Opposition had hoped to throw the **Presidential Election** of 1836 into the House, but did not succeed in doing so, for a majority of Van Buren electors were chosen. The White electors carried the States of Georgia and Tennessee. The Whig vote was largely increased since the last election.

---

[1] This distribution amounted to $28,000,000, none of which was ever recalled. It ceased in 1837 (p. 125).

12. **Congress met December 5th, 1836. XXIVth Congress, 2d Session.** January 26th, 1837, Michigan became a State of the Union In the Senate this Session was noteworthy for the final success of the President's supporters. When Clay' Resolution of Censure, against which the President had protested, was passed, Senator Benton of Missouri, had given notice that he would offer a resolution each year to expunge it. At this Session his resolution was carried and put into effect at once.[1]

13. **Texas**, which had been bargained away by Southern votes in 1819, was now a prize which the South longed to regain, as an offset to the rapidly multiplying Northern States. It had become a part of the Mexican State of Coahuila, had been colonized by Americans, and had declared its independence. The President's Message advised Congress not to interfere in the struggle between Mexico and Texas. Nevertheless a resolution recognizing the independence of Texas was passed by the Senate, but failed in the House.

14. In 1833 the **National Anti-Slavery Society** had been formed, and its branches multiplied rapidly. The renewal of the Slavery question alarmed the Southern States and many of the Northern people who considered any attack upon Slavery dangerous to the peace of the Union. From this time dates the

---

[1] The Resolution of 1834 on the Senate Journal was marked around by broad black lines, with the inscription "Expunged by order of the Senate this 16th day of January, 1937."

existence of the party opposed to Slavery in the United States, at first known as **Abolitionists**. A requisition was made by Georgia upon the State of New York for a leading Abolitionist, who had been indicted by a Georgia jury, and rewards were offered by citizens' committees in the South for the bodies of others, dead or alive, but without success. Finally mob violence was resorted to in Boston and other Northern cities, to destroy Abolition printing presses, break up Abolition meetings, and intimidate Abolition orators. At least one person (Lovejoy) was shot to death.

15. These lawless outrages only increased the zeal of the Abolitionists in offering **Petitions to Congress** to abolish Slavery in the District of Columbia, and in sending Abolitionist books and papers to every part of the country. At its last Session the House had resolved to lay all future petitions on the subject of Slavery upon the table, without further action or notice. At this Session the President's Message made indignant reference to the practice of sending Abolition documents through the United States mails. He recommended a bill to prohibit the practice in future. A bill was consequently introduced in the Senate, prohibiting any postmaster from knowingly putting any Abolition newspapers or documents into the mails. The bill was rejected.

16. In February, 1837, the electoral votes were counted, and were found to be, for President, 170 for Van Buren, 73 for Harrison, 26 for White, 14 for Webster, and 11 for W. P. Mangum, of North Caro-

lina, and, for Vice-President, 147 for Johnson, 77 for Granger, 47 for Tyler, and 23 for William Smith, of Alabama.[1] **Van Buren** was therefore declared elected President. No candidate having received a majority of all the votes for Vice-President, the Senate chose **Richard M. Johnson.** President Jackson issued a Farewell Address to the American People before leaving office. March 3d, 1837, Congress adjourned, and March 4th Van Buren and Johnson were sworn into office.

---

[1] The three votes of Michigan for Van Buren and Johnson are included in the above count, though the State was not fully admitted until after the election. They did not affect the result

# CHAPTER XIV.

### THIRTEENTH ADMINISTRATION, 1837-1841.

Martin Van Buren, President. Richard M. Johnson, Vice-President XXVth and XXVIth Congresses.

*Popular vote for President in 1836: Dem. 761,549, Combined Opposition 736,656.*

1. **The New Administration** had taken Jackson's Cabinet, and the President had declared his intention "to follow in the footsteps of his illustrious predecessor." He therefore caught the first full effects of the storm produced by Jackson's financial policy, from which even Jackson's popularity and admitted honesty would hardly have saved him. The excessive amount of paper money in circulation had encouraged reckless speculation, and nominally raised property to more than its real value. The Specie Circular of 1836 by reviving the demand for gold and silver, had destroyed most of the banks which had not Government deposits at command. The demand for the deposits, for distribution among the States, completed the ruin of many of the "pet banks." They had treated the

deposits as capital, to be used in loans to business men and now had to return them.

2. The sudden calling in of these loans began the **Panic of 1837**, to which nothing comparable had before been seen in America. Early in May the New York City banks refused to pay gold or silver for their notes, and the New York Legislature authorized a suspension of specie payments throughout the State for one year. Banks in other cities at once suspended. May 15th, the President, by Proclamation, called an Extra Session of Congress, to meet September 4th, and consider and secure the financial interests of the Government. During the summer of 1837 the Panic continued its course, wrecking banks and corporations, bankrupting business men, and violently reducing fictitious fortunes to their real value.

3. Congress met September 4th, 1837. In the Senate there was an Administration majority. **XXVth Congress. Extra Session.** In the House James K. Polk, of Tennessee, a Democrat, was re-elected Speaker, though the vote (116–103) shows a great increase of Whig members. Most of the Calhoun Democracy were now supporting the Administration. The **President's Message** recommended that Government should not interfere directly with the Panic, believing that it would finally right itself more safely and easily. He also recommended the adoption by the Government of the "Sub-Treasury plan."[1] This was regarded by the Whigs, and by some of the Dem

---

[1] See page 119. It is otherwise called the "Independent Treasury Plan."

ocrats, as an endeavor to break down all the banks in the country. Its Democratic opponents formed a temporary party, calling themselves **Conservatives**, and generally voting with the Whigs on financial matters. A bill for the establishment of an Independent Treasury passed the Senate, but was tabled in the House by a combination of Whigs and Conservatives. Acts were passed to cease the distribution of revenue among the States, to authorize the issue of $10,000,000 in Treasury notes, and to give merchants further time on their revenue bonds. Congress adjourned October 16th.

4. **XXVth Congress, 1st Session.** Congress met December 4th, 1837. The bill for the establishment of an Independent Treasury was again pressed upon Congress by the Administration. It passed the Senate by a small majority, and was again defeated in the House by a Union of Whigs and Conservatives. The only measure for the relief of business passed at this Session was a joint resolution directing the Secretary of the Treasury to receive the notes of specie paying banks in payment for public lands, thus annulling the Specie Circular. The first open attempt to unite Texas to the United States was made at this Session, but failed. Congress adjourned July 9th, 1838.

5. **XXVth Congress, 2d Session.** Congress met December 3d, 1838. There was little party contest at this Session. Discussion was confined mainly to the Seminole War in Florida, for whose prosecution large amounts had been voted, with little ap

parent prospect of a successful termination. The apparent disinclination of Congress and the Administration to interfere in the financial troubles of the country, while it agreed with the strict constructionist theory of the powers of the Federal Government, operated to the disadvantage of the Democratic party. Many of its former supporters were now ready to try Whig government. Congress adjourned March 3d, 1839.

6. Congress met December 2d, 1839. Continuous **Whig Successes** had given them a fair prospect of a majority, in the House. Outside of New Jersey 119 Democrats and 118 Whigs had been returned to the House. In New Jersey members of the House were at that time elected on a general ticket by the whole State. The five Whig candidates had certificates of election under the broad seal of the State,[1] while the five Democratic candidates contested their election on the ground of a miscount in one county. The admission of either delegation would give its party a majority in the House. For three days a disorderly debate continued, there being no presiding officer until December 5th, when John Quincy Adams was spasmodically chosen chairman *pro tempore*. Unsucessful attempts to choose a Speaker were made for two weeks longer many motions being voted upon by both the New Jersey delegations. December 17th, R. M. T. Hunter, of Virginia, a Sub-Treasury Whig, was chosen Speaker The **New Jersey Question** was not settled until

---
[1] Hence this contest is often called the Broad Seal War.

March, 1840, when the Democratic delegation was seated, many Whigs not voting because of lack of time to examine the evidence in the case.

7. The party contest over the organization of the House took up so much time that few measures of general interest were passed at this Session. The most notable event was the final success of the **Independent Treasury Scheme,** which had twice been rejected by the previous Congress. It was passed by both Houses, and signed by the President.[1] The "divorce of bank and state," which the President had been laboring to accomplish, was thus successful. The strict constructionist policy of the President was also successful in the entire suspension of appropriations for Internal Improvements.[2] Congress adjourned July 21st, 1840.

8. The **Whig National Convention** met at Harrisburgh, Pa., December 4th, 1839. It adopted no platform. For the purpose of uniting the Anti-Masonic and other opposition elements it reluctantly abandoned Clay, and nominated William H. Harrison, of Ohio, and John Tyler, of Virginia.[3] The **Democratic National Convention** met at Baltimore,

---

[1] It will be seen that the Whigs at the next Session made unsuccessful attempts to substitute a National Bank for the "Sub-Treasury plan."

[2] The tools, etc., belonging to the Government were ordered to be sold at auction.

[3] Tyler was a Strict Constructionist, a Calhoun Democrat, who had refused to follow the rest of his faction in supporting the Administration. His nomination was intended to gratify the Southern portion of the Opposition by an office of much honor and little importance.

May 5th, 1840, and adopted a strict constructionist platform, denying the power of Congress to carry on Internal Improvements, to protect manufactures, to charter a National Bank, or to interfere with Slavery in he States. It unanimously renominated the President, but left nominations for the Vice-Presidency to be made by the various States. The Abolitionists, or **Liberty Party,** made Presidential nominations November 13th, 1839. The candidates were James G. Birney, of New York, and Francis Lemoyne, of Pennsylvania.

9. The nomination of General Harrison, and the Whig attacks upon Van Buren and his financial policy, created an enthusiasm which Van Buren's nomination did not meet. Log-cabins and hard cider, which were supposed to be typical of Harrison's frontier life, became popular with the Whigs, whose hopes were renewed by their success in the State elections of the summer and fall of 1840. At the **Presidential Election** in November the united opposition abundantly gratified their personal hostility to Van Buren. The Whig electors were overwhelmingly successful. Democratic electors were chosen by only two Northern, and five Southern States. The new Abolition party did not succeed in choosing any electors, but polled a popular vote of 7,609.

10. Congress met December 7th, 1840. There was **XXVIth Congress, 2d Session.** little party contest at this Session. In February, 1841, the electoral votes were counted, and were found to be, for

President, 234 for Harrison, and 60 for Van Buren, and for Vice-President, 234 for Tyler, 48 for Richard M. Johnson, of Kentucky, 11 for L. W. Tazewell, of Virginia, and 1 for James K. Polk, of Tennessee. **Harrison** and **Tyler** were therefore declared elected March 3d, 1841, Congress adjourned, and March 4th Harrison and Tyler were sworn into office.

# CHAPTER XV.

## FOURTEENTH ADMINISTRATION, 1841-1845.

**William Henry Harrison, President,  John Tyler, Vice-President  
XXVIIth and XXVIIIth Congresses.**

*Popular vote for President in* 1840: *Whig* 1,275,017, *Democratic*, 1,128,702.

1. **The President's Inaugural Address** condemned any excessive use of the veto power, the employment for political purposes of Executive control over public officials, and all Presidential experiments upon the currency. March 17th the President, by proclamation, called an Extra Session of Congress, to meet May 31st and consider the financial difficulties of the Government. Before any further developments of the President's policy could take place, a short illness resulted in his death, April 4th. According to law **John Tyler** became President. He retained President Harrison's Cabinet, and promised to carry out his policy.

2. Congress met May 31st, 1841.[1] In the House

---

[1] Senate, 28 Whig, 22 Dem. House, 133 Whig, 108 Dem.

**XXVIIth Congress, Extra Session.** John White, of Kentucky, a Whig, was chosen Speaker The Whigs at once began the change in financial policy to which they were pledged. A bill to abolish the Sub-Treasury of the previous Administration was passed by both Houses and signed by the President A bill to incorporate **The Fiscal Bank of the United States** was passed by both Houses. It was weeded of many of the objectionable features of the old United States Bank, but was hardly less odious to the Democrats. It was vetoed by the President. His objection was that the powers given to the Bank were such as he and the majority of the people believed it to be unwise and unconstitutional for Congress to grant. An effort to pass the bill over the veto did not receive a two-thirds majority.

3. The Whig leaders, anxious to prevent a party disaster, asked from the President an outline of a bill which he would sign. After consultation with the Cabinet, it was given, and passed by both Houses. September 9th the President vetoed this bill also, and an attempt to pass it over the veto did not receive a two-thirds majority. The action of the President, in vetoing a bill drawn according to his own suggestions, and thus apparently provoking a contest with the party which had elected him, roused the unconcealed indignation of the Whigs. The Cabinet, with one exception,[1] at once resigned. The Whig members of Congress issued **Addresses to the People**, in which

---

[1] Daniel Webster, of Massachusetts, Secretary of State.

they detailed the reforms designed by the Whigs and impeded by the President, and declared that "all political connection between them and John Tyler was at an end from that day forth." At this Session an Act was passed to distribute the proceeds of the sales of public lands among the States. Congress adjourned September 13th, 1841.

4. **The President** filled the vacancies in the Cabinet by appointing Whigs and Conservatives. His position was one of much difficulty. His strict constructionist opinions, which had prevented him from supporting Van Buren, would not allow him to approve a National Bank, and yet he had accepted the Vice-Presidency from a party pledged to establish one. The over hasty declaration of war by the Whigs put a stop to his vacillations, and compelled him to rely upon support from the Democrats. But only a few members of Congress, commonly known as "the corporal's guard," recognized Tyler as a leader. The Democrats only supported him as a means to success, and were encouraged in so doing by the State elections of 1841, which were unfavorable to the Whigs.

5. Congress met December 6th, 1841. Although Congress had decided to refuse consideration to petitions for the abolition of Slavery, they continued to be sent. John Quincy Adams, of Massachusetts, made himself prominent in presenting them to the House, and an unsuccessful attempt was made to censure him In March, 1842, in the House, **Giddings**, of Ohio

**XXVIIth Congress, 1st Session.**

presented a set of resolutions which are noteworthy as containing the basis for the subsequent resistance to the extension of Slavery to the Territories. They declared that Slavery, being an abridgment of the natural rights of man, can exist only by force of positive municipal law, and is necessarily confined to the territorial jurisdiction of the power creating it. For offering these resolutions the House censured their author. He resigned his seat, was re-elected at a special election in April, and again took his seat in the House early in May.

6. The reduction of duties by the Compromise Tariff of 1833 had gone so far that the Government revenues were less than expenses. A new tariff became necessary and this brought on the struggle between Strict Constructionists and Loose Constructionists. The Whig majority passed a bill continuing for the present the duties under the Tariff of 1833, and providing for the distribution of any surplus revenue among the States. The President vetoed it, on the ground that it was in violation of the Compromise of 1833 by which Protection was to cease after 1842. A Tariff designed to afford a revenue was then passed by both Houses, still continuing the objectionable provision for the distribution of the surplus. This was also vetoed. In the House the Veto Message was referred to a committee, whose report condemned the President's undue assumption of power. Against this the President sent a formal protest. The bill was then passed by both Houses, without the distributing c'ause, signed by the President, and

became the **Tariff of 1842.** The distributing clause was passed as a separate bill, and disposed of by a "pocket veto." Congress adjourned August 31st, 1842.

7. Congress met December 5th, 1842. There was little party contest at this Session. On its last day a few Anti-Slavery Whigs issued an address to the people, warning them that the scheme for the annexation of **Texas** had never been abandoned, but was still in progress, and that its success would result in and justify a dissolution of the Union. Congress adjourned March 3d, 1843.

**XXVIIth Congress, 2d Session.**

8. Congress met December 4th, 1843. In the House John W. Jones, of Virginia, a Democrat, was chosen Speaker. The majority in the Senate was Whig, and in the House Democratic,[1] and the consequent disagreement prevented united action, and encouraged the President in his reliance upon the Democrats. The **President's Message** had recommended that any appropriations for Internal Improvements should be made for the benefit of the Western States. Two bills were passed, the Eastern Harbor Bill, and the Western Harbor Bill. The President signed the Western Bill, and vetoed the Eastern Bill. An attempt to pass it over the veto did not receive a two-thirds majority. The Administration concluded a treaty with Texas, providing for annexation. It was rejected by the Senate

**XXVIIIth Congress, 1st Session.**

---

[1] Senate, 28 Whig, 24 Dem. House, 142 Dem., 81 Whig.

by a strong vote (35–16), all the Whigs and 7 Democrats voting against it. Congress adjourned June 17th 1844.

9. The **Annexation of Texas** was now rapidly becoming a party question. The South was determined to accomplish it. It was felt that if the South must stop at the Sabine (the Eastern boundary of Texas), while the North might spread unchecked beyond the Rocky Mountains, "the Southern scale must kick the beam," and the existence of Slavery would be endangered. Before the National Conventions met the views of the leading candidates upon the question of annexation had been asked and given. Van Buren guardedly announced himself as opposed to the *present* annexation of Texas. Clay expressed himself more plainly to the same effect.

10. The National Convention of the **Liberty Party** met at Buffalo, August 30th, 1843. It adopted a long series of resolutions, denouncing Slavery, and calling upon the Free States for penal laws to stop the return of fugitive slaves. It nominated James G. Birney, of Michigan, and Thomas Morris, of Ohio. The **Whig National Convention** met at Baltimore, May 1st, 1844, and adopted a concise loose constructionist platform, advocating a national currency, a protective tariff, and a distribution of surplus revenue among the States. It nominated Henry Clay, of Kentucky, and Theodore Frelinghuysen, of New York. The **Democratic National Convention** met at Baltimore, May 27th, 1844, and again adopted its strict constructionist plat

form of 1840, with an additional article demanding the re-occupation of Oregon, and the re-annexation of Texas. A large majority of the delegates came pledged o vote for Van Buren, whose views on tne Texas uestion did not satisfy the Southern delegates. They succeeded in destroying his chances of a nomination by the adoption of the rule of two former Democratic Conventions, that nominations must be made by a two-thirds vote.[1] Van Buren had a majority, but not two-thirds. After eight ballots his name was withdrawn, and the Convention nominated James K. Polk, of Tennessee, and Silas Wright, of New York. Wright declined, and George M. Dallas, of Pennsylvania, was substituted. An abortive Convention of office-holders at Baltimore renominated Tyler. He accepted the nomination but soon withdrew.

11. The Democratic party was thus committed to the annexation of Texas, though the demand for the Tariff of 1842, and for "the whole of Oregon or none, with or without war with England" helped to gain votes. Nevertheless Whig success seemed probable until the appearance of an unfortunate letter of Clay's, in which he tried to conciliate Southern Democrats by saying that he would be "glad to see" the annexation take place at some future time. By this ill-judged piece of diplomacy he gained no Democratic votes, for Polk was a warm advocate of annexation, and lost those of the extreme Anti-Slavery Whigs and Abolitionists, who purposely threw away on Birney and

---

[1] This has since been the rule in Democratic National Conventions.

Morris a number of votes which would have carried New York and thus elected Clay. They were therefore the real agents in the election of Polk, the annexation of Texas, and the extension of Slavery to a vast amount of new territory.

12. The **Presidential Election** in November resulted in Democratic success. But it was the most closely contested election in our history, except those of 1800 and 1876. The result in 14 of the 26 States was doubtful for two days, and most of these chose Polk electors by very slender majorities. In several of them the small Abolition vote would have turned the scale, and chosen Clay electors. A majority of the members chosen to the XXIXth Congress were in favor of a lower Tariff than that of 1842.

13. **XXVIIIth Congress, 2d Session.** Congress met December 2d, 1844. A bill to organize a territorial government for Oregon, up to the line of 54° 40' North latitude, and beyond the line claimed by England as the true boundary, was passed by the House, but, as it prohibited Slavery, the Senate declined to consider it. The annexation of **Texas** took up most of the time of this Session. Mexico had abolished Slavery twenty years before, and therefor Texas was by Mexican law free territory.[1] Propositions to prohibit Slavery in Texas were voted down. The Joint Resolution to annex Texas was passed by both Houses, and signed by the President. It prohibited Slavery in any States to be formed from the ter

---

[1] The Republic of Texas, however had re-established Slavery by law.

ritory of Texas north of the Missouri Compromise Line (36° 30' North latitude), and left the question to be settled by the people in States formed south of that line

14. Appropriations were made at this Session for both Eastern and Western harbors. The President disposed of them by a pocket veto. In February, 1845, the electoral votes were counted and were found to be, for Polk and Dallas 170, and for Clay and Frelinghuysen 105. **Polk and Dallas** were therefore declared elected. March 3d, **Florida** became a State of the Union, and arrangements were made for the future admission of Iowa. The same day the President sent a messenger to secure the consent of Texas to the annexation. March 3d, 1845, Congress adjourned, and **March 4th Polk and Dallas were sworn into office.**

# CHAPTER XVI.

### FIFTEENTH ADMINISTRATION, 1845–1849.

James K. Polk, President.　　George M. Dallas Vice-President.
XXIXth and XXXth Congress.

*Popular vote for President in* 1844　*Dem.* 1,337,243,
*Whig* 1,299,068, *Ab.* 62,300.

1. THE policy of **Rotation in Office,** laid down by Jackson in 1829 and accepted by the Whigs in 1841, was now finally established by the new Administration. It has been the rule since that time that every Presidential election shall be marked by a wholesale removal of office-holders, whose places are filled by friends of the new Administration.

2. **Annexation** had been accepted by the Congress of Texas and by a Popular Convention. Mexico was so occupied by intestine dissensions and revolution that her exhibition of resentment was at first confined to a formal protest, and the withdrawal of her Minister from Washington. No aggressive movement was made by her even when United States troops under General Taylor occupied the Eastern bank of the Nueces River,

beyond which Texas had never hitherto exercised jurisdiction.

3. **XXIXth Congress, 1st Session.** Congress met December 1st, 1845, with a Democratic majority in both branches.[1] In the House John W. Davis, of Indiana, a Democrat, was chosen Speaker. The President's Message condemned all Anti-Slavery agitation, recommended a Sub-Treasury and a Tariff for Revenue, and spoke of the annexation of Texas as a matter which concerned only Texas and the United States. December 29th **Texas** became a State of the Union. December 31st an Act was passed extending the United States revenue system over the doubtful territory beyond the Nueces River, and a revenue officer was appointed to reside in the new district. Even these steps did not induce hostilities; Mexico still declared her willingness to negotiate concerning the disputed territory between the Nueces and the Rio Grande.

4. In March, 1846, **Hostilities** were precipitated by an order from the President to General Taylor to advance from the Nueces to the Rio Grande, and occupy the debatable district. He obeyed, and was thus brought face to face with Mexican troops. Early in May Arista, with 6,000 Mexicans, crossed the Rio Grande, attacked Taylor and his force of 2,300 men at Palo Alto, and was badly beaten. On the following day Taylor assumed the offensive, attacked Arista at Resaca de la Palma, and drove him in headlong retreat across the Rio Grande.

---

[1] Senate, 30 Dem., 25 Whig. House, 142 Dem., 75 Whig, and 6 others.

5. May 11th, 1846, the President sent a **War Message** to Congress in which he detailed the preliminary skirmishes on the Rio Grande, declared that Mexican troops had at last shed the blood of American citizens on American soil, and asked for a Declaration of War. A bill to recognize the existence of war, and to appropriate $10,000,000 for its prosecution, was at once passed by both Houses. Its preamble was as follows: "Whereas, by the act of the Republic of Mexico, a state of war exists between that government and the United States." This was considered a falsehood by the Whigs. They thought that President Polk had provoked hostilities by ordering the army into Mexican territory. Nevertheless they generally voted, under protest, for the declaration, on the ground that the army had been forced into a perilous situation, and must be rescued. On the same ground they generally supported the war until its conclusion. The Liberty party, particularly in New England, opposed the war bitterly.[1]

6. August 8th a Special Message from the President asked for money with which to purchase territory from Mexico, that the war might thus be settled by negotiation. A bill appropriating $2,000,000 for this purpose at once brought up the Slavery question, for it was certain that any newly acquired territory would swarm with slave-holders, who would demand protection in the possession of their slaves. In the House Wilmot, of Pennsylvania, on behalf of many Northern Demo-

---

[1] Their feeling is represented by Lowell's "Biglow Papers."

crats, offered an addition to the bill, applying to any newly acquired territory the provision of the Ordinance of 1787,[1] that "neither Slavery nor involuntary servitude shall ever exist in any part of said territory, except for crime, whereof the party shall first be duly convicted." This was the celebrated **Wilmot Proviso.** The Whigs and Northern Democrats united in favor of it, and it passed the House, but was sent to the Senate too late to be acted upon.

7. During this Session war with England upon the **Oregon Question** seemed imminent. By the treaties of 1803 with France, and 1819 with Spain, the United States had acquired the rights of those powers on the Pacific coast, north of California. The Northern boundary of the ceded territory was unsettled. The United States claimed that the boundary was the line 54° 40' North latitude. England claimed that it followed the Columbia River. By a convention of 1827 the disputed territory had been held by both countries jointly, the arrangement being terminable by either country on twelve months' notice. The last Democratic Convention had demanded the "*re*-occupation" of the whole of Oregon (up to 54° 40'), with or without war with England.[2] The "*re*-annexation" of Texas having been accomplished, the Whigs now began to urge the Democrats to carry out their programme in regard to Oregon. Against the votes of the extreme Southern Democrats, the President was

---
[1] See page 57.
[2] Popularly summed up as "fifty four-forty-or-fight"

directed to give the requisite twelve months' notice to England.

8. June 15th, 1846, the Oregon question was settled by a **Treaty with England,** by which the United States abandoned the line of 54° 40', and accepted hat of 49° North latitude as the Northern boundary A bill to organize the Territory of Oregon, with the Wilmot Proviso attached, was passed by the House, against the votes of the Southern Democrats, but was not acted upon by the Senate.

9. At this Session the **Tariff of 1846** was passed by a party vote. It followed the strict constructionist theory in aiming at a list of duties sufficient only to provide revenue for the Government, without regard to Protection. A **River and Harbor Improvement Bill** was passed by both Houses. It was vetoed by the President on the ground that the Constitution did not, in his opinion, give the Federal Government any power to appropriate money for the purpose of making Internal Improvements within the States. Congress adjourned August 13th, 1846.

10. Congress met December 7th, 1846. December 28th, **Iowa** became a State of the Union. The **President's Message** announced the continued success of the American arms in Mexico, and argued that the Rio Grande should be considered the Western boundary of Texas. The necessary measures for the prosecution of the war took up most of the time of this Session. A bill appropriating $3,000,000 for the purchase

**XXIXth Congress, 2d Session.**

of territory from Mexico was passed by the House
with the Wilmot Proviso attached. The Senate passed
the bill, but without the Wilmot Proviso, and, after unavailing struggle by the Whigs, the House adopted the
bill as it came from the Senate. The bill to organize
the Territory of Oregon, with the Wilmot Proviso, was
again passed by the House, and again left without action by the Senate. A motion in the House by a
Southern member to recognize the Missouri Compromise Line (36° 30′) as extending to the Pacific was
lost by a sectional vote, South against North. A River
and Harbor Improvement Bill was again passed but so
near the end of the Session that the President was able
to dispose of it by a "pocket veto." Congress adjourned March 3d, 1847.

11. **XXXth Congress, 1st Session.** Congress met December 6th, 1847, with a Democratic majority in the Senate, and a Whig majority in the House.[1] Robert C. Winthrop, of Massachusetts, a Whig, was chosen Speaker of the House. The subject of **Internal Improvements** was again brought up, and the House resolved by a large majority that the General Government had the power to improve harbors and rivers for the advantage of commerce and fo the common defense. A resolution embodying the substance of the Wilmot Proviso was tabled. It did not nave, as in the last Congress, the whole Free State Democratic vote in its favor.[2]

---

[1] Senate, 35 Dem., 21 Whig. House, 117 Whig, 108 Dem. Twenty-five Free State Democrats voted against it.

12. **Peace** was made with Mexico in February, 1848, and a large increase of territory was thereby gained by the United States. As a compromise between the advocates and the opponents of the extension of Slavery, a bill was passed by the Senate, establishing territorial governments in Oregon, New Mexico and California, with a provision that all questions concerning Slavery in those Territories should be referred to the United States Supreme Court for decision. It was voted for by the members from Slave States, and lost in the House. A bill was then passed in the House, by a sectional vote, to organize the **Territory of Oregon**, without Slavery. This was passed by the Senate, with an amendment declaring that the Missouri Compromise Line extended to the Pacific Ocean. This would have divided the United States into two parts, the Northern free, and the Southern slave. The amendment was rejected by the House, again by a sectional vote, and, the Senate withdrawing, the bill passed. Congress adjourned August 14th, 1848. May 29th **Wisconsin** had become a State of the Union.

13. The **Democratic National Convention** met at Baltimore, May 22d, 1848. It renewed the strict constructionist platform of 1840 and 1844, and nominated Lewis Cass, of Michigan, and William O. Butler, of Kentucky. A resolution that Congress had no power to interfere with Slavery, either in the States or in the Territories, was voted down by a heavy majority. The **Whig National Convention** met at Philadelphia, June 7th, and nominated Zachary Taylor, o

Louisiana, and Millard Fillmore, of New York. No platform was adopted, and resolutions affirming the Wilmot Proviso as a party principle were repeatedly voted down. It was thus evident that the Whigs were not ready to become an Anti-Slavery party, nor were the Democrats ready to become a Pro-Slavery party. The State of New York had sent two delegations to the Democratic Convention, the "Hunkers," or Conservatives, who wished to leave the Slavery question in abeyance, and the "Barnburners,"[1] or Free Soil Democrats, who opposed any further extension of Slavery into the Territories. The Convention admitted both, dividing the vote of New York between them. The Barnburners withdrew, and attended the National Convention of a new party, the **Free Soilers,** at Buffalo, August 9th. It adopted a platform declaring that Congress had no more power to make a slave than to make a king, and that there should be no more Slave States, and no more Slave Territories. It nominated Martin Van Buren, of New York, and Charles Francis Adams, of Massachusetts.

14. The Free Soilers (or Free Democracy) were joined by the old Liberty party, and by many Democrats who were offended at the support given by Southern Democrats to the efforts to establish Slavery in the territory lately won from Mexico. In the South many former Democrats preferred a slave-holding candidate without a platform to a non slave-holding candidate

---

[1] This was originally a term applied by their opponents to their supposed revolutionary principles. It made no charge of practical arson.

on a platform in which support of Slavery had been voted down. The **Presidential Election** in November resulted in the success of the Whig electors in majority both of the Free and of the Slave States. The belief of the Northern Democrats that they had been betrayed by the Southern Democrats in the election had its natural effect in the next Session of Congress, where the Free State Democrats voted for every measure aimed at Slavery.

15. Congress met December 5th, 1848. A bill to organize the Territories of New Mexico and California, with the Wilmot Proviso, was passed by the House by a sectional vote, almost all the Free State Democrats voting for it. The Senate refused to consider it. The House then passed a resolution condemning the sale of slaves in Washington as "notoriously a reproach to our country throughout Christendom," which roused the indignation of Southern members. Late in the Session the Senate passed the General Appropriation Bill for government expenses, with a "rider,"[1] organizing the **Territories of New Mexico and California,** permitting Slavery. Its object was to compel the House to yield, or leave the Government penniless. The House threw this responsibility back upon the Senate by substituting for its rider a provision that until July 4th, 1850, the existing Mexican laws of those Territories should remain in force. As Mexico had

---

[1] That is, an addition having no reference to the subject matter of the original bi'l.

abolished Slavery this would have made the new Territories free. On the last night of the Session the Senate unwillingly struck out its "rider" and the House substitute, and passed the Appropriation Bill as it originally came from the House.

16. Another River and Harbor Improvement Bill was passed by the House, but was not acted upon by the Senate. In February, 1849, the electoral votes were counted and were found to be, for Taylor and Fillmore 163, and for Cass and Butler 127. **Taylor and Fillmore** were therefore declared elected. March 3d, 1849, Congress adjourned, and March 5th Taylor and Fillmore were sworn into office.

# CHAPTER XVII.

#### SIXTEENTH ADMINISTRATION, 1849-1853.

Zachary Taylor, President.    Millard Fillmore, Vice-President
XXXIst and XXXIId Congresses.

*Popular vote for President in* 1848: *Whig* 1,360,101 *Dem.* 1,220,544, *Free Soil* 291,263.

1. TAYLOR's Inauguration marks the beginning of a **Process of Change** which in a few years destroyed one of the two great parties, and changed the character of the other. The Free Soil Democrats, who opposed any extension of Slavery to the Territories, and had therefore abandoned the Democratic party, saw no reason for joining the Whig party, which had distinctly rejected the principle of the Wilmot Proviso. The consequent loss of the Democrats, in numbers, was more than balanced by the accession of Pro-Slavery Whigs who made their new party progressively more Pro-Slavery. The Whig losses had no compensating gains. The disintegration of the party continued from its success in electing a slave-holding President in 1848 until the rise of its anti-slavery successor in 1855-56.

2. The accession of Pro-Slavery Whigs soon brought prominently forward the doctrine which the last Democratic National Convention had voted down, that the Constitution gave Congress no power to interfere with Slavery in the Territories, and that the people of each Territory should allow or prohibit Slavery as they pleased. This was **Squatter Sovereignty.**[1] Of course it would follow from this that the Missouri Compromise of 1820 was illegal and unconstitutional, as it abolished Slavery in the Territories North of 36° 30'. But this consequence was not at first mentioned, and, perhaps, not thought of.

3. As Squatter Sovereignty was a strict constructionist theory, it was more easy to force it upon the Democratic than upon the Whig party. From this time, therefore, Southern leaders aimed to control the Democratic party more thoroughly, abandoning its opponent after an effort to use it as an instrument in completing the work of the Democracy.[2] The struggle between the advocates of the Wilmot Proviso, which forbade Slavery in the new territory, and of Squatter Sovereignty, which allowed its introduction, if desired by the people, was precipitated by the **Discovery of Gold in California.** The consequent rush of immigration increased the population of California so rapidly that a State constitution was formed June 3d, 1849, expressly prohibiting Slavery. This practical application of Squatter Sovereignty was equally surprising and unwelcome to its first advocates.

---

[1] Otherwise called Popular Sovereignty.
[2] At the Presidential Convention of 1852.

4. Congress met December 3d, 1849, with a Democratic majority in the Senate, and no party majority in the House, the Free Soilers holding the balance of power between the other two parties.[1] The Free Soilers refused to vote for either the Whig or the Democratic candidates for Speaker, and, after 62 unavailing ballots in which no one had a majority of all the votes, it was agreed that the highest number of votes should elect. The House then chose as Speaker Howell Cobb, of Georgia, a Democrat and an advocate of the extension of Slavery.

*XXXIst Congress, 1st Session.*

5. California applied for admission as a State February 13th, 1850. Shortly before the application Clay had submitted a proposition to compromise the conflicting claims of the advocates of Slavery extension and of Slavery restriction. His proposition included seven points: (1) the admission of any new States properly formed from Texas, (2) the admission of California, (3) the organization of the Territories of New Mexico and Utah, without the Wilmot Proviso (*i. e.*, with Squatter Sovereignty), (4) the passage of the last two measures in one bill, (5) the payment of a money indemnity to Texas, (6) a more rigid Fugitive Slave Law, (7) the abolition of the slave trade, but not of Slavery, in the District of Columbia. This was the basis of the **Compromise of 1850.** It was opposed by the Whigs and Free Soilers, who considered it a

---

[1] Senate, 35 Dem. 25 Whig, 2 Free Soilers. House, 110 Dem., 105 Whig, 9 Free Soilers.

surrender of free soil to the slave power, and by the extreme Southern Democrats, who considered it a surrender of the slave-holder's right to hold his property and slaves wherever he pleased to settle. But it was undoubtedly satisfactory to the great majority of the people, as averting civil war and disunion.

6. The Compromise of 1850 was originally united in one bill.[1] It was debated throughout the Session, and gradually divided into a number of separate bills. These were all passed, during the months of August and September, by both Houses, and became law. **California** thus became a State of the Union September 9th, 1850. Perhaps the most important, in its bearing upon future events, was the **Fugitive Slave Law**, which was much more stringent in its provisions than the one already in existence. It directed and encouraged the surrender of fugitive slaves by United States Commissioners in the North, without any trial by jury, and commanded all good citizens to aid in making arrests. The work of chasing and arresting fugitive slaves in the Northern States was at once begun, and carried on diligently, often inhumanly. The consequent disgust and horror caused the passage, by some Northern Legislatures, of **Personal Liberty Laws**, intended to protect free negroes falsely alleged to be fugitive slaves. Congress adjourned September 30th, 1850.

7. July 9th President Taylor died, and **Vice-President Fillmore** became President in his stead

---

[1] Commonly called the Omnibus Bill, from its all-embracing nature.

The change had no effect upon party contests, the Administration remaining Whig, as before

**XXXIst Congress, 2d Session.**
8. Congress met December 2d, 1850. There was little party contest at this Session. The questions of Tariff, internal Improvements, and a National Bank, had, for a time at least, disappeared. On the question of Slavery, which had so suddenly sprung into controlling interest, neither party was ready to take a decided stand. The business of this Session was therefore confined to routine, with occasional debates on Slavery. Congress adjourned March 3d, 1851.

**XXXIId Congress, 1st Session.**
9. Congress met December 1st, 1851, with a Democratic majority in both branches.[1] In the House Linn Boyd, of Kentucky, a Democrat, was chosen Speaker. The increased Democratic majority in Congress marks the satisfaction with which the people generally had received the Compromise of 1850, as they understood it. There was little party contest at this Session. The question of Slavery was considered settled, and the Democratic majority generally supported the measures recommended by the Administration for carrying on the government. This Session, however, is noteworthy for the first mention of a measure destined to transfer the conflict between Slavery and its opponents to the country west of Missouri, stretching to the Rocky Mountains, and called, from its principal river, **the Platte Country**.[2] It had be-

---

[1] Senate, 34 Dem., 23 Whigs, 3 Free Soilers. House, 140 Dem., 88 Whigs, 1 Free Soilers.
[2] Now called Kansas.

come a through route to California, and its population was increasing. It now applied for organization as a Territory, but the application was not acted upon. Congress adjourned August 31st, 1852.

10. The **Democratic National Convention** met at Baltimore, June 1st, 1852. It renewed the strict constructionist platforms of preceding Conventions, endorsed the Kentucky and Virginia Resolutions of 1798, and pledged the Democratic party to the faithful observance of the Compromise of 1850, including the Fugitive Slave Law, and to a steady opposition to any agitation of the Slavery question. It nominated Franklin Pierce, of New Hampshire, and William R. King, of Alabama. The **Whig National Convention** met at Baltimore, June 16th. It adopted a loose constructionist platform, more cautiously worded than those of former Conventions, and endorsed the Compromise of 1850 and the Fugitive Slave Law in terms very similar to those of the Democratic platform. After a session of six days it nominated Winfield Scott, of Virginia, and William A. Graham, of North Carolina. The **Free Soil Democratic Convention** met at Pittsburgh, August 11th. It adopted a platform declaring Slavery to be a sin against God and a crime against man, and denouncing the Compromise of 1850, and the two parties who supported it. It nominated John P. Hale, of New Hampshire, and George W. Julian, of Indiana.

11. The success of the Southern delegates in committing the Whig Convention to the support of the Compromise of 1850 did not injure the party so much

at the time as it did afterwards, when the real nature of that Compromise was declared.¹ At the **Presidential Election** in November its popular vote was slightly increased since the previous election, although most of the Free Soil vote was drawn from it Nevertheless the Whig electors carried only four States,² the other twenty-seven States choosing Democratic electors, though generally by very small majorities.

12. **XXXIId Congress, 2d Session.** Congress met December 6th, 1852. A bill was passed by the House to organize the **Territory of Nebraska**, with the same boundaries as the formerly proposed Territory of Platte. It was tabled in the Senate. The opposition to it came from Southern members who were preparing, but were not yet ready to announce, their next advanced claim, that the Compromise of 1850 had superseded and voided that of 1820, abolished the prohibition of Slavery in the territory North of the Missouri Compromise Line (36° 30' North latitude), and opened it to the operation of Squatter Sovereignty. In February, 1853, the electoral votes were counted, and were found to be, for Pierce and King 254, and for Scott and Graham 42. **Pierce** and **King** were therefore declared elected. March 3d, 1853, Congress adjourned, and March 4th Pierce was sworn into office.³

---

[1] The Whig party was then forcibly said to have died "of an attempt to swallow the Fugitive Slave Law."

[2] Massachusetts, Vermont, Kentucky, and Tennessee.

[3] Vice-President King, on account of illness, was sworn into office afterward.

# CHAPTER XVIII.

## SEVENTEENTH ADMINISTRATION, 1853-1857.

**Franklin Pierce, President.** **William R. King, Vice-President.**
**XXXIIId and XXXIVth Congresses.**

*Popular vote for President in* 1852: *Dem.* 1,601,474, *Whig* 1,386,578, *Free Soil* 156,149.

**XXXIIId Congress, 1st Session.**
1. CONGRESS met December 5th, 1853. The Democratic majority in both branches was increased.[1] In the House Speaker Boyd was again elected. The President's Message assured those who had elected him that he intended to carry out the Compromise of 1850, in all its parts. A Senate bill to organize the **Territory of Nebraska** was interfered with by a demand from a Southern Senator that the Missouri Compromise should not be so construed as to prohibit Slavery in the new Territory. The bill was at once dropped. But a sufficient number of Free State Democrats soon acquiesced in the Southern demand to make it a success.

---

Senate, 36 Dem., 20 Whigs, 2 Free Soilers. House, 159 Dem., 71 Whigs, 4 Free Soilers.

2. Jan. 23d, 1854, the famous **Kansas-Nebraska Bill** was introduced in the House. It divided the territory covered by the previous Nebraska bill into two Territories, one directly west of Missouri and between the parallels of 37° and 40°, to be called Kansas, and the other north of this and between the parallels of 40° and 43°, to be called Nebraska. According to the Compromise of 1820 both of these Territories were forever barred to Slavery. But this bill distinctly declared that the Compromise of 1820 was inconsistent with the constitutional principle of non-interference with Slavery by Congress, that it was therefore inoperative, void, and repealed by the Compromise of 1850, and that hereafter each Territory, whether north or south of the parallel of 36° 30', should admit or exclude Slavery as its people should decide. This bill was passed by the Senate, its only opponents being the Northern Whigs and Free Soilers.

3. The Kansas-Nebraska Bill did not come up in the House until about two months later. The Southern Democrats and Southern Whigs united in favor of it. The Northern Democrats were evenly divided,[1] and the Northern Whigs and Free Soilers united against it. The division between the Democratic opponents and advocates of the Kansas-Nebraska Bill was soon healed. The division between Northern and Southern Whigs was final. The Northern Whigs at once repudiated their old party name, and were called at first **Anti-Nebraska Men**. The Southern Whigs kept the party

---
[1] There were 88 Northern Democratic votes, 44 for, and 44 against t.

name alive a few years longer, but their principles on the controlling question of Slavery were so similar to those of the Southern Democracy that they can hardly be called a distinct party. Congress adjourned August 7th, 1854.

4. A new party had by this time risen to active importance in American politics. It appeared in 1852,[1] in the form of a secret, oath-bound organization, of whose name, nature, and objects, nothing was told even to its members until they had reached its higher degrees. Their consequent declaration that they knew nothing about it gave the society its popular name of **Know Nothings.** It accepted the name of the **American Party.** Its design was to oppose the easy naturalization of foreigners, and to aid the election of native-born citizens to office. Its nominations were made by secret conventions of delegates from the various lodges, and were voted for by all members under penalty of expulsion in case of refusal. At first, by endorsing the nominations of one or other of the two great parties, it decided many elections. After the passage of the Kansas-Nebraska Bill, the Know Nothing organization was adopted by many Southern Whigs, who were unwilling to unite with the Democracy, and became, for a time, a national party. It

---

[1] The Hartford Convention had complained of the easy naturalization of foreigners. A "Native American" party had existed in New York City in 1835, but it was only local, and soon disappeared. In 1843 a new "Native American" party had arisen in New York City, and extended to Philadelphia. Its Whig members left it in 1844 because of its refusal to vote for Clay, and it too disappeared.

carried nine of the State elections in 1855, and in 1856 nominated Presidential candidates. After that time its Southern members gradually united with the Democracy, and the Know Nothing party disappeared from politics.

5. Congress met December 4th, 1854. There was little party contest at this Session, which was chiefly noteworthy for a revival of the question of **Internal Improvements.** It secured Democratic votes by providing for detached public improvements. A River and Harbor bill was passed by both Houses, but was vetoed by the President. Congress adjourned March 3d, 1855.

*XXXIIId Congress, 2d Session.*

6. Congress met December 3d, 1855,[1] with a Democratic majority in the Senate. In the House the "Anti-Nebraska men" had a majority, but so many of them were Know Nothings that no candidate could control their entire vote. After 130 ballots for Speaker, lasting until February, 1856, it was agreed that the highest number of votes should elect, and N. P. Banks, Jr., of Massachusetts, an "Anti-Nebraska man," was chosen. The remaining time of this Session was occupied by the **Kansas Troubles,** which will be referred to hereafter. A House Committee was sent to Kansas, and reported that no free or fair election had ever taken place in that Territory. The House voted an appro

*XXXIVth Congress, 1st Session.*

---

[1] Senate, 34 Dem., 25 Opposition. House, 117 Anti-Nebraska 79 Dem., 31 Pro-Slavery Whigs.

priation for the army, with a proviso forbidding the use of the army to enforce the acts of the Pro-Slavery Kansas Legislature.[1] The Senate rejected the proviso, and during the disagreement between the Houses the time xed for adjournment arrived, and Congress adjourned August 18th, 1856, leaving the Army Bill unpassed. The President at once called an Extra Session of Congress, in which the Army Bill, without the proviso, was passed, and Congress again adjourned August 30th, 1856.

7. Early in 1856 the "Anti-Nebraska men" had adopted the name of the **Republican Party**.[2] The new name was at once recognized by the Democrats with the addition of a contemptuous adjective *(Black Republican)*. It will be seen that the new party was a loose constructionist party, inheriting the desire of the Federalists and Whigs for Protective Tariffs, Internal Improvements, and a system of National Bank Currency, and adding to them the further principle that the Federal Government had power to control Slavery in the Territories. The new party had therefore an assured existence from the first, for its additional loose constructionist principle was the only logical answer to the strict constructionist principle still avowed by the Democrats, that Congress had no constitutional power to interfere for or against Slavery in the Territories.

8. The attention of the whole country had now been

---

[1] See page 165.
[2] First proposed, it is said, by Governor Seward, of New York, late in 1855

turned to the struggle provoked by the Kansas-Nebraska Bill, and the repeal of the Missouri Compromise. The fertile soil of **Kansas** had been offered as a prize to be contended for by Free and Slave States, and both had accepted the contest. The Slave State settlers were first in the field. The slave-holders of Western Missouri, which shut off Kansas from the Free States, had crossed the border, pre-empted lands, and warned Free State immigrants not to pass through Missouri. The first election of a delegate to Congress took place November 29th, 1854, and was carried by organized bands of Missourians, who moved over the border or election day, voted, and returned at once to Missouri. The spring election of 1855, for a Territorial Legislature, was carried in the same fashion. In July, 1855 this Legislature, all Pro-Slavery, met at Pawnee, and adopted a State Constitution. To save trouble it adopted the laws of the State of Missouri entire, with a series of original statutes denouncing the penalty of death for nearly fifty offenses against Slavery.

9. All through the spring and summer of 1855 Kansas was the scene of almost continuous conflict, the **Border Ruffians** of Missouri endeavoring to drive out the **Free State Settlers** by murder and arson, and the Free State settlers retaliating. The cry of "bleeding Kansas" went through the North. Emigration societies were formed in the Free States to aid, arm, equip, and protect intending settlers. These, prevented from passing through Missouri, took a more Northern route through Iowa and Nebraska, and

moved into Kansas like an invading army. The Southern States also sent parties of intending settlers. But these were not generally slave-holders, but young men anxious for excitement. They did not go to Kansas, as their opponents did, to plow, sow, gather crops and build up homes. Therefore, though their first rapid and violent movements were successful, their subsequent increase of resources and numbers was not equal to that of the Free State settlers.

10. The Territory soon became practically divided into a Pro-Slavery district, and a Free State district. Leavenworth in the former, and Topeka and Lawrence in the latter, were the chief towns. September 5th, 1855, a **Free State Convention at Topeka** repudiated the Territorial Legislature and all its works, as the acts and deeds of Missourians alone. It also resolved to order a separate election for delegate to Congress, so as to force that body to decide the question,[1] and to form a State government. January 15th, 1856, the Free State settlers elected State officers under the Topeka Free State Constitution.[2]

11. **The Federal Executive** now entered the field. January 24th, 1856, the President, in a Special Message to Congress, endorsed the Pro-Slavery Legislature, and pronounced the attempt to form a Free State government, without the approval of the Federal authorities in the Territory, to be an act of rebellion.

---

[1] The question was decided by the admission of the Pro-Slavery delegate.

[2] Under this (Topeka) Constitution Kansas applied for admission as a State and was rejected.

He then issued a proclamation, warning all persons engaged in disturbing the peace of Kansas to retire to their homes, and placed United States troops at the orders of Governor Shannon to enforce the (Pro-Slavery) laws of the Territory.

12. The population of Kansas was now so large that very considerable armies were mustered on both sides, and a desultory civil war was kept up until nearly the end of the year. During its progress two Free State towns, Lawrence and Ossawattomie, were sacked. July 4th, 1856, the Free State Legislature attempted to assemble at Topeka, but was at once dispersed by a body of United States troops, under orders from Washington.[1] September 9th, a new Governor, Geary, of Pennsylvania, arrived and succeeded in keeping the peace to some extent by a mixture of temporizing and decided measures. By the end of the year he even claimed to have established order in the Territory.

13. The heat of the Kansas discussion in Congress was marked by an **Assault upon Charles Sumner,** Senator from Massachusetts. In a speech on the Kansas question he had criticised Senator Butler, of South Carolina. After the Senate's adjournment, May 22d, 1856, Representative Brooks, of South Carolina, a relative of Butler, entered the Senate chamber, struck Sumner senseless to the floor, and then beat him so cruelly that an absence of several years in Europe was necessary for his recovery. The House passed a resolution

---

[1] For the consequent attempt of the House to limit this use of the army see page 162.

of censure upon Brooks, who immediately resigned but was unanimously re-elected by his district. Massachusetts declined to choose another Senator, preferring to leave Sumner's empty chair as her silent protest against unpunished violence.

14. The **Know Nothing National Convention** met at Philadelphia, February 22d, 1856. It adopted a platform which declared that Americans must rule America, and that naturalization should only be granted after 21 years' residence, and condemned the repeal of the Missouri Compromise. The Anti-Slavery delegates (one-fourth of all the Convention) withdrew because of a refusal to endorse the right of Congress to re-establish the Missouri Compromise Line. The Convention then nominated Millard Fillmore, of New York, and Andrew Jackson Donelson, of Tennessee. These nominations (but not the platform) were accepted by a convention of delegates from the remnants of the great Whig wreck, held at Baltimore, September 17th. The **Democratic National Convention** met at Cincinnati, June 2d, and adopted the strict constructionist platform of former Conventions. It added to it a condemnation of Know Nothingism, and an approval of the Kansas-Nebraska Bill and the substitution of Squatter Sovereignty for the Compromise of 1820.[1] It nominated James Buchanan, of Pennsylvania, and John

---

[1] From this time party platforms become so long and ambiguous that only the most succinct abstract can be given. The reader is referred to Greeley's Political Text Book for 1860, and to the *Tribune, World,* and *Herald* Almanack since 1860, for the platforms in full.

C. Breckinridge, of Kentucky. The **Republican National Convention** met at Philadelphia, June 17th, and adopted a loose constructionist platform. It declared in favor of Internal Improvements (including a Pacific Railway', and of the right and duty of Congress to prohibit Slavery and Polygamy in the Territories and admit Kansas as a Free State, and against the repeal of the Missouri Compromise, the general policy of the Administration, and the extension of Slavery. Its nominations were John C. Fremont, of California, and William L. Dayton, of New Jersey.

15. The Know Nothings and Whigs had denounced both the Democrats and Republicans as sectional, or "geographical" parties. But Fillmore's supporters had no remedy to offer for the troubles caused by Slavery. In the **Presidential Election** in November, therefore, they carried but one State, Maryland. Democratic electors were chosen by the remaining fourteen Slave States, and by New Jersey, Pennsylvania, Indiana, Illinois, and California, giving them a majority of all. The remaining eleven Free States chose Republican electors.[1] No candidate had a majority of the popular vote.

16. Congress met December 1st, 1856.[2] The sudden crystallization of the various Anti-Slavery ele-

**XXXIVth Congress, 2d Session.**

---

[1] If Pennsylvania and Illinois had chosen Republican electors Fremont and Dayton would have been elected.

[2] Senate, 40 Dem., 15 Rep., 5 Kn. N. House, 108 Rep., 93 Dem. 43 Kn. N.

ments into the Republican party had slightly altered the political proportions of the House. There was no party majority there, though the Republicans still had the greatest number of votes. At this Session grants of public lands were made to various Western and Southern States to aid the construction of new railroads. The **Tariff of 1857** was passed by both Houses, and became law. It reduced duties on imports to a rate lower than those of any Tariff since that of 1816.

17. The **Kansas** troubles took up much of the time of this Session. January 6th, 1857, the Free State Legislature again attempted to meet at Topeka, and was again dispersed by Federal interference. Its presiding officer and many of its members were arrested by a United States deputy marshal. The Territorial, or Pro-Slavery, Legislature quarreled with Gov. Geary, who resigned, and Robert J. Walker, of Mississippi, was appointed in his stead. A resolution was passed by the House declaring the Acts of the Territorial Legislature cruel, oppressive, illegal, and void. It was tabled by the Senate.

18. In February, 1857, the electoral votes were counted. The 5 votes of Wisconsin had not been cast on the 3d of December, as required by law, but on th 4th, and many members were disposed to debate thei legality. But the presiding officer declared all debat out of order, and announced the votes, including those of Wisconsin to be 174 for Buchanan and Breckinridge, 114 for Fremont and Dayton, and 8 for Fillmore and Donelson. **Buchanan** and **Breckinridge** were

therefore declared elected. March 3d, 1857, Congress adjourned, and March 4th Buchanan and Breckinridge were sworn into office.

# CHAPTER XIX.

### EIGHTEENTH ADMINISTRATION, 1857–1861.

James Buchanan, President.  John C. Breckinridge, Vice-President
XXXVth and XXXVIth Congresses.

*Popular vote for President in* 1856: *Dem.* 1,838,169, *Rep.* 1,341,264, *Kn. N.* 874,534.

1. Two days after Buchanan's Inauguration the Supreme Court rendered final judgment in the **Dred Scott Case.** It had been decided in 1856, but it had been thought best to reserve judgment until the excitement of the Presidential election should subside. This, though one of the most important cases ever decided in the United States, was originally a case of simple assault and battery. Dred Scott was a Missouri slave. His owner took him in 1834 to Illinois, a State in which Slavery was prohibited by statute, allowed him to marry and live there until 1838, and then took him to Minnesota, a Territory in which Slavery was prohibited by the Act of Congress of 1820, known as the Missouri Compromise. Thence his owner took him back to Missouri. Here he was whipped for some offense, and brought suit for damages, claiming to have

become a free man by his residence in Illinois and Minnesota. The owner's demurrer denied that the plaintiff was a citizen, or could sue, since he was descended from slave ancestors, and never had been set free. This was decided against him by the State Circuit Court of Missouri, and judgment given in favor of Dred Scott. By successive appeals the case finally reached the United States Supreme Court.

2. The **Decision** of the Supreme Court startled the Northern States. It declared, in substance, that the ancestors of negro slaves were not regarded as persons by the founders of the government, but as chattels, as things, "who had no rights or privileges but such as those who held the power and the government might choose to grant them;" that Dred Scott, the plaintiff in error, was consequently no citizen of Missouri, but *a thing*, without standing in Court, and his case must be dismissed for want of jurisdiction; and that his residence in Minnesota could avail him nothing, because the Act of Congress of 1820, prohibiting Slavery north of the parallel of 36° 30', was unconstitutional and void, and could not prevent a slave-owner from settling in any Territory with all his property. The Court further took occasion to observe that Congress had no more right to prohibit the carrying of slaves into any State or Territory than it had to prohibit the carrying thither of horses or any other property, for slaves were property, whose secure possession was guaranteed by the Constitution.[1]

---

[1] On the contrary, the dissenting Justices of the Court, and the mass of the Northern people, considered slaves as a kind of property whose secure pos-

3. The Dred Scott decision marks the last attempt to decide the contest between **Slavery Extension** and **Slavery Restriction** by form of law, and from this time the course of events tends with increasing rapidity to a settlement by force. The first Compromise (in 1820) had prohibited Slavery in part of the Territories, leaving the question open as to the remainder. The next Compromise (in 1850–1852) had opened all the Territories to Slavery, if established by Popular Sovereignty. In both of these the whole people had agreed. But the Dred Scott decision, in its logical consequences, opened all the Territories and all the Free States to at least a temporary establishment of Slavery, wherever a slave-owner might see fit to carry his slaves. It was plain that this would never be received as law by the Free States. The only practical results of the Dred Scott decision, therefore, were to show the failure of the Supreme Court as an arbiter, and to call the attention of the North to the impracticable demands of the slave-owners. It will be seen that the Northern (or Douglas) Democrats, who had supported the South heretofore, refused at this point to follow the Southern lead further, and chose rather to divide the party.

4. By the representation given by the Constitution to three-fifths of the slave population,[1] the 300,000 slave-owners had grown into a **Slave Power**. In 1857 they

---

session was guaranteed only by the *State* laws which made them property. Leaving the State they lost the guarantee afforded by State laws.

[1] By which the owner of 1,000 slaves was equal in political power to 600 non-slave-holders.

controlled the South, the South controlled the Democratic party, and the Democratic party controlled the Union. They were becoming extremely doubtful of success in the Kansas struggle, where they were evidently overmatched by the superior power, resources, and enthusiasm of the Free States. They had not received the expected increase of Slave States and United States Senators from the territory wrested from Mexico.[1] Should they fail in making Kansas a Slave State, they saw but three available courses to pursue—to add Cuba to the Union as material for new Slave States, to acquire new and more populous territory south of Texas for the same purpose, or to re-open the African slave trade. Failing in all these, they desired a secession, or separation, from the Free States, and the formation of an independent government, in which Slavery would be secured from all attacks or restrictions.

5. The **Purchase of Cuba** had been vainly attempted at various times since the inauguration of President Polk, and a growing disposition was apparent in the South to take it from Spain by force. In 1853, therefore, England and France asked the United States to join in a tripartite agreement to guarantee Cuba to Spain forever. The proposition was rejected. In 1854

---

[1] By forming new Southern States to balance new Northern States, the two sections were carefully kept in equilibrium until 1845, when Texas was admitted, (See Appendices C and F). After that time five new Northern States were admitted, and others were evidently almost ready for application, while no new Southern States could be formed to counterbalance them. The consequent impossibility of maintaining a future equality in the Senate seems to have been the primary cause of alarm in the South. For the present proportion in the Senate see Appendix G.

the American Ministers to England, France, and Spain, meeting in the Belgian town of Ostend, had published the so-called **Ostend Manifesto,** which declared that there was no hope of safety or repose for the United States without the acquisition of Cuba. But, so long as England, France, and Spain were united in opposing it, there was little hope for the South in the direction of Cuba.

6. In 1851 began the **Era of Filibustering Expeditions** against Cuba and Central America, with the ultimate design of adding slave territory to the United States. Lopez, a Cuban, with 500 men, sailed from New Orleans to conquer Cuba. He was defeated and executed, and his men imprisoned. In 1855 William Walker, of Tennessee, sailed from New Orleans to conquer Central America. He was repeatedly defeated, but repeatedly renewed his expeditions until 1858, when he was captured by the President of Honduras, and shot. This ended filibustering.

7. The re-opening of the **African Slave Trade** was already seriously demanded by many slave-owners. They believed that the South had been overpowered in the Kansas struggle because of her inability to pour slaves into the new Territory at once. There seemed a strong probability that Southern leaders would endeavor to obtain from the next Democratic Convention a declaration in favor of renewing the slave trade with Africa.

8. Congress met December 7th, 1857 with a Dem-

**XXXVth Congress, 1st Session.** ocratic majority in both branches.[1] In the House James L. Orr, of South Carolina, a Democrat, was chosen Speaker. The debates of this Session were mainly upon the last scene in the Kansas struggle. Governor Walker had succeeded in persuading the Free State settlers to recognize the Territorial Legislature so far as to take part in the election which it had ordered. The result gave them control of the Legislature. But a previously elected Pro-Slavery Convention, sitting at Lecompton, went on to form a State Constitution. This was to be submitted to the people, but only votes "For the Constitution *with* Slavery," or "For the Constitution *without* Slavery" were to be received. Not being allowed in either event to vote against the Constitution, the Free State settlers refused to vote at all, and the **Lecompton Constitution** *with* Slavery received 6,000 majority. The new Territorial Legislature, however, ordered an election at which the people could vote for or against the Lecompton Constitution, and a majority of 10,000 was cast against it.[2]

9. On the first day of the Session the Republican Congressmen united in publishing a protest against any effort to make Kansas a Slave State against the wish of her people. The **President's Message** argued in favor of receiving Kansas as a State under the Le-

---

[1] Senate, 39 Dem., 20 Rep., 5 Kn. N. House, 131 Dem., 92 Rep., 14 Kn. N.

[2] But this vote was considered worthless by the advocates of the Lecompton Constitution, on the ground that the Territorial Legislature had no power to order it.

compton Constitution with Slavery, on the ground that the delegates had been chosen to form a State Constitution, and were not obligated to submit it to the people at all. This view was supported by the Southern members of Congress, and opposed by the Republicans and by a part of the Democrats, headed by Senator Douglas, of Illinois.[1] The Senate passed a bill admitting Kansas as a State, under the Lecompton Constitution. The House passed the bill, with the proviso that the Constitution should again be submitted to a popular vote. The Senate rejected the proviso. A conference committee recommended that the bill of the House should be adopted, with an additional proviso making large grants of public lands to the new State, if the people of Kansas should vote to adopt the Lecompton Constitution. In this form the bill was passed by both Houses, and became law. An attempt was made without success to appropriate public lands to the States for educational purposes. Congress adjourned June 1st, 1858.

10. **Minnesota** had become a State of the Union May 11th, 1858. In the case of **Kansas** the proffered inducement of public lands was a failure, and in August the Lecompton Constitution was rejected by 10,000 majority. Kansas, therefore, still remained a Territory. In 1859, at an election called by the Territorial Legislature, the people decided in favor of another Conven-

---

[1] "It is not satisfactory to me to have the President say, in his Message that that Constitution is an admirable one. That is none of my business, and none of yours. You have no right to force an unexceptionable Constitution upon a people."—(*Douglas, Speech in Senate.*)

tion to form a State Constitution. This body met at Wyandot, in July, 1859, and adopted a State Constitution prohibiting Slavery. The **Wyandot Constitution** was submitted to the people and received a majority of 4,000 in its favor.

11. **XXXVth Congress, 2d Session.** Congress met December 6th, 1858.[1] Party contest at this Session centred upon the **Homestead Bill**, which gave heads of families the right to purchase 160 acres of public lands at $1.25 per acre. It was passed by the House, but postponed by the Senate. The bill to appropriate public lands for educational purposes was passed, but vetoed by the President. Congress adjourned March 3d, 1859. February 14th, 1859, **Oregon** had become a State of the Union.

12. In 1859 some of the extreme Abolitionists determined to try the Southern policy of filibustering. **John Brown**, a native of Connecticut,[2] had gone to Kansas in 1855, and settled in the town of Ossawattomie. Here he became so noted as a leader in carrying the war into the Pro-Slavery district that rewards for his arrest were offered by the Governor and the President. He thereupon left Kansas, and in July, 1859, settled at Harper's Ferry, Md., with the desperate intention of beginning a general insurrection of the slave race. His family and some of his Kansas associates were with him. October 17th, having matured

---

[1] Party strength was unchanged except that 11 members of the House now classed as Anti-Lecompton Democrats, and 116 supported the Administration

[2] He had for some time lived in ' John Brown's Tract" in New York.

their plans and prepared arms, they seized the town of Harper's Ferry, and the United States Arsenal, with all the arms contained in it. The news created a wild alarm in the South. Virginia and Maryland militia were hurried to Harper's Ferry. After a spirited defense, most of Brown's associates were shot, and their wounded leader and a few others were taken prisoners, tried, and hanged by the State of Virginia. John Brown's execution took place December 2d, 1859.

13. Congress met December 5th, 1859,[1] with a **XXXVIth Congress,** Democratic majority in the 1st Session. Senate. In the House the Republican vote was the largest, but there was no party majority. **Balloting for a Speaker** was continued for eight weeks, interrupted by angry debates upon a recently published Abolitionist[2] book called "The Impending Crisis in the South," and upon the Harper's Ferry insurrection. February 1st, 1860, William Pennington, of New Jersey, a Republican, was chosen Speaker. In the Senate resolutions were at once introduced affirming, in substance, that Congress and Territorial Legislatures had no power to prohibit Slavery in the Territories. They were debated, at intervals, for nearly four months, and then passed by a party vote.

14. A most unpleasant feature of this Session was

---

[1] Senate, 38 Dem., 25 Rep., 2 Kn. N. House, 109 Rep., 86 Dem., 13 Anti Lecompton Dem., 22 Kn. N.

[2] The term "Abolitionist" was then one of reproach. It is hardly necessary to say that it is not so used in the text.

the so-called **Covode Investigation** by a committee of the House. Two members of the House[1] had declared in debate that they had been offered inducements by the Administration to vote for the Lecompton Bill, and a committee of five was appointed, on motion of Covode, of Pennsylvania, to investigate the charge. The President protested against the investigation. After a tedious investigation of three months the Republican majority reported that the Administration had been guilty of bribing members of Congress and editors of newspapers to favor the Lecompton Bill. The Democratic minority defended and exonerated the President. No further action was taken in the matter.

15 The **Homestead Bill,** which was passed at the last Session, was again passed by the House. The Senate passed a substitute, to which the House agreed, giving public lands to actual settlers at 25 cents per acre. It was vetoed by the President on the ground that it was unjust to the older States in really giving away lands to the newer States.[2] The application of Kansas for admission as a State under the Wyandot Constitution[3] was approved by the House, but rejected by the Senate. Consequently Kansas still remained a Territory. Congress adjourned June 18th, 1860.

16. The **Democratic National Convention** met

---
[1] Hickman and G. B. Adrain.
[2] The Senate substitute seems to have been purposely drawn so as to provoke a veto, if possible. The Southern opposition to a Homestead Bill seems to have come from the apprehension that it would increase immigration in the North-West, and thus increase the Free State representation in the Senate.
[3] See page 177.

at Charleston, S. C., April 23d, 1860. The proceedings were stormy, and resulted in the splitting of the Convention and the party into two distinct fragments, through the refusal of the Northern (or Douglas) Democrats to agree to the demands of the Southern wing Both factions re-affirmed the strict constructionist platforms of past Conventions, and declared for a Pacifi Railway and for the acquisition of Cuba. The Southern delegates offered additional resolutions affirming the doctrine of the Dred Scott decision, that neither Congress nor the Territorial Legislatures had a right to prohibit Slavery in the Territories. The Douglas Democrats, refusing to abandon Popular Sovereignty openly, offered a resolution that the party would abide by the decisions of the Supreme Court. The Convention adopted the Douglas platform, whereupon the delegations from many Southern States successively protested and withdrew. The Convention then proceeded to ballot fifty-seven times for candidates without a choice, and adjourned to meet again at Baltimore, June 18th. When it re-assembled several new Douglas delegations were admitted, whereupon the few remaining Southern delegates also withdrew. The Convention then nominated Stephen A. Douglas, of Illinois, and Herschel V. Johnon, of Georgia.

17. **The Seceding Delegates** had a once organized a new Convention in Charleston, adopted their platform, and adjourned to meet again in Richmond, Va., June 11th. Here they adjourned again, re-assembled at Baltimore, June 28th, and nominated John

C. Breckinridge, of Kentucky, and Joseph Lane, of Oregon. The former American (or Know Nothing) party, now calling itself the **Constitutional Union Party,** held its National Convention at Baltimore, May 19th, and adopted an evasive platform, declaring as its political principles "The Constitution of the country, the Union of the States, and the enforcement of the laws." It nominated John Bell, of Tennessee, and Edward Everett, of Massachusetts. The **Republican National Convention** met at Chicago, May 16th, and adopted a loose constructionist platform. This outspoken document quoted the Declaration of Independence as to the freedom and equality of all men; denounced Democratic threats of disunion, and Democratic administration in Kansas and at Washington; declared that freedom was the normal condition of the Territories, which Congress was bound to preserve and defend; and pronounced in favor of Protection, Internal Improvements, the Homestead Bill, and a Pacific Railway. It nominated Abraham Lincoln, of Illinois, and Hannibal Hamlin, of Maine.

18. **Four Parties** were now in the field. The Bell platform meant simply to evade the question of Slavery altogether. The Lincoln platform avowed a purpose to exclude Slavery from the Territories at any cost. The Breckinridge platform avowed a purpose to carry Slavery into the Territories at any cost. The Douglas platform aimed to throw the responsibility of a decision of the Slavery question upon the Supreme Court, or upon the people of the Territories, or anywhere, in short, except upon the Democratic party

The discordant efforts of the three parties opposed to the Republicans only made Lincoln's election more certain, and at the **Presidential Election** in November Republican electors were chosen by every Free State but one,[1] giving them a majority of all the electoral votes. No candidate had a majority of the popular vote. Breckinridge electors were chosen by most of the Southern States.

19. The South Carolina Legislature, which had met to choose electors,[2] remained in session until Lincoln's election was assured. It then called a State Convention and adjourned. The South Carolina Senators and office-holders in the Federal service at once resigned. December 20th the Convention unanimously passed an **Ordinance of Secession**, entitled "An Ordinance to dissolve the union between the State of South Carolina and other States united with her in the compact entitled the Constitution of the United States of America." Copies of this Ordinance were sent to the other Slave States, and commissioners appointed to treat for the division of national property and of the public debt.

20. This bold step of the little State of South Carolina was relied upon, and with good reason, by the disunionists of the South to "fire the Southern heart," and urge on **Secession by other States.** Under the spur of an unwillingness to abandon their smaller sister, other Slave States rapidly came abreast with her. Before the end of January, 1861, Georgia, Alabama,

---

[1] New Jersey, where four Lincoln and three Douglas electors were chosen
[2] See page 102.

Florida, Mississippi, Louisiana, and Texas had passed Ordinances of Secession. Tennessee, North Carolina. Arkansas, and the Border States still refused to join their more Southern neighbors.

21. **XXXVIth Congress, 2d Session.** Congress met December 3d, 1860. The President's Message stated his inability to find judges or officers in the South to issue or execute process against offenders, and his own opinion, and that of the Attorney-General, that under such circumstances it was impossible legally to compel a State's obedience. The Message argued against the right of Secession much as did Jackson's Nullification Proclamation in 1832. But the latter closed with a warning, to which the known character of its author added convincing force, that blood would flow if the laws were resisted. President Buchanan's Message, on the contrary, summed up the whole matter by saying, in effect, that he knew not what to do, for he did not believe that Congress could constitutionally make war upon a State.

22. It would be wearisome to detail the long list of propositions for compromise and conciliation with which this Session was chiefly occupied. The one which seemed most likely to succeed was the **Crittenden Compromise.**[1] Its main provisions were that Slavery should be prohibited north of the parallel of 36° 30′, and recognized and never interfered with by Congress south of that line, and that the Federal Government should pay for slaves rescued from officers after arrest. These provisions were to be made a part

---

[1] So called from its proposer, John J. Crittenden, of Kentucky.

of the Constitution, and were never to be altered or amended while the Union existed. This measure failed to receive the Republican vote, without which the Southern members refused to entertain it.

23. February 4th, 1861, a **Peace Congress**, composed of delegates from 13 Free and 7 Border States met at Washington at the request of the Virginia Legislature. It adopted and reported to Congress a number of resolutions making various concessions to Southern demands. Congress threw all these aside, and passed, as a substitute, an Amendment to the Constitution proposed by Senator Douglas, which forbade Congress ever to interfere with Slavery in the States.[1]

24. While these measures were being uselessly debated, the work of **Secession** was pressed with energy and ability. Time which should have been spent in making the Federal Government ready to assert its supremacy was wasted in dallying with theoretical cures for incurable evils. Even during the debates the occasional farewells and departures of Southern Senators and Representatives would announce that another State had seceded without waiting to be conciliated. In February, 1861, a Convention of delegates from the seceding States met at Montgomery, Ala., and formed a government called the **Confederate States of America**. Its organization was a tribute to the excellence of the Constitution of 1787, for it mainly copied that instrument, except that it recognized Slavery, and forbade Protective Tariffs. Jefferson Davis,

---

[1] This Amendment was never adopted by the necessary number of States

of Mississippi, and Alexander H. Stephens, of Georgia were chosen President and Vice-President. A Cabinet was at once appointed, and arrangements were hastily made to organize an army, navy, and treasury. United States forts, arsenals, and arms were seized, and batteries were prepared for the reduction of the forts which resisted, particularly Fort Sumter, in Charleston Harbor.

25. As soon as a sufficient number of Southern members of Congress had withdrawn to give the Republicans a majority in both Houses, **Kansas** was admitted as a State under the Wyandot Free State Constitution, and the **Territories** of **Nevada, Colorado,** and **Dakota** were organized without mention of Slavery, thus giving the South the benefit of the Dred Scott decision therein. The so-called **Morrill Tariff of 1861** was also passed by both Houses and became law. Its great object was the protection of manufactures, revenue being a secondary consideration.[1] In February, 1861, the electoral votes were counted, and were found to be, for Lincoln and Hamlin 180, for Breckinridge and Lane 72, for Bell and Everett 39, and for Douglas and Johnson 12. **Lincoln** and **Hamlin** were therefore declared elected. After authorizing a loan and an issue of Treasury notes, this dismal Session of Congress adjourned March 3d, 1861, and March 4th Lincoln and Hamlin were sworn into office.

---

[1] From this time the subject of Internal Improvements drops out of politics. Both parties appear to recognize the right of Congress to appropriate money for isolated public improvements, and the project of a connected system of canals, etc., has not yet been formally revived.

# CHAPTER XX.

## NINETEENTH ADMINISTRATION, 1861-1865.

**Abraham Lincoln, President. Hannibal Hamlin, Vice-President.**
**XXXVIIth and XXXVIIIth Congresses.**

*Popular vote for President in* 1860: *Rep.* 1,866,352, *Const. Union* 589,581, *Dem.* 2,220,920 *(Douglas* 1,375,157, *Breckinridge* 845,763*).*

1. WHEN the **New Administration** entered office affairs seemed almost desperate. Seven States had already revolted, and others were notoriously ready to join them upon the first attempt to exert the National authority. Part of the Federal army had surrendered, and most of the remainder were beleaguered in isolated forts. The Federal ships of war had generally been sent to distant seas. Many of the experienced officers of the army and navy had taken service under the rebellious Confederacy. A large part of the Federal munitions of war, having been previously transferred to Southern arsenals, had fallen into the hands of the insurgents. The Federal Treasury, by defalcation and peculation, was nearly bankrupt. The public servants

like those of a dying king, seemed anxious only to secure as much plunder as possible and decamp. In the South the numbers of those who desired a permanent Southern Confederacy were being increased daily by accessions from those who had at first intended only to remain out of the Union long enough to secure guarantees for the future safety of Slavery. And yet men of all parties in the North, blind to the certainty of approaching war, were still busied with plans to conciliate the revolted States by any concession except that of nationalizing Slavery.

2. The announced purpose of the President to resupply **Fort Sumter** precipitated an attack upon it by the rebel forces around it. After a bombardment of thirty hours, the American flag, for the first time in its history, was lowered under the fire of insurgent citizens, and the fort surrendered, April 14th, 1861. The news woke the North as if from a trance. The mass of the Democracy were even more furious than the Republicans. The Southern States were no longer "erring sisters," to be gently conciliated. The whole North clamored for arms, for leaders, for legal authorization to bring the South back to law, order, and obedience, at the point of the bayonet.

3. **Civil War** had fairly begun. For the first time the government, in time of war, was under the control of a loose constructionist party, for the war Democrats soon became absorbed into the Republican organization, and the resulting fusion frequently took the name of the **Union Party**. The experiment was hazard

ous. In previous wars the Democratic party, though trammeled by its strict constructionist theories, had been driven to strain the Constitution to conform to the necessities of the hour. But the sobering responsibilities of power, and the active (though often ill-timed) opposition of the Peace Democrats, checked the loose constructionist theories of the dominant party, and brought the Constitution through a dreadful struggle of four years with less change than might have been anticipated.

4. The President at once called for 75,000 volunteers, and called an Extra Session of Congress. Through the spring of 1861 the State governments of Virginia, North Carolina, Tennessee, and Arkansas, which had hitherto refused to secede, followed the same general line of action. **Military Leagues** were made with the Confederacy; Confederate troops were then allowed to swarm over their territory; and finally, by their aid and countenance, Ordinances of Secession were passed. Efforts to carry out this plan in Delaware, Maryland, Kentucky, and Missouri, were not successful. By the time set for the meeting of Congress the line had been distinctly drawn, and the rebellion was general in the States of Virginia, North Carolina, South Carolina, Georgia, Florida, Alabama, Mississippi, Louisiana, Texas, Arkansas, and Tennessee.[1]

---

[1] About 40 Counties of *Western Virginia* refused to be bound by the action of the rest of the State, and formed a Legislature which claimed to be the real Legislature of Virginia. This body gave the assent required by the Con

5. Congress met July 4th, 1861, with a Republican **XXXVIIth Congress,** majority in both branches.

**Extra Session.** Only the Free States and the Border States were represented. In the House Galusha A. Grow, of Pennsylvania, a Republican, was chosen Speaker. In the Senate three Senators, who had absented themselves to take part in the rebellion were expelled. The House voted to consider at this Session only bills concerning the military, naval, and financial operations of the Government. The energy of the proceedings was only stimulated by the disastrous battle of Bull Run, July 21st. **Bills** were passed by both Houses to close the Southern ports against commerce, to authorize a loan, to appropriate money for the army and navy, to call out 500,000 volunteers, to define and punish conspiracy against the United States, and to confiscate all private property, including slaves, employed against the United States. The Tariff Act of August 5th, 1861, again increased the duties on imports. The House, by a heavy majority (121-5), pledged itself to vote any amount of money and any number of men necessary to put down the rebellion. Propositions looking to negotiations for peace were constantly offered by extreme Democrats, and as constantly voted down by heavy majorities on the ground that negotiation with armed rebellion was

---

stitution to the formation of a new State, at first called Kanawha, afterwards West Virginia. Congress recognized their right to do so, and admitted the new State in 1862.

[1] Senate, Rep 31, Dem. 11, Union 5. House, Rep 106, Dem. 42, Union 28.

unconstitutional. Congress adjourned August 6th 1861.

6. From the beginning of the war the Federal Government was embarrassed by the question of **Fugitive Slaves.** August 31st General John C. Fremont had declared the slaves of Missouri rebels free men, but his was overruled and annulled by the President. In Virginia General Benjamin F. Butler had announced that slaves were "contraband of war," and consequently liable to confiscation by military law. Elsewhere in the Federal lines slave-owners, on proving property were generally given possession of their fugitive slaves The disposition of the North was to put down the rebellion, without any interference with the Southern "institution" of Slavery. But it was plain that any long continuance of the rebellion would inevitably rouse the temper of the Free States, and provoke hostility to Slavery itself.

7. Congress met December 2d, 1861. **Slavery and The Prosecution of the War** occupied the Session. Bills were passed by both Houses to punish reason, to free slaves employed against the Government, to provide for the construction of a Pacific Railway and Telegraph, and to donate public lands to the various States for the benefit of Agricultural Colleges. The army was forbidden to surrender fugitive slaves. The **Homestead Bill**[1] was brought up again and passed. Provision was made for the United States

**XXXVIIth Congress, 1st Session.**

---

[1] See page 170.

representation by consuls in the negro states of Hayti and Liberia. A stringent form of oath [1] was prescribed, to be taken by United States officials and beneficiaries. The Act of February 25th, 1862, provided for a legal-tender **National Paper Currency** (commonly called "greenbacks"). It more than took the place of the favorite measure of the Federalists and Whigs, a National Bank. Most of these measures were passed by party votes. The Tariff Act of December 24th, 1861, again increased the duties on imports. Congress adjourned July 17th, 1862.

8. During the summer of 1862 the President at last determined to use Slavery itself as a means either of coercion or of punishment. By proclamation, therefore, September 22d, 1862, he warned the revolting States that, unless they should return to their allegiance by January 1st, 1863, he would, as an act of military necessity, declare the slaves in those States to be free men. As this proclamation had no effect, he issued his **Emancipation Proclamation**, January 1st, 1863, in the terms previously announced.[2] The two years of civil war had so developed anti-slavery feeling in the North that the Emancipation Proclamation excited no such opposition as would have met it if proposed in 1861. Nevertheless, it caused a temporary falling off in the Republican vote.

---

[1] Commonly called the "Iron Clad Oath."

[2] It did not apply to the slaves in States not in rebellion, nor to the portions of rebellious States then conquered. For these an Amendment to the Constitution was necessary (see p. 195).

9. Congress met December 1st, 1862. Under the **XXXVIIth Congress, 2d Session.** pressure of **Military Necessity** the Acts of this Session were based upon a looser construction of the Constitution than those of the previous Session. An Act was passed to legitimate the suspension of the writ of **Habeas Corpus.** A Draft or Conscription Act, more sweeping than that proposed in 1814,[1] was adopted. It provided that a part of the able-bodied citizens should be drawn by lot for service in the army.[2] Land grants were made to Kansas, and the Secretary of the Treasury was authorized to obtain further loans. Appropriations for this year amounted to about $972,000,000. Congress adjourned March 3d, 1863. **West Virginia** had become a State of the Union, December 31st, 1862.

10. By the **Writ of Habeas Corpus**, in substance, an imprisoned person obtains an examination before the courts and a release, if his imprisonment is shown to be without warrant of law. Its **Suspension** was considered necessary on account of the number of Northern courts disposed to resist military arrests of suspected persons. It is certain, however, that the summary arrests and imprisonments in United States forts, the seizures of newspapers, and the dispersions of public meetings, which followed the suspension of the writ of Habeas Corpus, did much to increase the opposition vote for a time. The month of July, 1863,

---

[1] See p. 78.

was notable for the sickening scenes of the three days' **Draft Riot** in New York City, originating in resistance to the Conscription Act of the last Session. It was forcibly suppressed, and the draft was carried out.

11. Congress met December 7th, 1863, with a Republican majority in both branches.[1] In the House Schuyler Colfax, of Indiana, a Republican, was chosen Speaker. Both Houses passed the **Internal Revenue Law,** for the collection of a revenue from domestic manufactures, etc., the **Income Tax Law,** levying a tax of five per cent. on incomes over $600, and the **National Bank Law,** creating a system of banks to take the place of State banks. The Draft and Homestead Laws were amended and strengthened, and the Fugitive Slave Law of 1850 was abolished. A proposed XIIIth Amendment to the Constitution abolishing Slavery was adopted by the Senate, but did not receive a two-thirds majority in the House. Congress adjourned July 2d, 1864.

**XXXVIIIth Congress, 1st Session.**

12. A Convention of **Radical Men,** who considered President Lincoln timid and irresolute, and who wished to deal with rebellion and rebels more harshly, met at Cleveland, Ohio, May 31st, 1864, and nominated John C. Fremont, of California, and John C Cochrane, of New York.[2] The **Republican National Convention** met at Baltimore, June 7th, and

---

[1] Senate, 36 Rep., 14 Dem. House, 102 Rep., 75 Dem., 9 "Border State men."

[2] They afterwards withdrew in favor of the Republican candidates.

adopted a platform declaring war upon Slavery, and demanding that no terms but unconditional surrender should be given to the rebellious States. It nominated Abraham Lincoln, of Illinois, and Andrew Johnson, of Tennessee.[1] The **Democratic National Convention** met at Chicago, August 29th. It came under the control of the Peace Democracy,[2] and declared in its platform that it was the sense of the American people that, after four years of failure to restore the Union by war, during which the Constitution had been violated in all its parts under the plea of military necessity, a cessation of hostilities ought to be obtained. It nominated George B. McClellan, of New Jersey, and George H. Pendleton, of Ohio.

13. The Democratic party was thus committed to the declaration that the war was a failure. This drove the doubtful votes into support of the Republican candidates, and assured their success. In the **Presidential Election** in November Republican electors were chosen by all the States not in rebellion, except New Jersey, Delaware, and Kentucky. The members chosen to the XXXIXth Congress were also overwhelmingly Republican.

14. Congress met December 6th, 1864. In February, 1865, the House finally passed the XIIIth

**XXXVIIth Congress, 2d Session.**

---

[1] Johnson's nomination was exactly parallel with that of Tyler by the Whigs. Both were Strict Constructionists by nature, temporarily adrift without a party, and offered by the loose constructionist party a place rather of honor than importance, to secure Opposition votes.

[2] Called by the Union party ' Copperheads," from a well-known Northern snake.

Amendment which had failed at the last Session to receive a two-thirds majority.[1] It was modeled on the language of the Ordinance of 1787,[2] which thus, after a struggle of nearly eighty years, became the law of the land. A **Joint Resolution** was passed by both Houses, declaring that the rebellious States were in such condition that no valid election had been held in them for electors, and that no electoral votes from them should be counted. The electoral votes were counted, and were found to be for Lincoln and Johnson 212, and for McClellan and Pendleton 21. **Lincoln** and **Johnson** were therefore declared elected. At this Session the **Freedmen's Bureau Bill** was passed. It organized a bureau for the protection of freedmen and refugees from the South. March 3d, 1865, Congress adjourned, and March 4th Lincoln and Johnson were sworn into office.

---

[1] This was ratified by three-fourths of the States, and was proclaimed to be in force, December 18th, 1865.

[2] See page 193. This provision of the ordinance of 1787 had been imitated in 1820 (Missouri) and in 1846 (Wilmot Proviso).

# CHAPTER XXI.

## TWENTIETH ADMINISTRATION, 1865-1869.

**Abraham Lincoln, President.    Andrew Johnson, Vice-President
XXXIXth and XLth Congresses.**

*Popular vote for President in 1864: Rep.* 2,216,067
*Dem.* 1,808,725.

1. THE gentleness, kindliness, and greatness of mind of **President Lincoln** were just beginning to win general appreciation when he fell by assassination, April 14th, 1865. The rebel army of Northern Virginia had previously surrendered, and the other rebel armies rapidly followed its example. On the death of President Lincoln, **Andrew Johnson** succeeded to his office, and to his difficult task, the reconstruction of the rebellious States.

2. **The Constitution** had made no provision for the reception of a State which had formally claimed the right to secede, and renounced its membership in the Union. To admit them at once to their former position would have been to give the negro race to the control of their former masters. The claims of the

negroes to security in their lately granted freedom seemed to the mass of the Northern people superior to all theoretical arguments on the relations of the States to the Federal Government. They believed that the rebellious States should be kept in a position approaching that of Territories, until Congress should be satisfied of the safety of the negroes and re-admit them to the Union.

3. To President Johnson, a Strict Constructionist by nature, the idea that a State could be punished for treason by a Federal Congress was incomprehensible. His **Policy of Reconstruction** was to punish individuals, if necessary, for treason, but to re-install the States at once in all the powers held by them before rebellion, and this policy he endeavored to carry out by successive Proclamations. He declared all the Southern ports open to commerce, except four in Texas. He proclaimed amnesty and pardon to all persons engaged in the rebellion, except fourteen classes of leaders, who were to make special applications for pardon. He restored the writ of Habeas Corpus in the Northern States, and appointed Provisional Governors for the rebellious States, with the purpose of organizing permanent governments as soon as possible.

4. The **Republican State Conventions** of 1865 generally approved the President's policy, so far as it had been developed, but stipulated that the Southern States should be held under provisional governments until they should recognize and accept the results of the war, including the freedom and protection of the

negroes. Unfortunately, the license of camp life had left many of the Southern whites with but slight disposition to live on terms of political equality with the former slaves. Cases of outrage became common, so that the new Congress, which was overwhelmingly Republican, came together with a fixed determination to protect the negroes at any cost. The party leaders seem to have been suspicious of President Johnson's willingness to disregard "State Rights" in assisting them.

5. Congress met December 4th, 1865, with a Republican majority in both branches,[1] sufficient, if necessary, to carry any bill over the President's veto. In the House Speaker Colfax was re-elected. In February, 1866, the **First Freedmen's Bureau Bill** was passed by both Houses. It aimed at the protection and assistance of the freedmen at the South. It was vetoed by the President on the grounds that it provided for unlimited distribution of lands to freedmen, that it tended to keep the minds of the negroes restless and uneasy, and that it had been passed by a Congress which was without representatives from the Southern States. An effort to pass the bill over the veto did not receive the full party vote, and consequently did not obtain a two-thirds majority. It was now evident that there was at least a disagreement between the President and the party which had elected him.

**XXXIXth Congress, 1st Session.**

6. An open rupture followed the passage of the

---

[1] Senate, 40 Rep., 11 Dem.  House, 145 Rep., 40 Dem.

Civil Rights Bill in March. It was designed to make freedmen citizens of the United States,[1] (with the right to sue and be sued, to make contracts, etc.), and to punish by fine and imprisonment any person interfering with those rights. It gave Federal courts exclusive cognizance of offenses against the Act, and Federal officers the power of arresting and holding offenders to bail. The bill was vetoed. The reasons given were that it gave Federal citizenship to 4,000,000 human beings just released from bondage; that it attempted to give the law where the States had their own rights; that it overrode the State courts, and created a swarm of Federal officials charged with the power of arrest for the discriminating protection of the black race. The bill was passed over the veto and became law.

7. For the purpose of securing the principle aimed at in the Civil Rights Bill by making it a part of the Constitution, both Houses adopted the **XIVth Amendment** in June.[2] The President informed Congress of his disapproval of it. A **Homestead Bill** was passed, applying previous Homestead Bills to public lands in the South. It was agreed by both Houses that no delegation from any of the States lately in rebellion should be received by either House until both Houses should unite in declaring such State again a member of the Union.

---

[1] But this did not carry the right to vote. For that, another Amendment was necessary.

[2] Ratified by three-fourths of the States and declared in force July 28th, 1868.

8. In July the **Second Freedmen's Bureau Bill** was passed by both Houses. It continued the bureau for two years, provided for selling lands to the freedmen at a low rate, reserved the property of the late Confederate Government for their education, and ordered the President to give military protection to the negroes whenever they were molested. It was vetoed by the President. The reasons given were that it gave the President too much power; that the civil courts were perfectly able to do all that the bureau aimed at in the way of protection; and that the bureau had become a political machine, by which the negroes were used for the personal advantage of its officers. The bill was passed over the veto and became law. After reducing the army and the revenue tax, and reviving the grade of General of the Army, Congress adjourned July 28th, 1866.

9. The **Conflict** between the President and the Republican majority had now become open and angry. The Republican National Committee expelled its chairman and two of its members, who had sided with the President. It also issued an **Address to the Party,** defining the issues between Congress and the President. It called the attention of the people to the fact that the Constitution made no provisions for the treatment of insurgent States forcibly reduced to obedience,[1] and claimed that the Republican plan for tiding

---

[1] But this "break" would have been of little importance, but for the legacy left by Slavery, the freedmen. This was the element of the question which caused the trouble, and not the defect in the Constitution.

over this obstacle was wise and honest, inasmuch as it would "give loyalty a fair start." It asserted that, under the President's plan, the whites lately in rebellion would seize the reins of power, reduce the blacks to real slavery under some plausible name, and retain representation for them, while denying their political rights.

10. **XXXIXth Congress, 2d Session.** Congress met December 3d, 1866. The conflict between the Legislative and the Executive was renewed at once. The first bill of the Session, giving negroes the right to vote in the District of Columbia, was vetoed and passed over the veto. Early in the Session a Resolution to impeach President Johnson was adopted by the House, and a committee appointed to take testimony. But upon their report the House decided that the grounds of impeachment were not sufficient, and thus this resolution was finally lost.

11. The main feature of this Session was a persistent effort to **Limit the President's Power,** originating in the fear that he designed some attack upon the privileges, or perhaps the existence of the Legislative. In January, 1867, a bill was passed which took from the President the power given by the Act of July, 1862, to proclaim general amnesty.[1] Provision was made for the meeting of the XLth and all succeeding Congresses immediately after the adjournment of the preceding

---

[1] The President denied the right of Congress to do so, and proceeded to issue further Proclamations of Amnesty, claiming the right under the Constitution.

Congress. Authority was given to the clerk of the House, before its meeting, to make out a roll of regularly elected members, who alone should take part in the organization of the House.[2] The **Army Appropriation Bill** was passed with a "rider" which took from the President the command of the army by providing that his orders to it should only be given through the General of the Army, who should not be removed without the previous approval of the Senate. It also disbanded all the militia of the States lately in rebellion. The President informed Congress that he signed the bill that the appropriation might not be lost, but that he protested against the "rider," because it deprived him of the command of the army, and eleven States of their militia, both of which were guaranteed by the Constitution.

12. In February a bill for the admission of the State of **Nebraska** was passed over the veto. It provided that the new State should never deny the right of voting to any person because of his race or color. Bills were also passed to give Federal courts the power to issue writs of Habeas Corpus when any person was deprived of liberty.

13. March 2d, 1867, the **Bill to Provide Efficient Governments for the Insurrectionary States** was passed over the veto. It embodied all the claims

---

[1] This was done by the XLth Congress, but abandoned after President Johnson's term of office.

[2] To prevent the organization of any pseudo-Congress by Northern Democrats and Southern claimants of admission. Fortunately, this arrangement has not yet caused any dispute as to the organization of the House.

of Congress to control the re-admission of the Southern States. It divided them into military districts, each under the government of a Brigadier-General, who should protect the rights of all persons. Each State was to remain under this military government until a State Convention, chosen without regard to race or color, should form a State government and ratify the XIVth Amendment. When this should be done Congress engaged to re-admit the State to the Union.

14. The same day the so-called **Tenure of Office Bill** was passed over the veto. It reversed all previous legislation upon the doubtful point of the President's power to remove officials without the consent of the Senate. Hitherto, from the time of the Ist Congress, it had been held that the consent of the Senate was necessary in making an appointment, but that the power of removal was wholly in the President. Under this interpretation it was feared that there would be a wholesale removal of public officials after Congress should adjourn. This bill provided that civil officers should hold office until their successors should qualify; that the Cabinet should hold over the President's term of office, and should only be removable with the Senate's approval; that, while Congress was not in session, the President might *suspend* (not remove) any official, but that if the Senate at its next session did not concur in the suspension the suspended official should resume his office; and that the President might fill any vacancy by death or resignation while Congress was not in session. Every removal, appointment, or acceptance of

exercise of office contrary to the provisions of this Act, was declared to be "a high misdemeanor,"[1] and punishable by fine and imprisonment, or both. Congress adjourned March 3d, 1867. **Nebraska** had become a State of the Union March 1st.

15. Three **Extra Sessions of Congress** were held this year. The first met March 4th, and adjourned March 30th, 1867. The second met July 3d, and adjourned July 20th. The third met November 21st, and adjourned at the opening of the first Regular Session. The Republican majority in both branches was continued, and, though slightly reduced, was sufficient to overrule the veto, if necessary.[2] In the House Speaker Colfax was re-elected. These almost continuous Sessions were mainly for the purpose of keeping a check upon the Southern policy of the President. The work of reconstruction by Congress had been fully laid out by the last Session. It was only necessary for this Session to secure its accomplishment.

*XLth Congress, Extra Sessions.*

16. Congress met December 2d, 1867. The principal topic of interest at this Session was the train of events which led to the impeachment of the President. August 5th, 1867, he had notified **Edwin M. Stanton**, Secretary of War, whom he particularly disliked, that "public considerations of a high character" compelled him to ask the Secretary to resign. Stanton ironically replied

*XLth Congress, 1st Session.*

---

[1] Apparently with a view to future impeachment.
[2] Senate, Rep 42 Dem. 14. House, 138 Rep, 47 Dem.

that "public considerations of a high character" forbade him to resign. He was therefore suspended, under the provisions of the Tenure of Office Bill, until Congress should meet, and the General of the Army, U. S. Grant, was appointed Secretary of War *ad interim.* Stanton protested that he denied the President's right to remove him, but would yield to superior force.

17. January 14th, 1868, the Senate refused to agree to Stanton's removal. General Grant at once abandoned the office, and Stanton again took possession. The President now determined to disobey the Tenure of Office Bill, and force an issue with Congress. February 21st he again removed Stanton, and appointed General Lorenzo Thomas in his place. The same day the Senate voted that the removal was illegal. General Thomas, however, accepted the appointment, and gave Stanton notice to quit. Stanton held to his office, and sent the notice to the Speaker of the House. Thereupon the House, February 24th, resolved that the President be **Impeached** before the Senate for high crimes and misdemeanors.

18. March 5th **The Trial of the Impeachment** was begun before the Senate sitting as a Court of Impeachment, with Chief Justice Chase, of the Supreme Court, in the chair. The Articles of Impeachment were mainly for violation of the Tenure of Office Bill. During the early part of the trial the President made a tour of the North and West, and in many passionate speeches to the crowds which met him denounced the XLth Congress as "no Congress," referring to its re-

fusal to admit the delegations from Southern States. The House made these and other imprudent utterances the basis of additional Articles of Impeachment.

19. The trial lasted until May 16th, when three of he main Articles were voted on. The vote stood 35 for conviction and 19 for acquittal, 5 Republican Senators voting with 14 Democrats for acquittal. It was thus apparent that there was not a two-thirds majority for conviction. The Senate, therefore, not waiting to vote on the remaining Articles, adjourned *sine die*, and the trial was abandoned. Chief Justice Chase directed a verdict of acquittal to be entered, and Stanton resigned his office. Congress adjourned July 27th, 1868.

20. The Presidential contest between the two parties naturally turned upon the right of Congress to fill the gap in the Constitution, and lay down rules for the readmission of the revolting States. Its right to do so was inferred by the loose constructionist party, and denied by the strict constructionist party. The **Republican National Convention** met at Chicago, May 20th, 1868, and adopted a platform holding that the Southern States had abandoned and lost their positions in the Union by seceding, and could only be re-admitted on terms satisfactory to Congress. It approved he terms offered, and declared that it was the business of Congress to protect equal suffrage in the South. It nominated Ulysses S. Grant, of Illinois, and Schuyler Colfax, of Indiana. The **Democratic National Convention** met at New York City, July 4th, and adopted a platform demanding that the Southern States

should immediately and unconditionally be given the representation in Congress and the power of self-government guaranteed by the Constitution, and that the regulation of suffrage should be left to the States. It nominated Horatio Seymour, of New York, and Francis P. Blair, of Missouri.

21. At the **Presidential Election** in November Democratic electors were chosen by New York,[1] New Jersey, Oregon, and by five Southern States. All the other States which were allowed to vote[2] chose Republican electors. As the issue between the parties was distinctly made, the result of the election would seem to settle the rule that any State which formally casts off allegiance to the Federal Government, and is compelled to submit, must be re-admitted by Congress in much the same manner as a Territory applying for admission as a State.

22. Congress met December 7th, 1868. There was little party contest at this Session. In February, 1869, the electoral votes were counted, and were found to be, for Grant and Colfax 214, and for Seymour and Blair 80, if the vote of Georgia were allowed, and 71 without it. As the vote of Georgia did not affect the result the question was left undecided. **Grant** and **Colfax** were therefore declared elected. February 26th the **XVth Amendment** to the Constitution, guaranteeing the

**XLth Congress, 2d Session.**

---

[1] Alleged to have been carried by frauds in New York City.
[2] Virginia, Georgia, Mississippi, and Texas had not yet complied with the conditions of Congress and been re-admitted.

right of suffrage, without regard to race, color, or previous condition of servitude, was adopted by Congress.¹ March 3d, 1869, Congress adjourned, and March 4th Grant and Colfax were sworn into office.

---

[1] Ratified by three-fourths of the States, and declared in force March 30th 1870.

# CHAPTER XXII.

## TWENTY-FIRST ADMINISTRATION, 1869-1873.

**U. S. Grant, President.**  **Schuyler Colfax, Vice-President.**
XLIst and XLIId Congresses.

*Popular vote for President in* 1868 : *Rep.* 3,015,071, *Dem.* 2,709,613.

**XLIst Congress,** **Extra Session.** 1. CONGRESS met March 4th, 1869, with a Republican majority in both branches.[1] James G. Blaine, of Maine, a Republican, was chosen Speaker in the House. The principal business of the Session was the confirmation by the Senate of the new President's nominations to positions in the Cabinet,[2] and debate as to Mississippi, Texas, and Virginia, which had not yet ratified the XIVth Amendment or been reconstructed. April 10th a bill was passed authorizing the people of these

---

[1] Senate, 58 Rep., 10 Dem., 8 vacancies; House, 149 Rep., 64 Dem., 25 vacancies. Mississippi, Texas, Virginia, and Georgia were not represented.

[2] Except that of A. T. Stewart, of New York, as Secretary of the Treasury. He was ineligible by statute, being engaged in commerce, and his name was withdrawn.

States to vote upon the constitutions already prepared for them by State conventions, and to elect State officers and members of Congress. A new condition, however, was imposed upon their ultimate re-admission; their Legislatures were required to ratify the XVth as well as the XIVth Amendment. Congress adjourned April 10th. During the year the Supreme Court, in the important case of **Texas v. White**,[1] rendered a decision sustaining Reconstruction by Congress. The Court held that the ordinances of secession had been absolutely null; that the seceding States had never been "out of the Union;" that they had, however, during and after their rebellion, no State governments "competent to represent the State in its relations with the National Government;" and that Congress had the power to re-establish the broken relations of a rebellious State to the Union.

2. Congress met December 6th, 1869. The President's Message announced that Virginia had fulfilled the conditions precedent to recognition. Before the close of the Session, Mississippi, Texas, and Georgia had also fulfilled the conditions, and the formal work of Reconstruction was completed by the re-admission of the last-named State in July, 1870.[2] The ratifications

**XLIst Congress, 1st Session.**

---

[1] 7 Wall., 700.

[2] Tennessee was re-admitted July 24th, 1866, and Arkansas June 22d, 1868. The Act of June 25th, 1868, provided for the admission of North Carolina, South Carolina, Louisiana, Georgia, Alabama, and Florida, as soon as they should have fulfilled the conditions imposed by the Acts of March, 1867 (see p. 203); and these States (except Georgia) were successively admitted

of the XVth Amendment by these States made it a part of the Constitution,[1] and a bill was passed to enforce it by making penal any interference, by force or by fraud, with the exercise of the right of suffrage as extended by the Amendment, and by authorizing the President to use the army to prevent violations of the Act. An Act was also passed to amend the naturalization laws; it made it penal to obtain, use, dispose of, or register or vote upon a false or fraudulent certificate of naturalization, authorized the appointment of Federal supervisors of elections, in cities of over 20,000 inhabitants, with the power of summary arrest for any offence committed in their view, and extended the privilege of naturalization to alien Africans. Congress adjourned July 15th, 1870. At the December Term of 1869 the Supreme Court had decided that the action of Congress in 1862, in giving a **legal-tender** character to the paper currency,[2] was unconstitutional. In March, 1870, after the complexion of the Court had been changed by the appointment of two new Justices,[3] the legal-tender question was again

---

without further legislation. Virginia, as above stated, was re-admitted January 25th, 1870, Mississippi February 23d, 1870, and Texas March 30th, 1870. Georgia, after a partial re-admission, had declared negroes incapable of holding office; the State was therefore admitted by special Act, July 15th, 1870, after revoking her objectionable action and also ratifying the XVth Amendment.

[1] See p. 208.

[2] See p. 191. Chief Justice S. P. Chase, who delivered the opinion, had been Secretary of the Treasury in 1862, but had not originated the legal-tender feature of the currency.

[3] One was a new appointment under a law creating an additional Justiceship; the other was appointed in place of a Justice who had resigned.

introduced in another case, and the previous decision was reversed by the votes of the two new Justices.

3. The Reconstruction Acts of March, 1867, had prohibited persons disabled from holding office by the XIVth Amendment, as it was then proposed, from taking part in the State conventions held under the Act; and this disability had been extended and perpetuated in the new constitutions of some of the Southern States, particularly South Carolina, Louisiana, and Arkansas, by prohibiting the exercise of the suffrage by any person still under disability to hold office by the XIVth Amendment. Shortly before the Presidential election of 1868 it appears that a secret, oath-bound organization was formed in North Carolina under the name of the **Ku Klux Klan**,[1] mainly composed of persons under disabilities, and having for its object the terrorizing of white and colored Republican voters by murder, maiming, or whipping. The organization spread rapidly into other Southern States, but naturally found its most congenial location in the three States above named. Throughout the summer of 1870 a Senate committee took evidence on the subject, which convinced the Republican majority that "the issue between government and anarchy" in the South was fairly presented. The Democratic minority, while it deplored the "detestable and wicked outrages" which it had found, believed that their number had been grossly exaggerated for political purposes.

---

[1] Otherwise known as "The Invisible Empire" or "White League."

4. Congress met December 5th, 1870, and in January, 1871, by the admission of the Georgia members, all the States were represented in Congress for the first time since December, 1860.[1] The President's message dealt largely with a project for annexing to the United States the West Indian Republic of **San Domingo**, or Dominica. A treaty for that purpose had been negotiated between the Presidents of the two Republics, September 4th, 1869, but had been rejected by the Senate at its last Session; and President Grant now suggested an annexation by joint resolution, as in the case of Texas,[2] which would require only a majority vote in the Senate. A joint resolution was passed authorizing the President to appoint three commissioners to examine the condition of San Domingo and the desires of its people for or against annexation. An Act was passed to enforce the XVth Amendment; it extended the powers of Federal supervisors, marshals, and deputy-marshals over elections and registrations, gave Federal Circuit Courts exclusive jurisdiction over all cases arising under the Act, and empowered them to punish any State officer who should proceed in such cases in contempt of their jurisdiction. A Senate committee was appointed to investigate the condition of the Southern States, and

---

[1] Congress was now divided politically as follows: Senate, 61 Rep., 13 Dem.; House, 172 Rep., 71 Dem.

[2] To this it was objected that only a *State* could be annexed by joint resolution, and that a *Territory*, as San Domingo was intended to be, could be acquired only by treaty, if at all.

*XLIst Congress, 2d Session.*

Congress adjourned, March 4th, 1871. During this year the long-standing **Alabama Claims** of the United States upon Great Britain, arising from the depredations of Anglo-rebel privateers, were referred to arbitration by the Treaty of Washington of May 8th, 1871.[1]

**XLIId Congress, Extra Session.** 5. Congress met March 4th, 1871,[2] with a Republican majority in both branches.[3] In the House, James G. Blaine, of Maine, a Republican, was chosen Speaker. The main business of the Session was the appointment of a committee of seven Senators and fourteen Representatives to inquire into the condition of the late insurrectionary States,[4] and the passage of a very sweeping Act to enforce the XIVth Amendment.[5] This Act allowed suit in Federal courts by the party injured against any person who should in any way deprive another of the rights of a citizen; it made it a penal offence to conspire to take away from any person the rights of a citizen; it provided that inability, neglect, or refusal by any State to suppress such conspiracy, to protect the rights of its citizens,

---

[1] Ratified by the Senate, May 24th, 1871. The arbitrators, appointed by Brazil, Italy, Switzerland, Great Britain, and the United States, awarded the United States $15,500,000, in gross, as damages, September 14th, 1872.

[2] This was the last Congress which met by law immediately after the expiration of the preceding Congress (see p. 201).

[3] Senate, 57 Rep., 17 Dem.; House, 138 Rep., 103 Dem.

[4] Often called the "Ku Klux Committee."

[5] Often called the "Force Bill." There is a striking similarity between the second section of the Act and the first section of the Sedition Law of 1798. Both were passed on the same ground, the actual existence of war—foreign in 1798 (see p. 44), and domestic in 1871.

or to call upon the President for aid, should be
"deemed a denial by such State of the equal protection
of the laws" under the XIVth Amendment; it
declared such conspiracies, if not suppressed by the
authorities, "a rebellion against the Government of
the United States;" it authorized the President,
"when in his judgment the public safety shall require
it," to suspend the privilege of the writ of *habeas corpus*
in any district, and suppress the insurrection by
means of the army and navy;[1] and it excluded from
the jury-box any person "who shall, in the judgment
of the court, be in complicity with any such combination
or conspiracy." The authority to suspend the
privilege of the writ of habeas corpus was to cease
after the end of the next regular Session of Congress.
Congress adjourned April 20th, 1871.

6. The system of "rotation in office"[2] had, since
1829, taken from the people at large the ownership
of the offices filled by appointment of the President,
and vested it practically in the politicians, in and out
of Congress, who controlled the President's party.
An Act of March 3d, 1871, authorized the President
to begin a reform in the **Civil Service**, for which
thinking men of all parties had long been unanimously
anxious. Under its provisions the President appointed
a board of Civil Service Commissioners to
provide for the examination of applicants for minor

---

[1] In October and November, 1871, a number of counties in South Carolina were brought under the provisions of this section by the President's proclamation.   [2] See p. 105.

offices, and to relieve him and his Cabinet from the necessity of deciding upon such applications. The system was begun January 1st, 1872, and, though under many limitations and discouragements, continued in operation for nearly three years with the emphatic commendation of the Cabinet and the President; but in December, 1874, despite two direct appeals from President Grant, Congress refused to make any further appropriation for the system, and it was abandoned. It has not yet been revived to the full extent of its original design.

7. Congress met December 4th, 1871. Much of the time of the Session was consumed in efforts to pass a bill to remove the political disabilities imposed by the XIVth Amendment. It was introduced by the Democrats in various forms, but was regularly amended by the Republicans by the addition to it of Senator Sumner's Supplementary Civil Rights Bill, intended to prevent discrimination against negroes by common carriers and other licensed or chartered public servants. The combined bills (now requiring a two-thirds vote) were then as regularly voted down by the Democrats. It was not until May 22d, 1872, that a separate **Amnesty Bill** became law.[1] A general **Election Law** for the whole country, after being lost in the House, was placed by the Senate as a "rider"[2] upon the Civil Appropriation Bill, and so

**XLIId Congress,**
**1st Session.**

---

[1] About 350 persons, who had held the higher positions under the Confederacy, were excepted from its provisions. [2] See p. 149.

passed, but with a proviso that the Federal supervisors of elections appointed under it should have no power of arrest. A bill to extend the *habeas corpus* section of the Force Bill of the last Session until the end of the next Session was passed by the Senate, but lost in the House. Congress adjourned June 10th, 1872.

8. In 1870 the Republican party in Missouri had split into two parts. The "Radical" wing wished to maintain for the present the disqualifications imposed on the late rebels by the State Constitution during the war; the "liberal" wing, headed by B. Gratz Brown and Carl Schurz, wished to abolish these disqualifications and substitute "universal amnesty and universal enfranchisement." Supported by the Democrats, the **Liberal Republicans** carried the State, though opposed by the Federal office-holders and the influence of the Administration. This success stimulated a reaction in the National Republican party, many of whose members believed that the powers of the Federal Government over the local concerns of the States had already been enforced up to or beyond constitutional limits, that the various enforcement Acts were designed rather for the political advancement of President Grant's personal adherents than for the benefit of the country, the freedmen, or even of the Republican party; and that the efforts to police the Southern States by the force of the Federal Government ought to cease. In the spring of 1871 the Liberal Republicans and Democrats of Ohio began

to show symptoms of common feeling on these subjects, and during the summer the "Liberal" movement continued to develop within the Republican party. January 24th, 1872, the Missouri Liberals issued a call for a National Convention at Cincinnati in the following May.

9. The **Liberal Republican National Convention** met at Cincinnati May 1st, 1872, and adopted a platform pledging the party to maintain the Union of the States, emancipation, enfranchisement, the last three Amendments, universal amnesty, the writ of *habeas corpus*, and the duty of a thorough civil service reform. In respect to the relative merits of protection and free trade, the Convention confessed itself irreconcilably divided, and remitted the decision of the question to the people in their Congressional elections. So far, although the Convention was itself a revolt from the ordinary party methods, and although many of its members were inexperienced, unmanageable, and not representative of any important body of voters, its action had been very skilfully suited to its acceptance by the subsequent Democratic Convention. After six ballots, however, in most of which C. F. Adams, of Massachusetts, led, the friends of other candidates threw their votes for Horace Greeley,[1] of New York, and he was nominated by 482 votes to 187 for Adams. B. Gratz Brown, of

---

[1] He had been, during his whole political life, an ardent protectionist, and an unsparing critic of his Democratic opponents, through the columns of the newspapers of which he was editor.

Missouri, was nominated for Vice-President. Some
of the "Liberal" leaders endeavored afterward, without success, to substitute other candidates for those
nominated. The **Republican National Convention** met at Philadelphia, June 5th, renominated
President Grant unanimously, and nominated Henry
Wilson, of Massachusetts, for the Vice-Presidency by
$364\frac{1}{2}$ votes to $321\frac{1}{2}$ for Schuyler Colfax. The platform detailed the party's past achievements, approved civil service reform and the suppression of
disorders in the South, and demanded complete
equality for all men throughout the entire country.
The **Democratic National Convention** met at
Baltimore, June 9th, and by a nearly unanimous vote
adopted the Cincinnati platform and candidates. A
few recalcitrant Democrats[1] met at Louisville, Ky.,
September 3d, and nominated Charles O'Conor, of
New York, and John Quincy Adams, of Massachusetts.[2] The result of the election was the success of
the Republican candidates by an increased popular
and electoral majority, due mainly to the refusal of
very many Democrats to vote for Greeley.

10. Congress met December 2d, 1872.[3] In the
**XLIId Congress,** House, on the first day of the
    **2d Session.** Session, the Speaker called attention to the charges made by the Democrats, dur-

---

[1] Usually called "straight-outs."

[2] The candidates declined the nomination, but about 30,000 scattering votes were cast for them.

[3] Senate, 51 Rep., 23 Dem. and Lib.; House, 133 Rep., 110 Dem. and Lib.

ing the campaign, that the Vice-President, the Vice-President elect, the Secretary of the Treasury, several Senators, the Speaker of the House, and a large number of Representatives had been bribed, during the years 1867 and 1868, by presents of stock in a corporation known as the **Credit Mobilier**,[1] to vote and act for the benefit of the Union Pacific Railroad Company. On his motion, an investigating committee was appointed, L. P. Poland, of Vermont, being chairman. The **Poland Committee** reported February 18th, 1873, recommending the expulsion of Oakes Ames, of Massachusetts, for "selling to members of Congress shares of the stock of the Credit Mobilier below their real value, with intent thereby to influence the votes of such members," and of James Brooks, of New York, for receiving such stock. The House modified the proposed expulsion into an "absolute condemnation" of the conduct of both members.[2] An Act was passed to abolish the franking privilege, and another to increase the salaries of officers of the Government. The President's salary was increased from $25,000 to $50,000, and that of Senators and Representatives from $5,000 to $7,500 per annum. This last feature of the Act proved very unpopular, as it was made to apply to the salaries of the Congressmen who passed the bill,[3] and it was commonly known as the **Salary Grab**. In Febru-

---

[1] Organized to contract for building the Union Pacific R. R.
[2] Both members died within three months afterward.
[3] In so doing, however, it followed precedent.

ary, 1873, the Electoral votes were counted and were found to be, for President, Grant, 286, T. A. Hendricks, of Indiana, 42, and 21 scattering,[1] and, for Vice-President, Wilson 286, Brown 47, and 19 scattering. The votes of Louisiana and Arkansas were rejected by concurrence of both Houses.[2]

11. At this Session appeared the first case of conflict of State governments in the South. The reconstructed State constitutions, in order to guard against intimidation by disfranchised citizens, had generally provided for **Returning Boards**, usually composed of three State officers and two citizens specified by name in the constitution. The Returning Board was empowered to canvass the votes, to reject the votes of all counties (or parishes) where they should judge force or fraud had been used, and to declare the results of all elections. In Louisiana successive removals and appointments of State officers by the Governor, for the purpose of controlling the Returning Board, had resulted in the formation of two bodies, each claiming to be the legitimate Returning Board. Two State Legislatures and governments, one (Democratic) headed by Governor John McEnery, the other (Republican) headed by Governor W. P. Kellogg, were thus declared elected. Kellogg, who apparently controlled the Federal District Judge,

---

[1] Greeley died November 29th, 1872, and the Democratic and Liberal electors were compelled, on their day of voting, December 4th, to vote for other persons. Three electors in Georgia voted for Horace Greeley, but their votes were not counted, the Houses non-concurring. [2] See p. 227.

Durell, brought suit before him against his political opponents, and obtained an order, illegitimately given, that the Federal marshal should seize the building used as a State House and prevent the meeting of the McEnery Legislature. Both governments, however, were inaugurated, and each claimed recognition by Congress. The Senate committee reported that Durell's conduct was most reprehensible, that Louisiana had no real government, that the McEnery government was most nearly a government of right, and that the Kellogg government was most nearly a government in fact. A bill declaring the election of November 4th, 1872, null and void, and providing for a new election under the direction of Judge Woods, the Federal Circuit Judge, was introduced in the Senate, but was lost by a close vote. Congress adjourned March 3d, 1873, and March 4th Grant and Wilson were sworn into office.

# CHAPTER XXIII.

TWENTY-SECOND ADMINISTRATION, 1873-1877.

U. S. Grant, President.        Henry Wilson, Vice-President.
XLIIId and XLIVth Congresses.

*Popular vote for President in 1872 : Rep.* 3,597,070, *Dem.* 2,834,079.

1. PRESIDENT GRANT'S Inaugural stated that, while still believing in the advisability of the annexation of **San Domingo**, he had dropped the project since its rejection by the Senate. During this year the proposition was renewed in the form of an application by San Domingo for the establishment of a protectorate over it by the United States; but shortly afterward President Baez, who had been the chief Dominican advocate of annexation, was driven from San Domingo by a revolution, and this unpopular scheme came to an end. In April, 1873, the Supreme Court, in the **Slaughter-House Cases**,[1] began the authori-

---

[1] 16 Wall., 36. They were so called because they arose from the incorporation by Louisiana of a Slaughter-House Company, with an entire monopoly of the business in New Orleans and its vicinity.

tative construction of the XIVth and XVth Amendments. The opinion of the court held that these Amendments only placed the special privileges of citizens of the United States under the protection of the Federal Constitution and Government; that the powers of the States over the privileges of their own citizens had not been changed; and that the great objects of the Amendments were the freedom and protection of the former *slave* race.

2. Congress met December 1st, 1873, the Republican majority being continued in both branches.[1] In the House, Speaker Blaine was re-elected. The increase of pay to members of Congress at the preceding Congress was repealed. A bill which purported to "fix the amount of United States notes," but which increased their total amount, was passed by both Houses, but was vetoed by the President and failed to become law. The bill for the establishment of a republican form of government in Louisiana[2] was again introduced in the Senate, but came to no final action. Congress adjourned June 23d, 1874. In 1867 a secret order, known as **Patrons of Husbandry**, had been formed in Washington, and its subordinate lodges, or Granges,[3] had since spread all over the country. Its object was co-operation among farmers in purchasing and in other business interests. In its nature it was not political, but the

**XLIIId Congress,**
**1st Session.**

---

[1] Senate, 50 Rep., 24 Dem. and Lib.; House, 198 Rep., 93 Dem and Lib
[2] See p. 223.   [3] Hence, its members were often called **Grangers.**

high freight rates of Western railroads brought them into conflicts with its members, which colored the politics of Western States during the years 1873 and 1874, and led to several unsuccessful attempts to induce Congress to pass transportation laws for the regulation of inter-State commerce and freight rates.

3. During this and the subsequent four years, perjury became so fundamental a feature in the politics of **Louisiana** that it is extremely difficult to give any exact account of the continuing difficulties in that State.[1] It seems certain, on the one hand, that the Democrats, or McEnery party, had resolved themselves into a "white man's party," and that outrages and massacres of negroes, such as those of Colfax and Coushatta, had become a recognized factor in politics; and, on the other hand, that the Kellogg, or Republican, government was sustained only by the decisions of a Federal judge of very doubtful character, by the consequent support of Federal troops, by the scandalous execution of the registration laws, and by the reckless counting of a partisan Returning Board. In brief, the contest lay between force and fraud for the control of the State. September 14th, 1874, the McEnery party suddenly rose in arms, seized the State offices, and forced the Kellogg government to take refuge in the Custom House. On the same day Kellogg called upon the

---

[1] The fairest account available has been followed, the report of the subcommittee of the House of Representatives, consisting of two Republicans and one Democrat, January 14th, 1875.

President for Federal troops, which were furnished to him.[1] The McEnery government refused to resist Federal authority, and the Kellogg government was reinstalled at once. In January, 1875, the Legislature was organized. The McEnery party, in a hasty and disorderly fashion, seated their Representatives from contested districts, gained control of the House, and elected the Speaker, whereupon Kellogg sent United States soldiers, under General de Trobriand, who turned out the members just seated. The Kellogg party, then having a majority, elected their Speaker, the McEnery party withdrew, and again two Legislatures were organized.[2]

4. Congress met December 7th, 1874. The President's Message dealt largely with the case of Louisiana, and his Special Message of January 13th, 1875, went still more fully into the case, defended his action in it, and appealed to Congress to take some action which would relieve him from the "exceedingly unpalatable" duty of supporting Southern State governments by the use of Federal troops. At the close of the Session, therefore, by resolution, the House endorsed the Kellogg government, and the Senate

**XLIIId Congress,**
**2d Session.**

---

[1] This was justified by the President and his supporters under Art. IV., § 4, of the Constitution (see p. 792); his opponents generally admitted the justification so far, but denied that a political struggle in the Legislature was a case of "domestic violence" to be settled by Federal troops.

[2] The difficulty was left, as far as regarded the Legislature, to W. A. Wheeler (afterward Vice-President), and, after his "adjustment" of it, the party conflict smouldered until the summer of 1876, when it was renewed.

approved the President's course in Louisiana. An Act for the **Resumption of Specie Payments** was passed which provided that on and after January 1st, 1879, the Secretary of the Treasury should redeem United States legal-tender notes in coin; but it left open the question whether these legal-tender notes, up to $300,000,000, should be reissued after redemption. Senator Sumner's Supplementary **Civil Rights Bill** became law.[1] A large part of the Session was taken up in considering the mode of election of the President and Vice-President, a great part of whose possible dangers and difficulties, as they eventuated in 1876-77, were already plainly foreseen and discussed in the debates, but Congress did nothing to avoid them. Senator Morton, of Indiana,[2] introduced an Amendment to the Constitution, providing for the general choice of electors by districts, and a resolution to abolish the **Twenty-Second Joint Rule**,[3] under which the counting of electoral votes had been conducted since 1865, but neither was adopted. Congress adjourned March 4th, 1875. During the year an extensive **Whiskey Ring** was unearthed in the West; it was an association, or series of associations, of distillers and Federal offi-

---

[1] See p. 836. Senator Sumner, the original framer of the bill, had died, March 11th, 1874.

[2] His speeches in these debates are almost a history of the workings of the electoral system up to date.

[3] This, a rule adopted by both Houses, February 6th, 1865, provided in effect that any electoral vote, to which objection should be made by any member, should only be counted if both Houses agreed to count it: a non-concurrence, therefore, operated as a rejection of the vote (see p. 230).

cials for the purpose of defrauding the Government of a large amount of the tax imposed on distilled spirits, and, further, of employing a part of the proceeds in political corruption. On the trial of the indictments a number of Federal officers were convicted, and O. E. Babcock, the President's private secretary, was acquitted.

5. In the South the Democrats, generally taking the name of Conservatives, had by this time gained control of all the State governments except those of South Carolina, Florida, and Louisiana. In some of the States the Republican governments had, as in Louisiana, called upon the President for help before surrendering their positions. From Arkansas **calls for troops** had been made by Elisha Baxter, April 19th, 1874, and by Joseph Brooks, April 20th, each claiming to be the legitimate Governor. On the supersedure of both of them by the adoption of a new State Constitution, October 13th, 1874, V. V. Smith, Baxter's Lieutenant-Governor, claiming to be Governor by Baxter's abdication, called upon the President for troops; but, as he fled the State immediately afterward, no answer was given. In Mississippi the Legislature called upon the President for troops, December 18th, 1874, to suppress rioting in Warren County, and the President answered by a proclamation warning rioters to disperse. The call for troops was repeated, September 8th, 1875, by Governor A. Ames, but was refused. The Governor was advised to assemble the Legislature and make some effort to

preserve the peace of his own State, the President's language seeming to show that his patience had been exhausted.[1]

6. The State elections of 1874-75 and the elections for members of the XLIVth Congress, to meet in December, 1875, showed a sudden and remarkable change of political sentiment.[2] They resulted in the almost universal defeat of Republican candidates for State offices, even Massachusetts electing a Democratic Governor, and the election of a great majority of Democrats to the House of Representatives. The Republicans considered the result due largely to the violent suppression of the colored Republican vote in the South; the Democrats attributed it entirely to popular disgust in the North at the continuance of enforcement Acts and efforts to "dragoon" the South. Both causes seem to have been operative, assisted by the financial distress which began to be felt in 1873, and which is always apt to re-act upon the popular vote, to the prejudice of the party in power.

7. Congress met December 6th, 1875, with a Republican majority in the Senate and a Democratic majority in the House,[3] where M. C. Kerr, of Indiana, was

**XLIVth Congress, 1st Session.**

---

[1] "The whole public are tired out with these annual autumnal outbreaks in the South, and the great majority are ready now to condemn any interference on the part of the Government. I heartily wish that peace and good order may be restored without issuing the proclamation. But if it is issued. I shall instruct the commander of the forces to have no child's play."

[2] The elections were popularly called the "tidal wave."

[3] Senate, 42 Rep., 29 Dem., 2 Ind.; House, 182 Dem., 110 Rep.

chosen Speaker. The President's Message was devoted mainly to foreign affairs and to a natural recognition of the great material progress made by the nation during its first century of existence. The Session was marked by an evident increase of anxiety as to the possible occurrence of some occasion for dispute between the Democratic House and the Republican Senate about the result of the impending Presidential election; but party jealousy, and fear of losing any party advantage from the Southern situation, prevented any remedial action. **Morton's Amendment** to the Constitution,[1] and several other Amendments, with the same general object, were introduced, but not passed. Morton's bill to provide for the counting of the electoral votes met the same fate. The Senate abolished the Twenty-second Joint Rule, so that the electoral count was now left without any provisions whatever for its government. The so-called **Blaine Amendment**, prohibiting the appropriation of public school money by any State to sectarian schools, passed the House but did not secure a two-thirds vote in the Senate.[2] An unlimited **Amnesty Bill** failed to secure a two-thirds vote in the House. A bill to reduce the President's salary to $25,000 yearly after March 4th, 1877, passed both Houses, but was vetoed and failed to become law. An appropriation of $1,500,000 was made to the Centennial Exhibition at Philadelphia. The

---

[1] See p. 227.  [2] 28 to 16 in favor.

Secretary of War, W. W. Belknap, was impeached by the House on a charge of having received bribes for the appointment of a post-trader at Fort Sill. The general vote in the Senate was 36 to 25 for conviction,[1] and as this was not two thirds he was acquitted. Congress adjourned August 15th, 1876. The end of the first, and the beginning of the second, century of the separate national existence of the United States was marked by the opening of the **Centennial Exhibition** at Philadelphia,[2] and by an unusually general celebration, July 4th. **Colorado** became a State of the Union August 1st, 1876.

8. The **Independent National Convention** met at Indianapolis, May 17th, 1876. Its platform demanded the repeal of the act for resumption of specie payments, and the issue of United States notes ("greenbacks"[3]), convertible into bonds on demand, as the currency of the country. It nominated Peter Cooper, of New York, for President, and Samuel F. Cary, of Ohio, for Vice-President.[4] The **Republican National Convention** met at Cincinnati, June 14th, and adopted a platform which reviewed the party's past achievements, charged the Democratic party with treason, imbecility, falsehood,

---

[1] He had anticipated impeachment by resigning in the forenoon of the day on which he was impeached, and most of the Senators who voted Not Guilty stated that they did so on the ground that he was then a private citizen and not subject to impeachment. [2] May 10th, 1876.

[3] Hence this was usually called the **Greenback Party**.

[4] Newton Booth, of California, was first nominated for Vice-President, but declined.

and subservience to former rebels, commended the resumption of specie payments, and demanded the immediate and vigorous exercise of Federal powers to secure the rights of American citizens everywhere throughout the country. Much excitement had been caused by an alleged design of President Grant to secure for himself a **Third Term**, but his name was not presented to the Convention for the Presidential nomination. On the first six ballots James G. Blaine, of Maine, led all the other candidates; on the seventh ballot Rutherford B. Hayes, of Ohio, was nominated by 384 votes, to 351 for Blaine and 21 for B. H. Bristow, of Kentucky. William A. Wheeler, of New York, was nominated for Vice-President. The **Democratic National Convention** met at St. Louis, June 28th, and adopted a platform entirely occupied by denunciation of the Republican party for corruption, mismanagement, personal government and sectional hatred, and by demands for reform; included in these was a demand for the repeal of the specie resumption Act until proper preparation should be made for its successful enforcement. On the second Presidential ballot, Samuel J. Tilden had 535 votes to 203 for all others, and was nominated. His leading competitor, Thomas A. Hendricks, of Indiana, was nominated for Vice-President.

9. The nomination of Hayes sensibly strengthened the Republican party. A strong section of its members had held a preliminary meeting, May 15th,[1] and

---

[1] The so-called Fifth Avenue Hotel Conference.

resolved to support no candidate not pledged to civil service reform. Their warm support was at once gained by the unexpected emphasis with which the nominee advocated the cessation of the sale of appointments to office for party services. The Democratic chances were increased by the evident certainty of the choice of Democratic electors in all the Southern States excepting three. In one of these, South Carolina, the Legislature had long been extravagant and corrupt, and the Presidential campaign was complicated with a final and desperate effort by the whites to secure control of the State government. In the course of it a massacre of a negro militia force at Hamburgh,[1] and another at Ellenton, induced a call for Federal troops by the Governor, and these were placed at his disposal by the President. The **Presidential election** took place November 7th, 1876. Democratic electors were chosen by Connecticut, New York, New Jersey, and Indiana in the North, and by all the Southern States except South Carolina, Florida, and Louisiana; Republican electors were chosen by South Carolina[2] in the South, and by all the Northern States except those named above. The undisputed results[3] of the election were

---

[1] July 9th.

[2] This State was also claimed at first by the Democrats, but their members of the Congressional investigating committee agreed that the State had chosen Republican electors.

[3] The Republicans alleged that very many of the Southern electoral votes had been obtained for the Democratic candidates by the violent suppression of the colored vote, but did not formally dispute the count of these votes. The Democrats disputed the count of many individual Republican electoral votes

therefore 184 electoral votes for Tilden and Hendricks, and 172 for Hayes and Wheeler, and the whole result of the election hinged upon the final declaration of the results in Florida and Louisiana, that is, upon the decisions of the Returning Boards of those States, and upon the one disputed vote of Oregon.

10. As soon as the state of affairs in the doubtful States was discovered, a large number of prominent citizens from the North went to the State capitals to oversee the count, by invitation of President Grant and of the Democratic National Committee. The four electoral votes of **Florida** were decided by the Returning Board to be Republican by a majority of 926; this result was reached by casting out the votes of various precincts and counties. The State Supreme Court then ordered the Board to declare the result of "the face of the returns,"[1] without casting out any. The Board again met, cast out the votes of certain other precincts and counties, and declared a Repub-

---

in the North, on the ground that the electors who cast them were Federal office-holders; but in these cases the ineligible electors regularly resigned before acting and were re-chosen by the electoral colleges to fill the resulting vacancies. The statement above is therefore made as "undisputed." It does not include the single vote of Oregon.

[4] What the real "face of the returns" was is doubtful. Those acknowledged by the Board and those claimed by the Democrats agree very closely, except as to Baker County. From this county two returns were sent: (1) 130 Rep., 89 Dem., Rep. maj. 41; and (2) 143 Rep., 238 Dem., Dem. maj. 95. The former was taken by the Board, while the latter was claimed by the Democrats. As the sum total of the votes of all the other counties, as acknowledged by both parties, is almost an exact tie on the face of the returns, it will be seen that the gist of the difficulty lies in the double return from Baker County.

lican majority of 206. Before this was done, however, the day appointed for the voting of the electors had come, and the Republican electors met and voted. In **Louisiana** the Democratic electors protested without effect against the refusal of the Returning Board to add a Democrat to their number, as the law required, and against their refusal to canvass all the votes in public. After a three-weeks' session, and many changes in the returns, the Board declared the Republican electors successful by an average majority of about 4,000; the Democrats claimed 8,000 majority on the face of the returns.[1] McEnery, claiming to be Governor, gave the Democratic electors a certificate of election; in Florida the Attorney-General, as one of the Returning Board, signed the Democratic certificate. In both States the Republican Governor signed the certificates of the Republican electors. In **Oregon** the three Republican electors had a majority, but, on the claim that one of them was a Federal office-holder and ineligible, the Democratic Governor gave a certificate of the election of one Democratic and two Republican electors. The three Republican electors were certified by the Secretary of State, who was the canvassing officer of the State by statute.

11. **XLIVth Congress, 2d Session.** Congress met December 5th, 1876. The President's Message deprecated harsh judgment for any mis-

---

[1] (Returns, average) Rep., 75,759, Dem., 83,635, Dem. maj., 7,876; (Returning Board, average) Rep., 74,436, Dem., 70,505, Rep. maj. 3,931.

takes of judgment which he had made in his two terms of office, and attributed them mainly to the subordinates whose appointment had been forced upon him by Congressmen. In the House, S. J. Randall, of Pennsylvania, was chosen Speaker in place of Speaker Kerr, who had died during the summer. The Session was almost entirely taken up by the **Disputed Presidential Election**. It was evident that neither House would consent to the adoption of a joint rule for the count which should seem to operate against the candidates of its majority. Extreme Republicans were beginning to advance the idea that the Vice-President, who was to open the certificates, was also to decide between two returns; extreme Democrats argued the right of the House to decide when the emergency had arrived in which it was to elect a President. As a compromise, the **Electoral Commission** was created by Act of January 29th, 1877; it was to consist of five members chosen by the House, five by the Senate, and five Justices of the Supreme Court. Double returns, and all returns to which objection should be made, were to be referred to this Commission, whose decision was to be final unless reversed by the vote of *both* Houses. The general rule held by the Commission was that it was only empowered to canvass electoral votes, not popular votes, and to decide whether the Governor had certified those electors who had been declared elected by the canvassing authority of the State. It thus ascertained that in

Louisiana and Florida the Governors had certified the legitimate electors, while in Oregon the Governor had not. In all these cases the House voted to reject, and the Senate to sustain, the Commission's decision, and the decision was therefore sustained in favor of the Republican electors. In the case of South Carolina, and in those of electors objected to as Federal office-holders, the Commission also decided in favor of the Republican electors, and the decision was not reversed by concurrent vote of both Houses. All the thirteen doubtful votes[1] thus fell to the Republican candidates, and the result was declared[2] to be 185 votes for Hayes and Wheeler, and 184 votes for Tilden and Hendricks. Hayes and Wheeler were therefore declared elected. March 3d, 1877, Congress adjourned, and March 4th, Hayes and Wheeler were sworn into office.

---

[1] Florida 4, Louisiana 8, Oregon 1.
[2] After 4 o'clock in the morning of March 2d.

# CHAPTER XXIV.

### TWENTY-THIRD ADMINISTRATION, 1877–1881.

**Rutherford B. Hayes, President.**   **William A. Wheeler, Vice-President.**

### XLVth and XLVIth Congresses.

*Popular vote for President in* 1876: *Dem.* 4,284,757, *Rep.* 4,033,950.[1]

1. IN **Florida** the State Supreme Court had persisted in compelling a count upon the face of the returns of the votes for State officers, and the Democratic State government was thus finally declared elected and inaugurated, although the Returning Board had at first given the election to the Republican candidates. In **South Carolina** and **Louisiana** President Hayes, soon after his inauguration, ordered the Federal troops to be withdrawn,[2] and the Democratic State governments at once took possession without resistance. It was charged that the President had thereby impeached his own title to the Presidency, which "rested upon the action of the

---

[1] In Florida and Louisiana the Returning Board count has been taken.

[2] Similar orders were given in March by President Grant, but were not executed.

same Returning Boards which had declared the Republican Governors elected." It must be noted, therefore, that electors are to be chosen "in such manner as the Legislature of the State may direct," and that the power of a Legislature to commit the choice of electors to a Returning Board may be admitted without admitting its power to delegate the choice of State officers to the same hands. During the summer extensive **Railroad Strikes** and other disorders caused considerable alarm and loss of property and life, but were successfully suppressed by the State authorities, assisted, wherever necessary, by United States troops.

2. Congress met October 15th,[1] 1877, having been **XLVth Congress, 1st Session.** called to an early session by a proclamation of the President, in consequence of the failure of the preceding Congress to pass the appropriation for the army. The Senate was still Republican and the House Democratic. In the House Speaker Randall was re-elected by 149 votes to 132 for James A. Garfield, of Ohio. The most striking action of the Session was the passage of the **Bland Silver Bill.** The Act of July 14th, 1870, to refund the national debt, had made all bonds issued under it payable in "coin;" and the Act of February 12th, 1873, had "demonetized" the silver dollar, that is, had dropped it from the list of United States coins. Since that time the value of silver, as compared with gold, had been very

---

[1] Senate, Rep. 39, Dem. 36, Ind. 1; House, Dem. 153, Rep. 140.

steadily falling, and a strong feeling had grown up in both parties that the silver dollar should be restored to the list of coins and used, at least in part, for the payment of bonds. The Bland Bill provided for the resumption of the coinage of the silver dollar of 412½ grains (worth then about 92 cents), made it a legal tender for public and private debts, and directed its coinage at the rate of not less than $2,000,000 or more than $4,000,000 monthly. It was vetoed, and was passed over the veto by heavy majorities. An Act was passed forbidding the further retirement of United States notes. An Army Appropriation Bill was passed containing a proviso that it should not be lawful to employ any part of the army as a *posse comitatus*, except as expressly authorized by the Constitution or by Act of Congress. A House committee, commonly known as the **Potter Committee**,[1] was appointed to investigate the alleged frauds in the Southern States. Congress adjourned June 20th, 1878. An unexpected result of the Potter Committee's investigation was the discovery of a number of **Cipher Telegrams**[2] from persons nearly connected with Mr. Tilden, having for their object the bribery of the Returning Boards. Mr. Tilden denied that he was a party to these negotiations.

3. From the beginning of his Administration, President Hayes had not the hearty support of any party in Congress. To many of the Republicans, who had

---

[1] So-called from its chairman, Clarkson N. Potter, of New York.
[2] These were mainly translated in the office of the *New York Tribune*.

# 1877.] Hayes' Administration. 241

grown up under the enforcement system, his withdrawal of Federal troops from Southern States, and his efforts to conciliate the South in other ways, seemed to be weak, wavering, and "Sunday-school politics;" very great feeling was excited among the Democrats by his appointment of members of the Returning Boards to Federal offices; his partial efforts to free himself from the control which Congressmen had gradually acquired over appointments deprived him of much of a President's usual influence over Congress; and the sudden rise to prominence of financial questions, on which neither party was thoroughly united, left him without any general or coherent party support. Many Administration measures were defeated, and others were only carried by Democratic votes. Nevertheless, President Hayes' term of office was of incalculable benefit to the country as a breathing-spell, and a relief from the almost intolerable violence of party contest. During these two years the Greenback or **National Party,** which was mainly opposed to the proposed resumption of specie payments, had largely increased its popular vote. In 1876 it had polled 80,000 votes; in the State elections of 1878 this was increased to over 1,000,000. **Specie payments** for United States notes were resumed without difficulty, January 1st, 1879.

4. **XLVth Congress, 2d Session.** Congress met December 2d, 1878. The President's Message urged upon the attention of Congress the alleged continuance of intimidation of negro voters in

the South. The only important legislation of the Session was an Act authorizing the refunding of the national debt at four per cent. interest, and an Act giving arrears of pension to those who had not yet filed applications. Congress adjourned March 4th, 1879, without passing the **Army Appropriation Bill,** owing to an endeavor by the House to add as a "rider"[1] to it a bill to repeal the general election law.[2]

5. Congress met March 18th, 1879, having been **XLVth Congress,** summoned to an extra session **Extra Session.** by a proclamation of the President. Both branches had Democratic majorities,[1] and in the House Speaker Randall was re-elected. The **Warner Silver Bill,** providing for the unlimited coinage of silver, was passed by the House, but the Senate Finance Committee refused to report it. The main business of the Session was with the **Appropriation Bills,** to all of which the Democratic majority added "riders" for the purpose of carrying out a reduction of Federal power. To the Army Bill a rider was added repealing the existing permission to the army to "keep the peace at the polls;" to the Legislative Bill was added another, repealing the authority given to Federal supervisors to count the votes at Congressional elections, and to Federal marshals to arrest at the polls; and to the Judiciary Bill was added another, forbidding the pay-

---

[1] See p. 149.   [2] See p. 216.
[3] Senate, Dem. 42, Rep. 33, Ind. 1; House, Dem. 149, Rep. 130, Nat. 14.

ment of Federal marshals for "services in connection with elections." All these were opposed by the Republicans as efforts to coerce a co-ordinate branch of the Government by refusing appropriations, were vetoed by the President, and failed to become law. Having finally passed the Appropriation Bills without riders, Congress adjourned July 1st, 1879. During the summer a considerable **Negro Exodus** took place from the South to the Northwest. It was ascribed by Republicans to Southern ill-treatment of negroes, and by Democrats to the operations of railroad agents.

6. Congress met December 1st, 1879. The President's Message advised Congress not to legislate further at present in regard to the coinage, recommended the retirement of the legal tenders, and urged the necessity of reform in the civil service. No important political action was taken except the passage of a law to prevent the use of the army to keep the peace at the polls, but with the proviso that it should not be construed to prevent the constitutional use of the army to suppress domestic violence in a State. The "riders" of the last Session were again added to Appropriation and Deficiency Bills, but were again vetoed and failed to become law. The Democratic opposition to the **General Election Law** was very much weakened by a Supreme Court decision during the Session, upholding the constitutionality of the law. Congress adjourned June 16th, 1880. Not

**XLVIth Congress,**
    **1st Session.**

one effective step had yet been taken, by statute or amendment, to avoid the recurrence of a disputed electoral count such as that of 1876. The Republicans were unwilling to entrust the count entirely to the control of a Democratic Congress, and neither party was willing to entrust the final and absolute decision upon the validity of a State's electoral votes to the highest judicial authority of the State itself.[1] The attempted counting-out of the Republican majority in the Legislature of **Maine**, by the Governor and Council, in the winter of 1878–79, had emphasized the danger by showing the possibility of double returns from some Northern State; but nothing was done, nor has anything since been done in this direction.

7. The **Republican National Convention** met June 5th, 1880, at Chicago. The Grant majority in the State Conventions of New York, Pennsylvania, and Illinois had ordered their delegates to cast the entire vote of their States for ex-President Grant, without regard to the preferences of individual districts. The Convention, however, refused to recognize the unit rule, and absolved the delegates from obedience to it. The platform detailed the party's achievements in the past, denounced the Democratic party and the "Solid South," and favored a protective tariff, the protection of all citizens in all their rights by Federal power, and the restriction of

---

[1] This, the proposition of Senator Edmunds, of Vermont, would seem to be in strict pursuance of the intention of the electoral system.

Chinese immigration. On the thirty-sixth ballot, June 8th, James A. Garfield, of Ohio, was nominated for President. His nomination was the result of a sudden union of the Blaine, Sherman, and other delegates against those delegates, about 306 in number, who voted steadily for Grant to the end. Chester A. Arthur, of New York, was nominated for Vice-President. The **Greenback-Labor National Convention** met at Chicago, June 9th, and adopted a platform which claimed for the Government the entire control of the issue of money, and condemned the grant of any such power to corporations, the continuance of grants of lands to railroads, and the immigration of Chinese. It nominated James B. Weaver, of Iowa, for President, and B. J. Chambers, of Texas, for Vice-President. The **Democratic National Convention** met at Cincinnati, June 22d, and adopted a strict construction platform. It called for home rule, honest money ("gold and silver, and paper convertible into coin on demand" [1]), a revenue tariff, and permission to purchase ships abroad, and denounced the "fraud of 1876–77" and the Administration's "claim of a right to surround the ballot-boxes with troops." It nominated Winfield S. Hancock, of Pennsylvania, for President, on the second ballot, and William H. English, of Indiana, for Vice-President. In the **Presidential election** in November, Democratic electors were chosen by all the

---

[1] The latter part of this definition would hardly have been accepted by the original, or Jeffersonian, Democracy.

Southern States, and by New Jersey, California,[1] and Nevada in the North; all the other States chose Republican electors. On the entire popular vote the Republicans had a slight plurality,[2] neither party having a majority. The Greenback vote did not affect the result, except in California, Indiana, and New Jersey, where it prevented either party from having a majority. The Congressional elections gave the Republicans a majority of one over all in the House of Representatives,[3] which was to meet in December, 1881.

8. Congress met December 6th, 1880. The principal business of the Session was the count of the electoral votes, as to which there was, luckily, no doubtful question of vital importance to either party. Georgia had as yet neglected to alter her State law, as passed under the Confederacy, by which her electors met and voted on the second Wednesday of December instead of the first Wednesday, as required by Federal law. Both parties amicably agreed to count the vote of Georgia "in the alternative,"[4] declaring that Garfield and Arthur had 214 votes, that Hancock and English had 155 votes if the vote of Georgia were counted, and 144 votes if the vote of Georgia were not counted, and that in either case Garfield and Arthur were elected. Congress adjourned March 3d, 1881, and March 4th Garfield and Arthur were sworn into office.

**XLVIth Congress, 2d Session.**

---

[1] One Democratic elector in California was defeated.
[2] Rep. 4,442,950, Dem. 4,442,035. Grb. 306,867, Scat. 12,576; Rep. plur. 915.   [3] Rep. 147, Dem. 136, Grb. 9, Ind. 1.   [4] See p. 90.

9. An extra session of the Senate, to consider the new President's nominations to office, met immediately after the inauguration. In actual membership the parties were a tie,[1] but the casting vote of the Vice-President gave the Republicans a majority. They at once undertook to change the employees of the Senate, as the Democrats had done on obtaining control of the Senate. The Democrats resisted the attempt on the ground that the Senate, at its extra session, ought to attend only to the specific business for which it had been summoned; and, there being no rules in the Senate to limit debate, the dispute was prolonged for many weeks, to the neglect of all other business. The sudden resignation of the two Republican Senators from New York, because of a disagreement with the President as to certain appointments in their State, left the Democrats in the majority, and the Senate, having confirmed the President's nominations, adjourned May 24th, 1881. The attention of the whole people was again called to the necessity of **Civil-Service Reform**—which had long been formally approved by all parties and faithfully executed by none—by the crime of a disappointed office-seeker in shooting the President, with intent to kill him, July 2d, 1881. September 19th, President Garfield died, and Vice-President Arthur became President in his stead.

---

[1] Dem. 37, Rep. 37, Ind. 2. The independent vote was divided between the two parties.

# APPENDIX A.

## Articles of Confederation.

*Articles of Confederation and Perpetual Union between the States of New Hampshire, Massachusetts Bay, Rhode Island and Providence Plantations, Connecticut, New York, New Jersey, Pennsylvania, Delaware, Maryland, Virginia, North Carolina, South Carolina, and Georgia.*

ARTICLE I.—The style of this Confederacy shall be, "The United States of America."

ARTICLE II.—Each State retains its sovereignty, freedom, and independence, and every power, jurisdiction, and right, which is not by this Confederation expressly delegated to the United States in Congress assembled.

ARTICLE III.—The said States hereby severally enter into a firm league of friendship with each other, for their common defense, the security of their liberties, and their mutual and general welfare, binding themselves to assist each other against all force offered to or attacks made upon them, or any of them, on account of religion, sovereignty, trade, or any other pretense whatever.

Article IV.—The better to secure and perpetuate mutual friendship and intercourse among the people of the different States in this Union, the free inhabitants of each of these States, paupers, vagabonds, and fugitives from justice excepted, shall be entitled to all privileges and immunities of free citizens in the several States; and the people of each State shall have free ingress and regress to and from any other State, and shall enjoy therein all the privileges of trade and commerce subject to the same duties, impositions, and restrictions as the inhabitants thereof respectively; provided that such restrictions shall not extend so far as to prevent the removal of property imported into any State to any other State of which the owner is an inhabitant; provided also, that no imposition, duties, or restriction shall be laid by any State on the property of the United States or either of them. If any person guilty of, or charged with, treason, felony, or other high misdemeanor in any State shall flee from justice and be found in any of the United States, he shall, upon demand of the governor or executive power of the State from which he fled, be delivered up and removed to the State having jurisdiction of his offense. Full faith and credit shall be given in each of these States to the records, acts, and judicial proceedings of the courts and magistrates of every other State.

Article V.—For the more convenient management

of the general interests of the United States, delegates shall be annually appointed in such manner as the Legislature of each State shall direct, to meet in Congress on the first Monday in November, in every year with a power reserved to each State to recall its delegates, or any of them, at any time within the year, and to send others in their stead for the remainder of the year. No State shall be represented in Congress by less than two, nor by more than seven members; and no person shall be capable of being a delegate for more than three years in any term of six years; nor shall any person, being a delegate, be capable of holding any office under the United States for which he, or another for his benefit, receives any salary, fees, or emolument of any kind. Each State shall maintain its own delegates in any meeting of the States and while they act as members of the Committee of the States. In determining questions in the United States in Congress assembled, each State shall have one vote. Freedom of speech and debate in Congress shall not be impeached or questioned in any court or place out of Congress; and the members of Congress shall be protected in their persons from arrests and imprisonment during the time of their going to and from, and attendance on, Congress, except for treason, felony, or breach of the peace.

ARTICLE VI.—No State, without the consent of the United States, in Congress assembled, shall send any embassy to, or receive any embassy from, or enter into any conference, agreement, alliance, or treaty with any king, prince, or state; nor shall any person holding any office of profit or trust under the United States, or any of them, accept of any present, emolument, office, or title of any kind whatever from any king, prince, or oreign state; nor shall the United States, in Congress assembled, or any of them, grant any title of nobility.

No two or more States shall enter into any treaty, confederation, or alliance whatever between them, without the consent of the United States, in Congress assembled, specifying accurately the purposes for which the same is to be entered into, and how long it shall continue.

No State shall lay any imposts or duties which may interfere with any stipulations in treaties entered into by the United States, in Congress assembled, with any king, prince, or state, in pursuance of any treaties already proposed by Congress to the courts of France and Spain.

No vessels of war shall be kept up in time of peace by any State, except such number only as shall be deemed necessary by the United States, in Congress assembled, for the defense of such State or its trade, nor shall any body of forces be kept up by any State in time of peace, except such number only as, in the judgment of the United States, in Congress assembled, shall be deemed requisite to garrison the forts necessary for the defense of such State; but every State shall always keep up a well-regulated and disciplined militia, sufficiently armed and accoutered, and shall provide and constantly have ready for use in public stores a due number of field-pieces and tents, and a proper quantity of arms, ammunition and camp equipage.

No State shall engage in any war without the consent of the United States, in Congress assembled, unless such State be actually invaded by enemies, or sha have received certain advice of a resolution being formed by some nation of Indians to invade such State, and the danger is so imminent as not to admit of a delay till the United States, in Congress assembled, can be consulted; nor shall any State grant commissions to any ships or vessels of war, nor letters of marque or reprisal, except it be after a declaration of war by the United States, in Congress assembled, and then only against the kingdom or state, and the subjects thereof, against which war has been so declared, and under such regulations as shall be established by the United States, in Congress assembled, unless such State be infested by pirates, in which case vessels of war may be fitted out for that occasion, and kept so long as the danger shall continue, or until the United States, in Congress assembled, shall determine otherwise.

ARTICLE VII.—When land forces are raised by any State for the common defense, all officers of or under the rank of Colonel shall be appointed by the Legislature of each State respectively by whom such forces shall be raised, or in such manner as such State shall direct, and all vacancies shall be filled up by the State which first made the appointment.

ARTICLE VIII.—All charges of war, and all other expenses that shall be incurred for the common defense or general welfare, and allowed by the United States, in Congress assembled, shall be defrayed out of a common treasury, which shall be supplied by the several States in proportion to the value of all land within each State, granted to, or surveyed for, any person, as such land and the buildings and improvements thereon shal be estimated, according to such mode as the United States, in Congress assembled, shall, from time to time, direct and appoint. The taxes for paying that proportion shall be laid and levied by the authority and direction of the Legislatures of the several States, within the time agreed upon by the United States, in Congress assembled.

ARTICLE IX.—The United States, in Congress assembled, shall have the sole and exclusive right and power of determining on peace and war, except in the cases mentioned in the sixth Article; of sending and receiving ambassadors; entering into treaties and alliances, provided that no treaty of commerce shall be made, whereby the legislative power of the respective States shall be restrained from imposing such imposts and duties on foreigners as their own people are subjected to, or from prohibiting the exportation or importation of any species of goods or commodities whatever; of establishing rules for deciding, in all cases, what captures on land and water shall be legal, and in what manner prizes taken by land or naval forces in the service of the United States shall be divided or appropriated; of granting letters of marque and reprisal in times of peace; appointing courts for the trial of piracies and felonies committed on the high seas; and establishing courts for receiving and determining finally appeals in all cases of captures; provided that no member of Congress shall be appointed a judge of any of the said courts.

The United States, in Congress assembled, shall also be the last resort on appeal in all disputes and differences now subsisting, or that hereafter may arise between two or more States concerning boundary, jurisdiction, or any other cause whatever; which authority shall always be exercised in the manner following: Whenever the legislative or executive authority, or lawful agent of any State in controversy with another, shall present a petition to Congress, stating the matter in question, and praying for a hearing, notice thereof shall be given by order of Congress to the legislative or executive authority of the other State in controversy, and a day assigned for the appearance of the parties by their lawful agents, who shall then be directed to appoint, by joint consent, commissioners or judges to constitute a court for hearing and determining the matter in question; but if they cannot agree, Congress shall name three persons out of each of the United States, and from the list of such persons each party shall alternately strike out one, the petitioners beginning, until the number shall be reduced to thirteen; and from that number not less than seven nor more than nine names, as Congress shall direct, shall, in the presence of Congress, be drawn out by lot; and the persons whose names shall be so drawn, or any five of them, shall be com

## Articles of Confederation. 255

missioners or judges, to hear and finally dete mine the controversy, so always as a major part of the judges who shall hear the cause shall agree in the determination; and if either party shall neglect to attend at the day appointed, without showing reasons which Congress shall judge sufficient, or being present, shall refuse to strike, the Congress shall proceed to nominate three persons out of each State, and the secretary of Congress shall strike in behalf of such party absent or refusing; and the judgment and sentence of the court, to be appointed in the manner before prescribed, shall be final and conclusive; and if any of the parties shall refuse to submit to the authority of such court, or to appear or defend their claim or cause, the court shall nevertheless proceed to pronounce sentence or judgment, which shall in like manner be final and decisive; the judgment or sentence and other proceedings being in either case transmitted to Congress, and lodged among the acts of Congress for the security of the parties concerned; provided, that every commissioner, before he sits in judgment, shall take an oath, to be administered by one of the judges of the supreme or superior court of the State where the cause shall be tried, " well and truly to hear and determine the matter in question, according to the best of his judgment, without favor, affection, or hope of reward." Provided, also, that no State shall be deprived of territory for the benefit of the United States.

All controversies concerning the private right of soil claimed under different grants of two or more States, whose jurisdictions, as they may respect such lands and the States which passed such grants are adjusted, the said grants or either of them being at the same time claimed to have originated antecedent to such settlement of jurisdiction, shall, on the petition of either party to the Congress of the United States, be finally determined, as near as may be, in the same manner as is before prescribed for deciding disputes respecting territorial jurisdiction between different States.

The United States, in Congress assembled, shall also have the sole and exclusive right and power of regulating the alloy and value of coin struck by their own authority, or by that of the respective States; fixing the standard of weights and measures throughout the United States; regulating the trade and managing all affairs with the Indians, not members of any of the States; provided that the legislative right of any State, within its own limits, be not infringed or violated; establishing and regulating post offices from one State to another, throughout all the United States, and exacting such postage on the papers passing through the same as may be requisite to defray the expenses of the said office; appointing all officers of the land forces in the service of the United States, excepting regimental officers; appointing all the officers of the naval forces, and commissioning all officers whatever in the service of the United States; making rules for the government and regulation of the said land and naval forces, and directing their operations.

The United States in Congress assembled, shall have

authority to appoint a committee, to sit in the recess of Congress, to be denominated, "A Committee of the States," and to consist of one delegate from each State, and to appoint such other committees and civil officers as may be necessary for managing the general affairs of the United States under their direction; to appoint one of their number to preside; provided that no person be allowed to serve in the office of president more than one year in any term of three years; to ascertain the necessary sums of money to be raised for the service of the United States, and to appropriate and apply the same for defraying the public expenses; to borrow money or emit bills on the credit of the United States, transmitting every half year to the respective States an account of the sums of money so borrowed or emitted; to build and equip a navy; to agree upon the number of land forces, and to make requisitions from each State for its quota, in proportion to the number of white inhabitants in such State, which requisition shall be binding; and thereupon the Legislature of each State shall appoint the regimental officers, raise the men, and clothe, arm, and equip them in a soldier-like manner, at the expense of the United States; and the officers and men so clothed, armed, and equipped shall march to the place appointed, and within the time agreed on by the United States, in Congress assembled; but if the United States, in Congress assembled, shall, on consideration of circumstances, judge proper that any State should not raise men, or should raise a smaller number than its quota, and that any other State should raise a greater number of men than the quota thereof, such extra number shall be raised, officered clothed, armed and equipped in the same manner as the quota of such State, unless the Legislature of such State shall judge that such extra number can not be safely spared out of the same, in which case they shall raise, officer, clothe, arm, and equip as many of such extra number as they judge can be safely spared, and the officers and men so clothed, armed, and equipped shall march to the place appointed, and within the time agreed on by the United States, in Congress assembled.

The United States, in Congress assembled, shall never engage in a war, nor grant letters of marque and reprisal in time of peace, nor enter into any treaties or alliances, nor coin money, nor regulate the value thereof, nor ascertain the sums and expenses necessary for the defense and welfare of the United States, or any of them, nor emit bills, nor borrow money on the credit of the United States, nor appropriate money, nor agree upon the number of vessels of war to be built or purchased, or the number of land or sea forces to be raised, nor appoint a commander-in-chief of the army or navy, unless nine States assent to the same, nor shall a question on any other point, except for adjourning from day to day, be determined, unless by the votes of a majority of the United States, in Congress assembled

The Congress of the United States shall have power to adjourn to any time within the year, and to any place within the United States, so that no period of adjournment be for a longer duration than the space of six months, and shall publish the journal of their proceedings monthly, except such parts thereof relating to treaties, alliances, or military operations as in their judgment require secrecy; and the yeas and nays of the delegates of each State, on any question, shall be entered on the journal when it is desired by any delegate; and the delegates of a State, or any of them, at his or their request, shall be furnished with a transcript of the said journal except such parts as are above excepted, to lay before the Legislatures of the several States.

ARTICLE X.—The Committee of the States, or any nine of them, shall be authorized to execute, in the recess of Congress, such of the powers of Congress as the United States, in Congress assembled, by the consent of nine States, shall, from time to time, think expedient to vest them with; provided that no power be delegated to the said Committee, for the exercise of which, by the Articles of Confederation, the voice of nine States in the Congress of the United States assembled is requisite.

ARTICLE XI.—Canada, acceding to this Confederation, and joining in the measures of the United States, shall be admitted into, and entitled to all the advantages of this Union; but no other colony shall be admitted into the same, unless such admission be agreed to by nine States.

ARTICLE XII.—All bills of credit emitted, moneys borrowed, and debts contracted by or under the authority of Congress, before the assembling of the

United States, in pursuance of the present Confederation, shall be deemed and considered as a charge against the United States, for payment and satisfaction whereof the said United States and the public faith are hereby solemnly pledged.

ARTICLE XIII.—Every State shall abide by the determinations of the United States, in Congress assembled, on all questions which by this Confederation are submitted to them. And the Articles of this Confederation shall be inviolably observed by every State and the Union shall be perpetual; nor shall any alteration at any time hereafter be made in any of them, unless such alteration be agreed to in a Congress of the United States, and be afterwards confirmed by the Legislatures of every State.

AND WHEREAS it hath pleased the great Governor of the world to incline the hearts of the Legislatures we respectively represent in Congress to approve of, and to authorize us to ratify, the said Articles of Confederation and perpetual Union, know ye, that we, the undersigned delegates, by virtue of the power and authority to us given for that purpose, do, by these presents, in the name and in behalf of our respective constituents, fully and entirely ratify and confirm each and every of the said Articles of Confederation and perpetual Union, and all and singular the matters and things therein contained. And we do further solemnly plight and engage the faith of our respective constituents, that they shall abide by the determinations of the United States, in Congress assembled, on all questions which by the said Confederation are submitted to them; and that the Articles thereof shall be inviolably observed by the States we respectively represent, and that the Union shall be perpetual. In witness whereof, we have hereunto set our hands in Congress. Done at Philadelphia, in the State of Pennsylvania, the ninth day of July, in the year of our Lord 1778, and in the third year of the Independence of America.

# APPENDIX B.

## Constitution of the United States of America.

### PREAMBLE.[1]

WE the people of the United States, in order to form a more perfect union, establish justice, insure domestic tranquillity, provide for the common defense, promote the general welfare, and secure the blessings of liberty to ourselves and our posterity, do ordain and establish this Constitution for the United States of America.

### ARTICLE I. LEGISLATIVE DEPARTMENT.

#### *Section I.  Congress in General.*[2]

All legislative powers herein granted shall be vested in a Congress of the United States, which shall consist of a Senate and House of Representatives.

#### *Section II.  House of Representatives.*

1. The House of Representatives shall be composed of members chosen every second year by the people of the several States; and the electors in each State shall

---

[1] Compare the Preamble with Confederation Articles I and III.

[2] Compare Article I, §§ I-VII with Confed. Article V.

have the qualifications requisite for electors of the most numerous branch of the State Legislature.

2. No person shall be a representative who shall not have attained to the age of twenty-five years, and been seven years a citizen of the United States, and who shall not, when elected, be an inhabitant of that State in which he shall be chosen.

3. Representatives and direct taxes shall be apportioned among the several States which may be included within this Union, according to their respective numbers, which shall be determined by adding to the whole number of free persons, including those bound to service for a term of years, and excluding Indians not taxed, three-fifths of all other persons. The actual enumeration shall be made within three years after the first meeting of the Congress of the United States, and within every subsequent term of ten years, in such manner as they shall by law direct. The number of representatives shall not exceed one for every thirty thousand, but each State shall have at least one representative; and until such enumeration shall be made, the State of New Hampshire shall be entitled to choose three, Massachusetts eight, Rhode Island and Providence Plantations one, Connecticut five, New York six, New Jersey four, Pennsylvania eight, Delaware one Maryland six, Virginia ten, North Carolina five, South Carolina five, and Georgia three.

4. When vacancies happen in the representation from any State, the executive authority thereof shall issue writs of election to fill such vacancies.

5. The House of Representatives shall choose their speaker and other officers, and shall have the sole power of impeachment.

*Section III. Senate.*

1. The Senate of the United States shall be composed of two senators from each State, chosen by the Legislature thereof for six years, and each senator shall have one vote.

2. Immediately after they shall be assembled in consequence of the first election, they shall be divided, as equally as may be, into three classes. The seats of the senators of the first class shall be vacated at the expiration of the second year, of the second class at the expiration of the fourth year, and of the third class at the expiration of the sixth year, so that one-third may be chosen every second year; and if vacancies happen, by resignation or otherwise, during the recess of the Legislature of any State, the executive thereof may make temporary appointments until the next meeting of the Legislature, which shall then fill such vacancies.

3. No person shall be a senator who shall not have attained to the age of thirty years, and been nine years a citizen of the United States, and who shall not, when elected, be an inhabitant of that State for which he shall be chosen.

4. The Vice-President of the United States shall be President of the Senate, but shall have no vote, unless they be equally divided.

5. The Senate shall choose their officers, and also a

president *pro tempore*, in the absence of the Vice President, or when he shall exercise the office of President of the United States.

6. The Senate shall have the sole power to try all impeachments. When sitting for that purpose, they shall be on oath or affirmation. When the President of the United States is tried, the chief justice shall preside; and no person shall be convicted without the concurrence of two-thirds of the members present.

7. Judgment in case of impeachment shall not extend farther than to removal from office, and disqualification to hold and enjoy any office of honor, trust, or profit under the United States; but the party convicted shall, nevertheless, be liable and subject to indictment, trial, judgment, and punishment according to law.

### Section IV. Both Houses.

1. The times, places, and manner of holding elections for senators and representatives shall be prescribed in each State by the Legislature thereof; but the Congress may at any time, by law, make or alter such regulations, except as to the place of choosing senators.

2. The Congress shall assemble at least once in every year, and such meeting shall be on the first Monday in December, unless they shall by law appoint a different day.

### Section V. The Houses Separately.

1. Each house shall be the judge of the elections, returns, and qualifications of its own members, and a

majority of each shall constitute a quorum to do business; but a smaller number may adjourn from day to day, and may be authorized to compel the attendance of absent members, in such manner and under such penalties as each house may provide.

2. Each house may determine the rules of its proceedings, punish its members for disorderly behavior, and, with the concurrence of two-thirds, expel a member.

3. Each house shall keep a journal of its proceedings, and from time to time publish the same, excepting such parts as may in their judgment require secrecy; and the yeas and nays of the members of either house, on any question, shall, at the desire of one-fifth of those present, be entered on the journal.

4. Neither house during the session of Congress shall, without the consent of the other, adjourn for more than three days, nor to any other place than that in which the two houses shall be sitting.

*Section VI. Disabilities of Members.*

1. The senators and representatives shall receive a compensation for their services, to be ascertained by law, and paid out of the treasury of the United States. They shall in all cases, except treason, felony, breach of the peace, be privileged from arrest during their attendance at the session of their respective houses, and in going to or returning from the same; and for any speech or debate in either house, they shall not be questioned in any other place.

2. No senator or representative shall, during the time for which he was elected, be appointed to any civil office under the authority of the United States, which shall have been created, or the emoluments whereof shall have been increased, during such time; and no person holding any office under the United States shall be a member of either house during his continuance in office.

*Section VII. Mode of Passing Laws.*

1. All bills for raising revenue shall originate in the House of Representatives; but the Senate may propose or concur with amendments, as on other bills.

2. Every bill which shall have passed the House of Representatives and the Senate shall, before it become a law, be presented to the President of the United States; if he approve, he shall sign it; but if not, he shall return it, with his objections, to that house in which it shall have originated, who shall enter the objections at large on their journal, and proceed to reconsider it. If, after such reconsideration, two-thirds of that house shall agree to pass the bill, it shall be sent, together with the objections, to the other house, by which it shall likewise be reconsidered, and if approved by two-thirds of that house, it shall become a law. But in all such cases the votes of both houses shall be determined by yeas and nays, and the names of the persons voting for and against the bill shall be entered on the journal of each house respective'y. If any bill shall not be returned by the President within ten

days (Sundays excepted) after it shall have been presented to him, the same shall be a law in like manner as if he had signed it, unless the Congress by their adjournment prevent its return, in which case it shall not be a law.

3. Every order, resolution, or vote to which the concurrence of the Senate and House of Representatives may be necessary (except on a question of adjournment) shall be presented to the President of the United States; and before the same shall take effect, shall be approved by him, or, being disapproved by him, shall be repassed by two-thirds of the Senate and House of Representatives, according to the rules and limitations prescribed in the case of a bill.

*Section VIII. Powers granted to Congress.*[1]

The Congress shall have power:

1. To lay and collect taxes, duties, imposts, and excises, to pay the debts and provide for the common defense and general welfare of the United States; but all duties, imposts, and excises shall be uniform throughout the United States;

2. To borrow money on the credit of the United States;

3. To regulate commerce with foreign nations, and among the several States, and with the Indian tribes;

4. To establish a uniform rule of naturalization, and uniform laws on the subject of bankruptcies, throughout the United States;

---

[1] Compare §§ VIII and IX with Confed. Art. IX; clause 1 of § VIII with Confed. Art. VIII; and clause 12 of § VIII with Confed. Art. VII.

5. To coin money, regulate the value thereof and of foreign coin, and fix the standard of weights and measures;

6. To provide for the punishment of counterfeiting the securities and current coin of the United States;

7. To establish post-offices and post-roads;

8. To promote the progress of science and useful arts, by securing for limited times to authors and inventors the exclusive right to their respective writings and discoveries;

9. To constitute tribunals inferior to the Supreme Court;

10. To define and punish felonies committed on the high seas, and offenses against the law of nations;

11. To declare war, grant letters of marque and reprisal, and make rules concerning captures on land and water;

12. To raise and support armies; but no appropriation of money to that use shall be for a longer term than two years;

13. To provide and maintain a navy;

14. To make rules for the government and regulation of the land naval forces;

15. To provide for calling forth the militia to execute the laws of the Union, suppress insurrections, and repel invasions;

16. To provide for organizing, arming, and disciplining the militia, and for governing such part of them as may be employed in the service of the United States, reserving to the States respectively the appointment of

the officers, and the authority of training the militia according to the discipline prescribed by Congress;

17. To exercise exclusive legislation. in all cases whatsoever, over such district (not exceeding ten miles square) as may, by cession of particular States and the acceptance of Congress, become the seat of government of the United States, and to exercise like authority over all places purchased, by the consent of the Legislature of the State in which the same shall be, for the erection of forts, magazines, arsenals, dock-yards, and other needful buildings; and

18. To make all laws which shall be necessary and proper for carrying into execution the foregoing powers, and all other powers vested by this Constitution in the government of the United States, or in any department or office thereof.

*Section IX. Powers denied to the United States.*

1. The migration or importation of such persons as any of the States now existing shall think proper to admit shall not be prohibited by the Congress prior to the year one thousand eight hundred and eight; but a tax or duty may be imposed on such importation, not exceeding ten dollars for each person.

2. The privilege of the writ of *habeas corpus* shall not be suspended unless when, in case of rebellion or invasion, the public safety may require it.

3. No bill of attainder, or *ex-post-facto* law, shall be passed.

4. No capitation or other direct tax shall be laid

unless in proportion to the census or enumeration herein before directed to be taken.

5. No tax or duty shall be laid on articles exported from any State.

6. No preference shall be given by any regulation of commerce or revenue to the ports of one St.te over those of another; nor shall vessels bound to or from one State be obliged to enter, clear, or pay duties in another.

7. No money shall be drawn from the treasury but in consequence of appropriations made by law; and a regular statement and account of the receipts and expenditures of all public money shall be published from time to time.

8. No title of nobility shall be granted by the United States; and no person holding any office of profit or trust under them shall, without the consent of the Congress, accept of any present, emolument, office, or title of any kind whatever, from any king, prince, or foreign state.

*Section X. Powers denied to the States.*[1]

. No State shall enter into any treaty, alliance, or confederation; grant letters of marque and reprisal; coin money; emit bills of credit; make any thing but gold and silver coin a tender in payment of debts; pass any bill of attainder, *ex-post-facto* law, or law impairing the obligation of contracts; or grant any title of nobility.

2. No State shall, without the consent of the Con

---

[1] Compare Article I, § X with Confed. Art. VI.

gress, lay any imposts or duties on imports or exports except what may be absolutely necessary for executing its inspection laws; and the net produce of all duties and imposts laid by any State on imports or exports shall be for the use of the treasury of the United States, and all such laws shall be subject to the revision and control of the Congress.

3. No State shall, without the consent of Congress, lay any duty of tonnage, keep troops or ships of war in time of peace, enter into any agreement or compact with another State or with a foreign power, or engage in war unless actually invaded, or in such imminent danger as will not admit of delays.

## ARTICLE II. EXECUTIVE DEPARTMENT.[1]

### *Section I. President and Vice-President.*

1. The executive power shall be vested in a President of the United States of America. He shall hold his office during the term of four years, and, together with the Vice-President, chosen for the same term, be elected as follows:

2. Each State shall appoint, in such manner as the Legislature thereof may direct, a number of electors, equal to the whole number of senators and representatives to which the State may be entitled in the Congress; but no senator or representative, or person holding an office of trust or profit under the United States, shall be appointed an elector.

3. [The electors shall meet in their respective States.

---

[1] Compare Article II with Confed. Art. X.

and vote by ballot for two persons, of whom one at least shall not be an inhabitant of the same State with themselves. And they shall make a list of all the persons voted for, and of the number of votes for each; which list they shall sign and certify, and transmit sealed, to the seat of the government of the United States, directed to the President of the Senate. The President of the Senate shall, in the presence of the Senate and House of Representatives, open all the certificates, and the votes shall then be counted. The person having the greatest number of votes shall be the President, if such number be a majority of the whole number of electers appointed; and if there be more than one who have such majority, and have an equal number of votes, then the House of Representatives shall immediately choose by ballot one of them for President; and if no person have a majority, then, from the five highest on the list, the said House shall in like manner choose the President. But in choosing the President, the votes shall be taken by States, the representation from each State having one vote; a quorum for this purpose shall consist of a member or members from two-thirds of the States, and a majority of all the States shall be necessary to a choice. In every case, after the choice of the President, the person having the greatest number of votes of the electors shall be the Vice-President. But if there should remain two or more who have equal votes, the Senate shall choose from them by ballot the Vice-President.] [1]

---

[1] Altered by the XIIth Amendment.

4. The Congress may determine the time of choosing the electors, and the day on which they shall give their votes, which day shall be the same throughout the United States.

5. No person except a natural-born citizen, or a citizen of the United States at the time of the adoption of this Constitution, shall be eligible to the office of President; neither shall any person be eligible to that office who shall not have attained to the age of thirty-five years, and been fourteen years a resident within the United States.

6. In case of the removal of the President from office, or of his death, resignation, or inability to discharge the powers and duties of the said office, the same shall devolve on the Vice-President; and the Congress may by law provide for the case of removal, death, resignation, or inability, both of the President and Vice-President, declaring what officer shall then act as President; and such officer shall act accordingly, until the disability be removed or a President shall be elected.

7. The President shall, at stated times, receive for his services a compensation, which shall neither be increased nor diminished during the period for which he shall have been elected, and he shall not receive within that period any other emolument from the United States, or any of them.

8. Before he enter on the execution of his office, he shall take the following oath or affirmation:

"I do solemnly swear (or affirm) that I will faith

fully execute the office of President of the United States, and will, to the best of my ability, preserve, protect, and defend the Constitution of the United States."

## Section II. Powers of the President.

1. The President shall be commander-in-chief of the army and navy of the United States, and of the militia of the several States when called into the actual service of the United States; he may require the opinion in writing of the principal officer in each of the executive departments upon any subject relating to the duties of their respective offices; and he shall have power to grant reprieves and pardons for offenses against the United States, except in cases of impeachment.

2. He shall have power, by and with the advice and consent of the Senate, to make treaties, provided two-thirds of the senators present concur; and he shall nominate, and by and with the advice and consent of the Senate, shall appoint ambassadors, other public ministers and consuls, judges of the Supreme Court, and all other officers of the United States, whose appointments are not herein otherwise provided for and which shall be established by law; but the Congress may by law vest the appointment of such inferior officers as they think proper in the President alone, in the courts of law, or in the heads of departments.

3. The President shall have power to fill up all vacancies that may happen during the recess of the Senate, by granting commissions, which shall expire at the end of their next session.

### Section III. Duties of the President.

He shall, from time to time, give to the Congress information of the state of the Union, and recommend to their consideration such measures as he shall judge necessary and expedient; he may, on extraordinary occasions, convene both houses, or either of them; and in case of disagreement between them, with respect to the time of adjournment, he may adjourn them to such time as he shall think proper; he shall receive ambassadors and other public ministers; he shall take care that the laws be faithfully executed, and shall commission all the officers of the United States.

### Section IV. Impeachment of the President.

The President, Vice-President, and all civil officers of the United States shall be removed from office on impeachment for and conviction of treason, bribery, or other high crimes and misdemeanors.

## ARTICLE III. JUDICIAL DEPARTMENT.[1]

### Section I. United States Courts.

The judicial power of the United States shall be vested in one Supreme Court, and in such inferior courts as Congress may from time to time ordain and establish. The judges, both of the supreme and inferior courts, shall hold their offices during good behavior; and shall, at stated times, receive for their services a compensation, which shall not be diminished during their continuance in office.

---

[1] The Confederacy had no such provision as Article III of the Constitution except the attempt to make a Congressional Court in Con.fed. Art. IX.

## Section II. *Jurisdiction of the United States Courts.*

1. The judicial power shall extend to all cases in law and equity arising under this Constitution, the laws of the United States, and treaties made or which shall be made, under their authority; to all cases affecting ambassadors, other public ministers, and consuls; to all cases of admiralty and maritime jurisdiction; to controversies to which the United States shall be a party; to controversies between two or more States; between a State and citizens of another State; between citizens of different States; between citizens of the same State claiming lands under grants of different States; and between a State, or the citizens thereof, and foreign states, citizens, or subjects.[1]

2. In all cases affecting ambassadors, other public ministers, and consuls, and those in which a State shall be a party, the Supreme Court shall have original jurisdiction. In all the other cases before mentioned, the Supreme Court shall have appellate jurisdiction, both as to law and fact, with such exceptions and under such regulations as the Congress shall make.

3. The trial of all crimes, except in cases of impeachment, shall be by jury; and such trial shall be held in he State where the said crimes shall have been committed; but when not committed within any State, the trial shall be at such place or places as the Congress may by law have directed.

## Section III. *Treason.*

1. Treason against the United States shall consist

---

[1] Altered by XIth Amendment.

only in levying war against them, or in adhering to their enemies, giving them aid and comfort. No person shall be convicted of treason unless on the testimony of two witnesses to the same overt act, or on confession in open court.

2. The Congress shall have power to declare the punishment of treason; but no attainder of treason shall work corruption of blood, or forfeiture, except during the life of the person attainted.

### ARTICLE IV. THE STATES AND THE FEDERAL GOVERNMENT.[1]

#### *Section I. State Records.*

Full faith and credit shall be given in each State to the public acts, records, and judicial proceedings of every other State. And the Congress may, by general laws, prescribe the manner in which such acts, records, and proceedings shall be proved, and the effect thereof.

#### *Section II. Privileges of Citizens, etc.*

1. The citizens of each State shall be entitled to all privileges and immunities of citizens in the several States.

2. A person charged in any State with treason, felony, or other crime, who shall flee from justice and be found in another State, shall, on demand of the executive authority of the State from which he fled, be delivered up, to be removed to the State having jurisdiction of the crime.

---

[1] Compare Article IV with Confed. Art. IV.

3. No person held to service or labor in one State under the laws thereof, escaping into another, shall, in consequence of any law or regulation therein, be discharged from such service or labor, but shall be delivered up on claim of the party to whom such service o labor may be due.

*Section III. New States and Territories.*[1]

1. New States may be admitted by the Congress into this Union; but no new State shall be formed or erected within the jurisdiction of any other State; nor any State be formed by the junction of two or more States, or parts of States, without the consent of the Legislatures of the States concerned, as well as of the Congress.

2. The Congress shall have power to dispose of, and make all needful rules and regulations respecting, the territory or other property belonging to the United States; and nothing in this Constitution shall be so construed as to prejudice any claims of the United States or of any particular State.

*Section IV. Guarantee to the States.*

The United States shall guarantee to every State in this Union a republican form of government, and shall protect each of them against invasion; and, on application of the Legislature, or of the executive (when the Legislature cannot be convened), against domestic violence.

---

[1] Compare Article IV, § III with Confed. Art. XI.

### Article V. Power of Amendment.[1]

The Congress, whenever two-thirds of both Houses shall deem it necessary, shall propose amendments to this Constitution, or, on the application of the Legislatures of two-thirds of the several States, shall call a convention for proposing amendments, which, in either case, shall be valid to all intents and purposes as part of this Constitution, when ratified by the Legislatures of three-fourths of the several States, or by conventions in three-fourths thereof, as the one or the other mode of ratification may be proposed by Congress; provided that no amendment which may be made prior to the year one thousand eight hundred and eight shall in any manner affect the first and fourth clauses in the ninth section of the first Article; and that no State, without its consent, shall be deprived of its equal suffrage in the Senate.

### Article VI. Public Debt, Supremacy of the Constitution, Oath of Office, Religious Test.[2]

1. All debts contracted and engagements entered into before the adoption of this Constitution shall be as valid against the United States under this Constitution as under the Confederation.

2. This Constitution, and the laws of the United States which shall be made in pursuance thereof, and all treaties made, or which shall be made, under the

---

[1] Compare Article V with Confed. Art. XIII (last sentence).

[2] Compare Article VI, clause 1, with Confed. Art. XII; and clauses 2 and 3 with Confed. Art. XIII and addendum, "And whereas," etc.

authority of the United States, shall be the supreme law of the land; and the judges in every State shall be bound thereby, anything in the Constitution or laws of any State to the contrary notwithstanding.

3. The senators and representatives before-mentioned, and the members of the several State Legislatures, and all executive and judicial officers, both of the United States and of the several States, shall be bound by oath or affirmation to support this Constitution; but no religious test shall ever be required as a qualification to any office or public trust under the United States.

ARTICLE VII. RATIFICATION OF THE CONSTITUTION.

The ratifications of the Conventions of nine States shall be sufficient for the establishment of this Constitution between the States so ratifying the same.

Done in Convention, by the unanimous consent of the States present, the seventeenth day of September, in the year of our Lord one thousand seven hundred and eighty-seven, and of the Independence of the United States of America the twelfth.

# AMENDMENTS TO THE CONSTITUTION.

## ARTICLE I.

Congress shall make no law respecting an establishment of religion, or prohibiting the free exercise thereof; or abridging the freedom of speech, or of the press or the right of the people peaceably to assemble, and to petition the government for a redress of grievances.

### ARTICLE II.

A well regulated militia being necessary to the security of a free state, the right of the people to keep and bear arms shall not be infringed.

### ARTICLE III.

No soldier shall, in time of peace, be quartered in any house, without the consent of the owner, nor in time of war, but in a manner to be prescribed by law.

### ARTICLE IV.

The right of the people to be secure in their persons, houses, papers, and effects, against unreasonable searches and seizures shall not be violated, and no warrants shall issue but upon probable cause, supported by oath or affirmation, and particularly describing the place to be searched, and the persons or things to be seized.

### ARTICLE V.

No person shall be held to answer for a capital, or otherwise infamous crime, unless on a presentment or indictment of a grand jury, except in cases arising in the land or naval forces, or in the militia when in active service in time of war or public danger; nor shall any person be subject for the same offense to be twice put in jeopardy of life or limb; nor shall be compelled, in any criminal case, to be a witness against himself; nor be deprived of life, liberty, or property, without due process of law; nor shall private property be taken for public use without just compensation.

## Article VI.

In all criminal prosecutions, the accused shall enjoy he right to a speedy and public trial, by an impartial jury of the State and district wherein the crime shall have been committed, which district shall have been previously ascertained by law, and to be informed of the nature and cause of the accusation; to be confronted with the witnesses against him; to have compulsory process for obtaining witnesses in his favor; and to have the assistance of counsel for his defense.

## Article VII.

In suits at common law, where the value in controversy shall exceed twenty dollars, the right of trial by jury shall be preserved; and no fact tried by a jury shall be otherwise re-examined in any court of the United States than according to the rules of the common law.

## Article VIII.

Excessive bail shall not be required, nor excessive fines imposed, nor cruel and unusual punishment inflicted.

## Article IX.

The enumeration in the Constitution of certain rights shall not be construed to deny or disparage others retained by the people.

## Article X.[1]

The powers not granted to the United States by the Constitution, nor prohibited by it to the States, are reserved to the States respectively or to the people.

## Article XI.[2]

The judicial power of the United States shall not be construed to extend to any suit in law or equity, commenced or prosecuted against one of the United States by citizens of another State, or by citizens or subjects of any foreign State.

## Article XII.[3]

1. The electors shall meet in their respective States, and vote by ballot for President and Vice-President, one of whom, at least, shall not be an inhabitant of the same State with themselves; they shall name in their ballots the person voted for as President, and in distinct ballots the person voted for as Vice-President, and they shall make distinct lists of all persons voted for as President, and of all persons voted for as Vice-President, and of the number of votes for each, which lists they shall sign and certify, and transmit sealed to the seat of government of the United States, directed to the President of the Senate; the President

---

[1] Compare the Xth Amendment with Confed. Art. II. The first ten Amendments were proposed by Congress, September 25th, 1789, and declared in force, December 15th, 1791.

[2] Proposed by Congress March 5th, 1794, and declared in force January 8th, 1798.

[3] Proposed by Congress December 12th, 1803, and declared in force September 25th, 1804.

of the Senate shall, in the presence of the Senate and House of Representatives, open all the certificates, and the votes shall then be counted; the person having the greatest number of votes for President shall be the President, if such number be a majority of the whole number of electors appointed; and if no person have such majority, then from the persons having the highest numbers, not exceeding three, on the list of those voted for as President, the House of Representatives shall choose immediately by ballot the President. But in choosing the President, the votes shall be taken by States, the representation from each State having one vote; a quorum for this purpose shall consist of a member or members from two-thirds of the States, and a majority of all the States shall be necessary to a choice. And if the House of Representatives shall not choose a President, whenever the right of choice shall devolve upon them, before the fourth day of March next following, then the Vice-President shall act as President, as in the case of death or other constitutional disability of the President.

2. The person having the greatest number of votes as Vice-President shall be the Vice-President, if such number be a majority of the whole number of electors appointed, and if no person have a majority, then from the two highest numbers on the list the Senate shall choose the Vice-President; a quorum for the purpose shall consist of two-thirds of the whole number of senators, and a majority of the whole number shall be necessary to a choice.

3. But no person constitutionally ineligible to the office of President shall be eligible to that of Vice-President of the United States.

## Article XIII.[1]

1. Neither slavery nor involuntary servitude, except as a punishment for crime whereof the party shall have been duly convicted, shall exist within the United States, or any place subject to their jurisdiction.

2. Congress shall have power to enforce this article by appropriate legislation.

## Article XIV.[2]

1. All persons born or naturalized in the United States, and subject to the jurisdiction thereof, are citizens of the United States and of the State wherein they reside. No State shall make or enforce any law which shall abridge the privileges or immunities of citizens of the United States; nor shall any State deprive any person of life, liberty, or property, without due process of law, nor deny to any person within its jurisdiction the equal protection of the laws.

2. Representatives shall be apportioned among the several States according to their respective numbers, counting the whole number of persons in each State, excluding Indians not taxed. But when the right to vote at any election for the choice of electors for Presi-

---

[1] Proposed by Congress February 1st, 1865, and declared in force December 18th, 1865.

[2] Proposed by Congress June 16th, 1866, and declared in force July 28th, 1868.

dent and Vice-President of the United States, representatives in Congress, the executive and judicial officers of a State, or the members of the Legislature thereof, is denied to any of the male members of such State, being twenty-one years of age, and citizens of the United States, or in any way abridged, except for participation in rebellion or other crime, the basis of representation therein shall be reduced in the proportion which the number of such male citizens shall bear to the whole number of male citizens twenty-one years of age in such State.

3. No person shall be a senator or representative in Congress, or elector of President and Vice-President, or holding any office, civil or military, under the United States, or under any State, who, having previously taken an oath, as a member of Congress, or as an officer of the United States, or as a member of any State Legislature, or as an executive or judicial officer of any State, to support the Constitution of the United States, shall have engaged in insurrection or rebellion against the same, or given aid and comfort to the enemies thereof. But Congress may, by a vote of two-thirds of each House, remove such disability.

4. The validity of the public debt of the United States, authorized by law, including debts incurred for payment of pensions and bounties for services in suppressing insurrection or rebellion, shall not be questioned. But neither the United States nor any State shall assume or pay any debt or obligation incurred in aid of insurrection or rebellion against the United States

or any claim for the loss or emancipation of any slave but all such debts, obligations, and claims shall be held illegal and void.

5. The Congress shall have power to enforce by appropriate legislation the provisions of this article.

## Article XV.[1]

1. The right of the citizens of the United States to vote shall not be denied or abridged by the United States or any State on account of race, color, or previous condition of servitude.

2. The Congress shall have power to enforce the provisions of this article by appropriate legislation.

---

[1] Proposed by Congress February 26th, 1869, and declared in force March 30th, 1870.

# APPENDIX C.

## Admission of the States.[1]

1. Delaware,[2] Dec. 7, 1787.
2. Pennsylvania,[2] Dec. 12, 1787.
3. New Jersey,[2] Dec. 18, 1787.
4. Georgia,[2] Jan. 2, 1788.
5. Connecticut,[2] Jan. 9, 1788.
6. Massachusetts,[2] Feb. 7, 1788.
7. Maryland,[2] April 28, 1788.
8. South Carolina,[2] May 23, 1788.
9. New Hampshire,[2] June 21, 1788.
10. Virginia,[2] June 26, 1788.
11. New York,[2] July 26, 1788.
12. North Carolina,[2] Nov. 21, 1789.
13. Rhode Island,[2] May 29, 1790.
14. Kentucky, June 1, 1792.
15. Vermont, March 4, 1791.
16. Tennessee, June 1, 1796.
17. Ohio, Nov. 29, 1802.
18. Louisiana, April 30, 1812.
19. Indiana, Dec. 11, 1816.
20. Mississippi, Dec. 10, 1817.
21. Illinois, Dec. 3, 1818.
22. Alabama, Dec. 14, 1819.
23. Maine, March 15, 1820.
24. Missouri, Aug. 10, 1821.
25. Arkansas, June 15, 1836.
26. Michigan, Jan. 26, 1837.
27. Florida, March 3, 1845.
28. Texas, Dec. 29, 1845.
29. Iowa, Dec. 28, 1846.
30. Wisconsin, May 29, 1848.
31. California, Sept. 9, 1850.
32. Minnesota, May 11, 1858.
33. Oregon, Feb. 14, 1859.
34. Kansas, Jan. 29, 1861.
35. West Virginia, June 19, 1863.
36. Nevada, Oct. 31, 1864.
37. Nebraska, March 1, 1867.
38. Colorado, Aug. 1, 1876.

---

[1] The dates given, after the first thirteen States, are those upon which the admissions took effect.

[2] Ratified the Constitution and became States.

# APPENDIX D.

## SUMMARY OF POPULAR AND ELECTORAL VOTES IN PRESIDENTIAL ELECTIONS, 1789–1876.

| Year. | Number of States. | Total Elect. Votes. | Party. | Candidates.[1] | States. | Popular Vote. | Electoral Vote. |
|---|---|---|---|---|---|---|---|
| 1789 | 10[2] | 73 | | George Washington, | | | 69 |
| | | | | John Adams, | | | 34 |
| | | | | John Jay, | | | 9 |
| | | | | R. H. Harrison, | | | 6 |
| | | | | John Rutledge, | | | 6 |
| | | | | John Hancock, | | | 4 |
| | | | | George Clinton, | | | 3 |
| | | | | Samuel Huntington, | | | 2 |
| | | | | John Milton, | | | 2 |
| | | | | Benjamin Lincoln, | | | 1 |
| | | | | James Armstrong, | | | 1 |
| | | | | Edward Telfair, | | | 1 |
| | | | | Vacancies, | | | 4 |
| 1792 | 15 | 135 | Federalist, | George Washington, | | | 132 |

For the conditions of the Presidential elections previous to 1804 see page 102.
[2] Three States not voting, viz.: New York, which had not yet passed an electoral law: and North Carolina and Rhode Island which had not yet ratified the Constitution

## Votes for President, 1789-1876.

| Year | | | Votes |
|---|---|---|---|
| 1796 | John Adams, | Federalist, | 71 |
| | Thomas Jefferson, | Republican, | 68 |
| | Thomas Pinckney, | Federalist, | 59 |
| | Aaron Burr, | Republican, | 30 |
| | Samuel Adams, | | 15 |
| | Oliver Ellsworth, | | 11 |
| | George Clinton, | | 7 |
| | John Jay, | | 5 |
| | James Iredell, | | 3 |
| | George Washington, | | 2 |
| | John Henry, | | 2 |
| | S. Johnson, | | 2 |
| | Charles C. Pinckney, | | 1 |
| | | | 138 |
| | | (electors) | 16 |
| 1800 | Thomas Jefferson, | Republican, | ¹73 |
| | Aaron Burr, | " | 73 |
| | John Adams, | Federalist, | 65 |
| | Charles C. Pinckney, | " | 64 |
| | John Jay, | | 1 |
| | | | 138 |
| | | (electors) | 16 |

¹ The disputed election of 1800; see page 49.

## APPENDIX D.—Continued.

| Year | No. of States | Total Elect. Votes | Party | For President | States | Popular Vote. | Electoral | For Vice-President | Electoral |
|---|---|---|---|---|---|---|---|---|---|
| 1804 | 17 | 176 | Republican, Federalist, | Thomas Jefferson, Chas. C. Pinckney, | 15 2 | | 162 14 | George Clinton, Rufus King, | 162 14 |
| 1808 | 17 | 176 | Republican, " Federalist, | James Madison, George Clinton, Chas. C. Pinckney, Vacancy, | 12 5 | | 122 6 47 1 | George Clinton, James Madison, Rufus King, John Langdon, James Monroe, | 113 3 47 9 3 1 |
| 1812 | 18 | 218 | Republican, Federalist, | James Madison, De Witt Clinton, Vacancy, | 11 7 | | 128 89 1 | Elbridge Gerry, Jared Ingersoll, | 131 86 1 |
| 1816 | 19 | 221 | Republican, Federalist, | James Monroe, Rufus King, Vacancies. | 16 3 | | 183 34 4 | D. D. Tompkins, John E. Howard, James Ross, John Marshall, Robt. G. Harper, | 183 22 5 4 3 4 |

## Votes for President, 1789–1876.

| Year | | Total | Party | Candidate | Electoral | Popular | | VP Candidate | VP Votes |
|---|---|---|---|---|---|---|---|---|---|
| 1820 | 24 | 235 | Republican, | James Monroe, | 231 | | | D. D. Tompkins, | 218 |
| | | | | John Q. Adams, | 1 | | | Rich. Stockton, | 8 |
| | | | | | | | | Daniel Rodney, | 4 |
| | | | | | | | | Robt. G. Harper, | 1 |
| | | | | | | | | Richard Rush, | 1 |
| | | | | Vacancies, | 3 | | | | 3 |
| 1824 | 24 | 261 | Republican, | Andrew Jackson, | 99 | 155,872 | 10 | John C. Calhoun, | 182 |
| | | | " | John Q. Adams, | 84 | 105,321 | 8 | Nathan Sanford, | 30 |
| | | | " | Wm. H. Crawford, | 41 | 44,282 | 3 | Nathaniel Macon, | 24 |
| | | | " | Henry Clay, | 37 | 46,587 | 3 | Andrew Jackson, | 13 |
| | | | | | | | | M. Van Buren, | 9 |
| | | | | | | | | Henry Clay, | 2 |
| | | | | Vacancy, | | | | | 1 |
| 1828 | 24 | 261 | Democratic, | Andrew Jackson, | 178 | 647,231 | 15 | John C. Calhoun, | 171 |
| | | | Nat. Republican, | John Q. Adams, | 83 | 509,097 | 9 | Richard Rush, | 83 |
| | | | | | | | | William Smith, | 7 |
| 1832 | 24 | 288 | Democratic, | Andrew Jackson, | 219 | 687,502 | 15 | M. Van Buren, | 189 |
| | | | Nat. Republican, | Henry Clay, | 49 | 530,189 | 7 | John Sergeant, | 49 |
| | | | Anti-Mason, | William Wirt, | 7 | 33,108 | 1 | Amos Ellmaker, | 7 |
| | | | | John Floyd, | 11 | | 1 | Henry Lee, | 11 |
| | | | | Vacancies, | 2 | | | William Wilkins, | 30 |
| | | | | | | | | | 2 |

[1] The disputed election of 1824; see page 92.

## APPENDIX D.—Continued.

| Year. | No. of States. | Total Elect. Votes. | Party. | For President. | State. | Popular Vote. | Electoral. | For Vice-President. | Electoral. |
|---|---|---|---|---|---|---|---|---|---|
| 1836 | 26 | 294 | Democratic, Whig, | Martin Van Buren, Wm. H. Harrison, Hugh L. White, Daniel Webster, W. P. Mangum, | 15 7 2 1 1 | 761,549 736,656 | 170 73 26 14 11 | R. M. Johnson, Francis Granger, John Tyler, William Smith, | [1]147 77 47 23 |
| 1840 | 26 | 294 | Whig, Democratic, Liberty, | Wm. H. Harrison, Martin Van Buren, James G. Birney, | 19 7 | 1,275,017 1,128,702 7,059 | 234 60 | John Tyler, R. M. Johnson, | 234 48 |
|  |  |  |  |  |  |  |  | L. W. Tazewell, James K. Polk, | 11 1 |
| 1844 | 26 | 275 | Democratic, Whig, Liberty, | James K. Polk, Henry Clay, James G. Birney, | 15 11 | 1,337,243 1,299,068 62,300 | 170 105 | Geo. M. Dallas, T. Frelinghuysen, | 170 105 |
| 1848 | 30 | 290 | Whig, Democratic, Free Soil, | Zachary Taylor, Lewis Cass, Martin Van Buren, | 15 15 | 1,360,101 1,220,544 291,263 | 163 127 | Millard Fillmore, Wm. O. Butler, Chas. F. Adams, | 163 127 |

[1] R. M. Johnson chosen by the Senate; see page 124.

## Votes for President, 1789–1876.

| Year | | | Party | Candidates | | Popular Vote | Electoral | VP Candidates | Electoral |
|---|---|---|---|---|---|---|---|---|---|
| 1852 | 31 | 296 | Democratic, Whig, Free Democracy, | Franklin Pierce, Winfield Scott, John P. Hale, | 27 4 | 1,601,474 1,386,578 156,149 | 254 42 | Wm. R. King, Wm. A. Graham, Geo. W. Julian, | 254 42 |
| 1856 | 31 | 296 | Democratic, Republican, American, | James Buchanan, John C. Fremont, Millard Fillmore, | 19 11 1 | 1,838,169 1,341,264 874,534 | 174 114 8 | J. C. Breckinridge, Wm. L. Dayton, A. J. Donelson, | 174 114 8 |
| 1860 | 33 | 303 | Republican, Democratic, Democratic, "Const. Union," | Abraham Lincoln, J. C. Breckinridge, S. A. Douglas, John Bell, | 17 11 2 3 | 1,866,352 845,763 1,375,157 589,581 | 180 72 12 39 | Hannibal Hamlin, Joseph Lane, H. V. Johnson, Edward Everett, | 180 72 12 39 |
| 1864 | 36 | 314 | Republican, Democratic, | Abraham Lincoln, Geo. B. McClellan, Vacancies,[1] | 22 3 11 | 2,216,067 1,808,725 | 212 21 81 | Andrew Johnson, Geo. H. Pendleton, | 212 21 81 |
| 1868 | 37 | 317 | Republican, Democratic, | Ulysses S. Grant, Horatio Seymour, Vacancies,[2] | 26 8 3 | 3,015,071 2,709,613 | 214 80 23 | Schuyler Colfax, F. P. Blair, Jr., | 214 80 23 |
| 1872 | 37 | 366 | Republican, Dem. and Lib. Rep., Democratic, | Ulysses S. Grant, Horace Greeley, Chas. O'Conor, | 31 6 | 3,597,070 2,834,079 29,408 | 286 47 | Henry Wilson. B. Gratz Brown, John Q. Adams, | 286 47 |

[1] Not voting, Alabama, Arkansas, Florida, Georgia, Louisiana, Mississippi, North Carolina, South Carolina, Tennessee, Texas, and Virginia.
[2] Not voting, Mississippi, Texas, and Virginia.

## APPENDIX D.—Continued.

| Year | No. of States | Total Elect. Votes | Party | For President | States | Popular Vote | Electoral | For Vice-President | Electoral |
|---|---|---|---|---|---|---|---|---|---|
| | | | Temperance, | James Black, | | 5,608 | | A. H. Colquite, | 5 |
| | | | | T. A. Hendricks, | | | 42 | John M. Palmer, | 3 |
| | | | | B. Gratz Brown, | | | 18 | Geo. W. Julian, | 5 |
| | | | | Chas. J. Jenkins, | | | 2 | T. E. Bramlette, | 3 |
| | | | | David Davis, | | | 1 | W. S. Groesbeck, | 1 |
| | | | | | | | | Willis B. Machen, | 1 |
| | | | | Not Counted,[1] | | | 17 | N. P. Banks, | 14 |
| 1876 | 38 | 369 | Republican, | R. B. Hayes, | 21 | 4,033,950 | 185 | Wm. A. Wheeler, | 185 |
| | | | Democratic, | S. J. Tilden, | 17 | 4,284,885 | 184 | T. A. Hendricks, | 184 |
| | | | "Greenback," | Peter Cooper, | | 81,740 | | S. F. Cary, | |
| | | | "Prohibition," | Green C. Smith, | | 9,522 | | R. T. Stewart, | |
| 1880 | 38 | 369 | Republican, | James A. Garfield, | 19 | 4,442,950 | 214 | Chester A. Arthur, | 214 |
| | | | Democratic, | W. S. Hancock. | 19 | 4,442,035 | 155 | Wm. H. English, | 155 |
| | | | "Greenback," | James B. Weaver, | | 306,867 | | B. J. Chambers, | |
| | | | | Scattering, | | 12,576 | | | |

[1] Seventeen votes rejected, viz.: 3 from Georgia for Horace Greeley (dead), and 8 from Louisiana and 6 from Arkansas for U. S. Grant.

## APPENDIX E.

### POPULATION OF THE SECTIONS, 1790-1860.

| Year. | Free States. | Slave States. |
|---|---|---|
| 1790 | 1,968,453 | 1,961,374 |
| 1800 | 2,684,616 | 2,621,316 |
| 1810 | 3,758,910 | 3,480,902 |
| 1820 | 5,152,372 | 4,485,819 |
| 1830 | 7,006,399 | 5,848,312 |
| 1840 | 9,733,922 | 7,334,433 |
| 1850 | 13,599,488 | 9,663,997 |
| 1860 | 19,128,418 | 12,315,372 |

## APPENDIX F.

### CONGRESSIONAL REPRESENTATION OF THE SECTIONS 1790–1860.

| Year | Senate. | | House. | |
|---|---|---|---|---|
| | Free States. | Slave States. | Free States. | Slave States. |
| 1790 | 14 | 12 | 35 | 30 |
| 1792 | 16 | 14 | 57 | 48 |
| 1796 | 16 | 16 | 57 | 49 |
| 1800 | 16 | 16 | 57 | 49 |
| 1804 | 18 | 16 | 77 | 65 |
| 1808 | 18 | 16 | 77 | 65 |
| 1812 | 18 | 18 | 103 | 79 |
| 1816 | 20 | 18 | 104 | 79 |
| 1820 | 24 | 24 | 105 | 82 |
| 1824 | 24 | 24 | 123 | 90 |
| 1828 | 24 | 24 | 123 | 90 |
| 1832 | 24 | 24 | 141 | 99 |
| 1836 | 26 | 26 | 142 | 100 |
| 1840 | 26 | 26 | 142 | 100 |
| 1844 | 26 | 26 | 135 | 98 |
| 1848 | 30 | 30 | 139 | 91 |
| 1852 | 32 | 30 | 144 | 90 |
| 1856 | 32 | 30 | 144 | 90 |
| 1860 | 36 | 30 | 147 | 90 |

☞ To find the Electoral Votes, add together the number of Senators and Representatives.

## APPENDIX G.

### THE SECTIONS IN 1870.

| Sections. | Population in 1870. | Senate. | House. | Elect Votes. |
|---|---|---|---|---|
| THE SOUTH: (Ala., Ark., Fla., Ga., Ky., La., Md., Miss., N. C., S. C., Tenn., Tex., Va., W. V.), | 12,032,225 | 28 | 92 | 120 |
| THE NORTH-WEST: (Ill., Ia., Ind., Ks., Mich., Minn., Mo., Neb., O., Wis.), | 12,702,299 | 20 | 98 | 118 |
| THE MIDDLE STATES: (Del., N. J., N. Y., Penn.), | 8,941,625 | 8 | 68 | 76 |
| NEW ENGLAND: (Conn., Mass., Me., N. H., R. I., Vt.), | 3,187,924 | 12 | 28 | 40 |
| THE PACIFIC: (Cal., Col., Nev., Or.), | 889,789 | 8 | 7 | 15 |
| Total, | 38,925,598 | 76 | 293 | 369 |

☞ The total population includes territories and Indians.

### THE SECTIONS IN 1880.

| Sections. | Population in 1880. | Senate. | House. | Elect Votes. |
|---|---|---|---|---|
| THE SOUTH, | 16,188,757 | 28 | 92 | 120 |
| THE NORTH-WEST, | 17,229,810 | 20 | 98 | 118 |
| THE MIDDLE STATES, | 10,644,233 | 8 | 68 | 76 |
| NEW ENGLAND, | 4,010,438 | 12 | 28 | 40 |
| THE PACIFIC, | 1,296,367 | 8 | 7 | 15 |
| Total, | 50,152,866 | 76 | 293 | 369 |

☞ The total population includes Territories and Indians. In December, 1881, an Apportionment Act is not yet passed, so that Representatives and Electoral Votes remain as in 1870-80.

# APPENDIX H.

## Cabinet Officers of the Administrations.

### I. and II.; 1789–1797 (page 18).

**Secretary of State**, Thomas Jefferson, Virginia, September 26th, 1789; Edmund Randolph, Virginia, January 2d, 1794; Timothy Pickering, Pennsylvania, December 10th, 1795. **Secretary of Treasury**, Alexander Hamilton, New York, September 11th, 1789; Oliver Wolcott, Connecticut, February 2d, 1795. **Secretary of War**, Henry Knox, Massachusetts, September 12th, 1789; Timothy Pickering, Pennsylvania, January 2d, 1795; James McHenry, Maryland, January 27th, 1796. **Attorney-General**, Edmund Randolph, Virginia, September 26th, 1789; William Bradford, Pennsylvania, January 27th, 1794; Charles Lee, Virginia, December 10th, 1795. **Postmaster-General**,[1] Samuel Osgood, Massachusetts, September 26th, 1789; Timothy Pickering, Pennsylvania, August 12th, 1791; Joseph Habersham, Georgia, February 25th, 1795.

### III.; 1797–1801 (page 41).

**Secretary of State**, Timothy Pickering, continued; John Marshall, Virginia, May 13th, 1800. **Secretary of Treasury**, Oliver Wolcott, continued; Samuel Dexter, Massachusetts,

---

[1] Not a Cabinet officer, but a subordinate of the Treasury Department until 1829.

## Cabinet Officers of the Administrations. 301

January 1st, 1801. **Secretary of War,** James McHenry, continued; Samuel Dexter, Massachusetts, May 13th, 1800; Roger Griswold, Connecticut, February 3d, 1801. **Secretary of Navy,**[1] George Cabot, Massachusetts, May 3d, 1798; Benjamin Stoddert, Maryland, May 21st, 1798. **Attorney-General,** Charles Lee, continued; Theophilus Parsons, Massachusetts, February 20th, 1801. **Postmaster-General,** Joseph Habersham, continued.

### IV. AND V.; 1801-1809 (page 52).

**Secretary of State,** James Madison, Virginia, March 5th, 1801. **Secretary of Treasury,** Samuel Dexter, continued; Albert Gallatin, Pennsylvania, May 14th, 1801. **Secretary of War,** Henry Dearborn, Massachusetts, March 5th, 1801. **Secretary of Navy,** Benjamin Stoddert, continued; Robert Smith, Maryland, July 15th, 1801; Jacob Crowninshield, Massachusetts, May 3d, 1805. **Attorney-General,** Levi Lincoln, Massachusetts, March 5th, 1801; Robert Smith, Maryland, March 3d, 1805; John Breckinridge, Kentucky, August 7th, 1805; Cæsar A. Rodney, Pennsylvania, January 20th, 1807. **Postmaster-General,** Joseph Habersham, continued; Gideon Granger, Connecticut, November 28th, 1801.

### VI. AND VII.; 1809-1817 (page 69).

**Secretary of State,** Robert Smith, Maryland, March 6th, 1809; James Monroe, Virginia, April 2d, 1811. **Secretary of Treasury,** Albert Gallatin, continued; George W. Campbell, Tennessee, February 9th, 1814; A. J. Dallas, Pennsyl-

---

[1] Naval affairs were under the control of the Secretary of War until a separate Navy Department was organized by Act of April 30th, 1798. The Acts organizing the other Departments were of the following dates: **State,** September 15th, 1789; **Treasury,** September 2d, 1789; **War,** August 7th, 1789. The Attorney-General's duties were regulated by the Judiciary Act of September 24th, 1789.

vania, October 6th, 1814; William H. Crawford, Georgia, October 22d, 1816. **Secretary of War,** William Eustis, Massachusetts, March 7th, 1809; John Armstrong, New York, January 13th, 1813; James Monroe, Virginia, September 27th, 1814; William H. Crawford, Georgia, August 1st, 1815. **Secretary of Navy,** Paul Hamilton, South Carolina, March 7th, 1809; William Jones, Pennsylvania, January 12th, 1813; B. W. Crowninshield, Massachusetts, December 19th, 1814. **Attorney-General,** C. A. Rodney, continued; William Pinckney, Maryland, December 11th, 1811; Richard Rush, Pennsylvania, February 10th, 1814. **Postmaster-General,** Gideon Granger, continued; Return J. Meigs, Ohio, March 17th, 1814.

### VIII. AND IX.; 1817–1825 (page 83).

**Secretary of State,** John Quincy Adams, Massachusetts, March 5th, 1817. **Secretary of Treasury,** William H. Crawford, continued. **Secretary of War,** George Graham, Virginia, April 7th, 1817; John C. Calhoun, South Carolina, October 8th, 1817. **Secretary of Navy,** B. W. Crowninshield, continued; Smith Thompson, New York, November 9th, 1818; John Rogers, Massachusetts, September 1st, 1823; Samuel L. Southard, New Jersey, September 16th, 1823. **Attorney-General,** Richard Rush, continued; William Wirt, Virginia, November 13th, 1817. **Postmaster-General,** R. J. Meigs, continued; John McLean, Ohio, June 26th, 1823.

### X.; 1825–1829 (page 96).

**Secretary of State,** Henry Clay, Kentucky, March 7th, 1825. **Secretary of Treasury,** Richard Rush, Pennsylvania, March 7th, 1825. **Secretary of War,** James Barbour, Virginia, March 7th, 1825; Peter B. Porter, New York, May 26th, 1828. **Secretary of Navy,** S. L. Southard, continued. **Attorney-General,** William Wirt, continued. **Postmaster-General,** John McLean, continued.

# Cabinet Officers of the Administrations. 303

## XI. AND XII.; 1829-1837 (page 102).

**Secretary of State**, Martin Van Buren, New York, March 6th, 1829; Edward Livingston, Louisiana, May 24th, 1831; Louis McLane, Delaware, May 29th, 1833; John Forsyth, Georgia, June 27th, 1834. **Secretary of Treasury**, Samuel D. Ingham, Pennsylvania, March 6th, 1829; Louis McLane, Delaware, August 8th, 1831; William J. Duane, Pennsylvania, May 29th, 1833; Roger B. Taney, Maryland, September 23d, 1833; Levi Woodbury, New Hampshire, June 27th, 1834. **Secretary of War**, John H. Eaton, Tennessee, March 9th, 1829; Lewis Cass, Michigan, August 1st, 1831; Benjamin F. Butler, New York, March 3d, 1837. **Secretary of Navy**. John Branch, North Carolina, March 9th, 1829; Levi Woodbury, New Hampshire, May 23d, 1831; Mahlon Dickerson, New Jersey, June 30th, 1834. **Attorney-General**, John M. Berrien, Georgia, March 9th, 1829; Roger B. Taney, Maryland, July 20th, 1831; Benjamin F. Butler, New York, November 15th, 1833. **Postmaster-General**, William T. Barry, Kentucky, March 9th, 1829; Amos Kendall, Kentucky, May 1st, 1835.

## XIII.; 1837-1841 (page 125).

**Secretary of State**, John Forsyth, continued. **Secretary of Treasury**, Levi Woodbury, continued. **Secretary of War**, Joel R. Poinsett, South Carolina, March 7th, 1837. **Secretary of Navy**, Mahlon Dickerson, continued; James K. Paulding, New York, June 25th, 1838. **Attorney-General**, Benjamin F. Butler, continued; Felix Grundy, Tennessee, July 5th, 1838; Henry D. Gilpin, Pennsylvania, January 11th, 1840. **Postmaster-General**, Amos Kendall, continued; John M. Niles, Connecticut, May 19th, 1840.

## XIV.; 1841-1845 (page 132).

**Secretary of State**, Daniel Webster, Massachusetts, March 5th, 1841; Hugh S. Legare, South Carolina, May 9th, 1843;

A. P. Upshur, Virginia, July 24th, 1843; John C. Calhoun, South Carolina, March 6th, 1844. **Secretary of Treasury,** Thomas Ewing, Ohio, March 5th, 1841; Walter Forward, Pennsylvania, September 13th, 1841; John C. Spencer, New York, March 3d, 1843; George M. Bibb, Kentucky, June 15th, 1844. **Secretary of War,** John Bell, Tennessee, March 5th, 1841; John McLean, Ohio, September 13th, 1841; John C. Spencer, New York, October 12th, 1841; James M. Porter, Pennsylvania, March 8th, 1843; William Wilkins, Pennsylvania, February 15th, 1844. **Secretary of Navy,** G. E. Badger, North Carolina, March 5th, 1841; A. P. Upshur, Virginia, September 13th, 1841; David Henshaw, Massachusetts, July 24th, 1843; T. W. Gilmer, Virginia, February 15th, 1844; John Y. Mason, Virginia, March 14th, 1844. **Attorney-General,** John J. Crittenden, Kentucky, March 5th, 1841; Hugh S. Legare, South Carolina, September 13th, 1841; John Nelson, Maryland, July 1st, 1843. **Postmaster-General,** Francis Granger, New York, March 6th, 1841; Charles A. Wickliffe, Kentucky, September 13th, 1841.

### XV.; 1845-1849 (page 141).

**Secretary of State,** James Buchanan, Pennsylvania, March 6th, 1845. **Secretary of Treasury,** Robert J. Walker, Mississippi, March 6th, 1845. **Secretary of War,** William L. Marcy, New York, March 6th, 1845. **Secretary of Navy,** George Bancroft, Massachusetts, March 10th, 1845; John Y. Mason, Virginia, September 9th, 1846. **Attorney-General,** John Y. Mason, Virginia, March 5th, 1845; Nathan Clifford, Maine, October 17th, 1846. **Postmaster-General,** Cave Johnson, Tennessee, March 6th, 1845.

### XVI.; 1849-1853 (page 151).

**Secretary of State,** John M. Clayton, Delaware, March 7th, 1849; Daniel Webster, Massachusetts, July 22d, 1850;

## Cabinet Officers of the Administrations. 305

Edward Everett, Massachusetts, December 6th, 1852. **Secretary of Treasury**, W. M. Meredith, Pennsylvania, March 8th, 1849; Thomas Corwin, Ohio, July 23d, 1850. **Secretary of War**, George W. Crawford, Georgia, March 8th, 1849; Winfield Scott (*ad interim*), July 23d, 1850 ; Charles M. Conrad, Louisiana, August 15th, 1850. **Secretary of Navy**, William B. Preston, Virginia, March 8th, 1849; William A. Graham, North Carolina, July 22d, 1850; J. P. Kennedy, Maryland, July 22d, 1852. **Secretary of Interior**,[1] Thomas H. Ewing, Ohio, March 8th, 1849; A. H. H. Stuart, Virginia, September 12th, 1850. **Attorney-General**, Reverdy Johnson, Maryland, March 8th, 1849; John J. Crittenden, Kentucky, July 22d, 1850. **Postmaster-General**, Jacob Collamer, Vermont, March 8th, 1849; Nathan K. Hall, New York, July 23d, 1850; S. D. Hubbard, Connecticut, August 31st, 1852.

XVII.; 1853-1857 (page 158).

**Secretary of State**, William L. Marcy, New York, March 7th, 1853. **Secretary of Treasury**, James Guthrie, Kentucky, March 7th, 1853. **Secretary of War**, Jefferson Davis, Mississippi, March 7th, 1853. **Secretary of Navy**, James C. Dobbin, North Carolina, March 7th, 1853. **Secretary of Interior**, Robert McClelland, Michigan, March 7th, 1853; Jacob Thompson, Mississippi, March 6th, 1856. **Attorney-General**, Caleb Cushing, Massachusetts, March 7th, 1853. **Postmaster-General**, James Campbell, Pennsylvania, March 7th, 1853.

XVIII.; 1857-1861 (page 170).

**Secretary of State**, Lewis Cass, Michigan, March 6th. 1857; J. S. Black, Pennsylvania, December 17th, 1860. **Secretary of Treasury**, Howell Cobb, Georgia, March 6th, 1857 ; Philip F. Thomas, Maryland, December 12th, 1860; John A. Dix,

---

[1] Organized by Act of March 3d, 1849.

New York, January 11th, 1861. **Secretary of War**, John B. Floyd, Virginia, March 6th, 1857; Joseph Holt, Kentucky, January 18th, 1861. **Secretary of Navy**, Isaac Toucey, Connecticut, March 6th, 1857. **Secretary of Interior**, Jacob Thompson, continued. **Attorney-General**, J. S. Black, Pennsylvania, March 6th, 1857; E. M. Stanton, Pennsylvania, December 20th, 1860. **Postmaster-General**, Aaron V. Brown, Tennessee, March 6th, 1857; Joseph Holt, Kentucky, March 14th, 1859; Horatio King, Maine, February 12th, 1861.

## XIX. AND XX.; 1861-1869 (page 186).

**Secretary of State**, William H. Seward, New York, March 5th, 1861. **Secretary of Treasury**, S. P. Chase, Ohio, March 5th, 1861; W. P. Fessenden, Maine, July 1st, 1864; Hugh McCulloch, Indiana, March 7th, 1865. **Secretary of War**, Simon Cameron, Pennsylvania, March 5th, 1861; Edwin M. Stanton, Pennsylvania, January 15th, 1862; U. S. Grant (*ad interim*),[1] August 12th, 1867; Edwin M. Stanton (reinstated), January 14th, 1868; J. M. Schofield, Illinois, May 28th, 1868. **Secretary of Navy**, Gideon Welles, Connecticut, March 5th, 1861. **Secretary of Interior**, Caleb P. Smith, March 5th, 1861; John P Usher, Indiana, January 8th, 1863; James Harlan, Iowa, May 15th, 1865; O. H. Browning, Illinois, July 27th, 1866. **Attorney-General**, Edward Bates, Missouri, March 5th, 1861; Titian J. Coffee, June 22d, 1863; James Speed, Kentucky, December 2d, 1864; Henry Stanbery, Ohio, July 23d, 1866; William M. Evarts, New York, July 15th, 1868. **Postmaster-General**, Montgomery Blair, Maryland, March 5th, 1861; William Dennison, Ohio, September 24th, 1864; Alexander W. Randall, Wisconsin, July 25th, 1866.

---

[1] See p. 205.

## Cabinet Officers of the Administrations.

### XXI. AND XXII.; 1869–1877 (page 209).

**Secretary of State,** E. B. Washburne, Illinois, March 5th, 1869; Hamilton Fish, New York, March 11th, 1869. **Secretary of Treasury,** George S. Boutwell, Massachusetts, March 11th, 1869; William A. Richardson, Massachusetts, March 17th, 1873; Benjamin H. Bristow, Kentucky, June 2d, 1874; Lot M. Morrill, Maine, June 21st, 1876. **Secretary of War,** John A. Rawlins, Illinois, March 11th, 1869; William T. Sherman, Ohio, September 9th, 1869; William W. Belknap, Iowa, October 25th, 1869; Alphonso Taft, Ohio, March 8th, 1876; J. D. Cameron, Pennsylvania, May 22d, 1876. **Secretary of Navy,** Adolph E. Borie, Pennsylvania, March 5th, 1869; George M. Robeson, New Jersey, June 25th, 1869. **Secretary of Interior,** Jacob D. Cox, Ohio, March 5th, 1869; Columbus Delano, Ohio, November 1st, 1870; Zachariah Chandler, Michigan, October 19th, 1875. **Attorney-General,** E. R. Hoar, Massachusetts, March 5th, 1869; Amos T. Akerman, Georgia, June 23d, 1870; George H. Williams, Oregon, December 14th, 1871; Edwards Pierrepont, New York, April 26th, 1875; Alphonso Taft, Ohio, May 22d, 1876. **Postmaster-General,** J. A. J. Creswell, Maryland, March 5th, 1869; Marshall Jewell, Connecticut, August 24th, 1874; James M. Tyner, Indiana, July 12th, 1876.

### XXIII.; 1877–1881 (page 223).

**Secretary of State,** William M. Evarts, New York, March 12th, 1877. **Secretary of Treasury,** John Sherman, Ohio, March 8th, 1877. **Secretary of War,** George W. McCrary, Iowa, March 12th, 1877; Alexander Ramsey, Minnesota, December 12th, 1879. **Secretary of Navy,** Richard W. Thompson, Indiana, March 12th, 1877; Nathan Goff, Jr., West Virginia, January 6th, 1881. **Secretary of Interior,** Carl Schurz, Missouri, March 12th, 1877. **Attorney-General,** Charles Devens, Massachusetts, March 12th, 1877. **Postmaster-**

General, David M. Key, Tennessee, March 12th, 1877; Horace Maynard, Tennessee, August 25th, 1880.

### XXIV.; 1881–1885 (page 247).

**Secretary of State**, James G. Blaine, Maine, March 5th, 1881; Frederick T. Frelinghuysen, New Jersey, December 12th, 1881. **Secretary of Treasury**, William H. Windom, Minnesota, March 5th, 1881; Charles J. Folger, New York, October 27th, 1881. **Secretary of War**, Robert T. Lincoln, Illinois, March 5th, 1881. **Secretary of Navy**, W. H. Hunt, Louisiana, March 5th, 1881. **Secretary of Interior**, S. J Kirkwood, Iowa, March 5th, 1881. **Attorney-General**, Wayne MacVeagh, Pennsylvania, March 5th, 1881; Benjamin H. Brewster, Pennsylvania, December 16th, 1881. **Postmaster-General**, Thomas L. James, New York, March 5th, 1881; Timothy O. Howe, Wisconsin, December 20th, 1881.

ABOLITIONISTS, THE, 123, 177, 178 (*note*).
Abolition of Slavery, 195.
Adams, C. F., 148, 218.
Adams, John, 18, 27, 39, 40, 47, 49.
Adams, John Quincy, 67, 91, 95, 101, 128, 134.
Adams, J. Q., Jr., 219.
Admission of the States, 289.
Alabama Claims, 214.
Alien Law, 44.
American Party, 160.
American Whigs, 5.
Ames, Oakes, 220.
Ames, Fisher, 37.
Amnesty, 201, 216, 230.
Annexation of Louisiana, 55; of Florida, 85, of Texas, 137–140.
Anti-Federal Party (see *Democratic-Republican Party*).
Anti-Masonic Party, 102.
Anti-Nebraska Men, 159.
Arthur, C. A., 245, 246, 247.
Articles of Confederation, 7, 248.

BANK, NATIONAL, 23, 70; the second, 81; overthrown by Jackson, 104-118; substitutes for, 133, 155, 191.
Banks, N. P., Jr., 161.
Barbour, P. P., 92.
Barnburners, 148.
Bell, John, 181, 185.
Birney, James G., 130, 137.

Black Cockade-Federalist, 53.
Black Republican, 162.
Blaine Amendment, 230.
Blaine, James G., 209, 214.
Blair, F. P., 207.
Bland Silver Bill, 239.
"Bloody Bill," 113.
Border Ruffians, 163.
Boyd, Linn, 155, 158.
Breckenridge, John C., 166, 168, 181, 185.
Bristow, B. H., 232.
Broad Seal War, 128.
Brooks, Preston S., 165.
Brooks, James, 220.
Brown, B. G., 217, 218, 221.
Brown, John, 177.
Buchanan, James, 166, 168, 179, 183.
Burr, Aaron, 27, 39, 49, 58, 59, 62, 64.
Butler, Benjamin F., 190.
Butler, William O., 147, 150.

CABINETS, 300.
Calhoun, John C., 71, 95, 98, 104, 108, 113.
Calls for Troops, 228.
Capital, The National, 23, 49.
Cary, S. F., 231.
Cass, Lewis, 147, 150.
Caucus Nominations, 49, 94.
Censure of Jackson, 117, 122; of Tyler, 135.
Centennial Exhibition, 230, 231.
Chambers, B. J., 245.

Chase, Salmon P., 192, 205, 211.
Chase Trial, 58, 59.
Cherokee Indian Case, 107, 112.
Chesapeake Case, 64.
Cipher Telegrams, 240.
Civil Rights Bill, 199, 216, 227.
Civil Service, 105, 141, 215, 247.
Clay, Henry, 71, 76, 81, 83, 84, 87, 88, 93, 95, 96, 103, 111, 114, 117, 129, 137, 140.
Clinton, De Witt, 72, 75.
Clinton, George, 27, 58, 59, 66, 68.
Cobb, Howell, 153.
Cochrane, John C., 193.
Colfax, Schuyler, 193, 198, 204, 206, 207, 219.
Compromise of 1820, 86, 159; of 1850, 153, 157, 163; Crittenden, 183.
Confederation, Articles of, 6, 248; revision, 9.
Confederate States, 184.
Congress, Peace, 184.
Congress, Powers of, 12.
Conservatives, 127.
Constitution, The, 11, 15, 196, 262; its Amendments, 20, 34, 58, 184, 193, 194, 199, 207, 281.
Constitutional Union Party, 181.
Convention of 1787, 10.
Conventions, Nominating, 111.
Cooper, Peter, 231.
Copperheads, 194 (*note*).
Corporal's Guard, 135.
Courts, United States, 12.
Covode Investigation, 179.
Crawford, William H., 71, 82, 94, 95, 104.
Crittenden, John J., 183.
Cuba, 173, 180.
Cumberland Road, 92.

DALLAS, GEORGE M., 138, 140.
Davis, Jefferson, 184.
Davis, John W., 142.
Dayton, Jonathan, 36, 42.
Dayton, William L., 169, 170.

Debt, Hamilton's Settlement of Public, 21.
Democrat, 26, 97.
Democratic Clubs, 30, 34.
Democratic Party, overthrows the United States Bank, 106–118; supports War with Mexico, 138; ruled by Southern members, 158; Division of, 180; opposes War against the Rebellion, 194; opposes Reconstruction by Congress, 207.
Democratic-Republican Party, 25, 45; first great success of, 49, 52; supports War with England, 71; division of, 80 (see thereafter *Democratic Party*).
Demonetization of Silver, 239.
Deposits, Removal of, 115.
Disputed Elections, 49, 95, 124, 236.
Dominica, 213, 223.
Donelson, A. J., 166, 168.
Dough Faces, 89 (*note*).
Douglas, S. A., 176, 180, 184, 185.
Draft Act (of 1814), 78; (of 1863), 192.
Dred Scott Case, 170, 180, 185.
Duane, William J., 115.

ELECTION LAWS, GENERAL, 211, 216, 242, 243.
Electoral Commission, 236.
Electoral Counts, 18, 27, 40, 50, 59, 68, 75, 82, 91, 95, 101, 114, 123, 131, 140, 150, 157, 168, 185, 195, 207, 221, 237, 246.
Electoral Votes, 290.
Electors, mode of choosing, 18, 102, 239.
Ellmaker, Amos, 111, 114.
Emancipation, 191.
Embargo Bill, 65, 67, 77.
England, 31, 63, 69; War against, 73; Difficulties with, 102.
English, Wm. H., 245, 246.
Era of Good Feeling, 92.
Everett, Edward, 181, 185.

# Index. 311

FARRWELL ADDRESS, Washington's, 38; Jackson's, 124.
Fauchet, Citizen, 34.
Federal Powers, 12.
Federalist, The, 16.
Federal Party, 14, 25, 27, 48; first great defeat, 49, 53; opposes the Embargo, 67; and War with England, 74; becomes extinct, 80.
Filibustering, 174.
Fillmore, Millard, 148, 150, 154, 166, 168.
Florida, 234, 238.
Florida Purchase, 85.
Floyd, John, 112, 114.
Foot's Resolution, 106.
Force Bill, 113, 214, 217.
France, 28, 41, 43; War with, 47; treaty with, 58; claims against, 102.
Freedmen's Bureau, 195, 198, 200.
Free Soil Party, 148, 156.
Free Trade, 88.
Frelinghuysen, Theodore, 137, 140.
Fremont, John C., 167, 168, 190, 193.
French Revolution, 25, 28.
Fugitive Slave Law, 154, 157, 193.

GARFIELD, JAMES A., 239, 244, 246, 247.
Genet, Citizen, 29, 31.
Gerry, Elbridge, 72, 75.
Giddings, J. R., 134.
Graham, William Alexander, 156, 157.
Granger, Francis, 120, 124.
Grangers, 224.
Grant, U. S., 205, 207, 209, 219, 221, 232, 244.
Greeley, Horace, 218, 221.
Greenback Party, 231, 241.
Greenbacks, 191, 211, 224.
Grow, G. A., 189.
Gunboat System, 60.

HABEAS CORPUS, 62, 192, 197, 215, 217.
Hale, John P., 156.
Hamilton, Alexander, 16, 19, 21, 23, 34, 35, 48, 49, 59, 81.
Hamlin, Hannibal, 181, 185.
Hancock, W. S., 245, 246.
Harper's Ferry, 177.
Harrison, Wm. H., 120, 123, 129, 131, 132.
Hartford Convention, 78, 160.
Hayes, R. B., 232, 234, 237, 242.
Helper's "Impending Crisis," 178.
Hendricks, T. A., 221, 232, 234, 237.
Henry Documents, 72.
Homestead Bill, 177, 179, 190, 199.
Hunkers, 148.
Hunter, R. M. T., 128.

IMPEACHMENT (of Judge Chase, 58, 59; (of Judge Peck), 109 (of President Johnson), 201 205; (of Secretary Belknap), 231.
"Impending Crisis," 178.
Income Tax Law, 193.
Independent Treasury, 118, 119, 126, 129.
Ingersoll, Jared, 72, 75.
Internal Improvements, 62, 92, 94, 98, 101, 104, 107, 109, 129, 133, 136, 145, 146, 155, 161, 185.
Internal Revenue Law, 193.

JACKSON, ANDREW, 85, 95, 97, 101, 111, 114, 117, 122, 124.
Jay, John, 16, 20, 30, 33, 35.
Jay's Treaty, 33, 35, 37, 41.
Jefferson, Thomas, 20, 25, 27, 32, 39, 40, 45, 49, 50, 53, 57, 71, 86, 105, 108.
Johnson, Andrew, 194, 195, 196, 200, 205.
Johnson, H. V., 180, 185.
Johnson, R. M., 120, 124, 131.

Jones, J. W., 136.
Juliau, Geo. W., 156.

KANSAS (Pawnee Constitution), 163; (Topeka Constitution), 164; (Lecompton Constitution), 175; (Wyandot Constitution), 177, 185.
Kentucky Resolutions (of 1798), 46; (of 1799), 47, 97, 100, 105, 182.
Kerr, M. C., 229.
King, Rufus, 30, 58, 59, 66, 68, 82.
King, Wm. R., 156, 157.
Kitchen Cabinet, 109.
Know Nothing, 160, 181.
Knox, Henry, 19.
Ku Klux Klan, 212.

LANE, JOSEPH, 181, 185.
Lecompton Constitution, 175.
Lee, Henry, 112, 114.
Legal Tender, 191, 211.
Lemoyne, Francis, 130.
Liberal-Republicans, 217.
Liberty Party, 130, 143.
Lincoln, Abraham, 181, 185, 191, 195, 196.
Loco-foco, 120 (note).
Loose Construction, 1, 14, 97, 162, 206.
Lopez Expedition, 174.
Louisiana, 221, 224, 225, 235, 238.
Louisiana Purchase, 55.

MACON, NATHANIEL, 54, 58, 60.
Madison, James, 10, 16, 45, 63, 66, 68, 72, 75, 105.
Maine, 244.
Mangum, W. P., 123.
Marshall, John, 64.
Mason and Dixon's Line, 86.
Maysville Road Bill, 107.
McClellan, G. B., 194, 195.
McLean, John, 111, 120, 124.
Mexico, War with, 141, 142.
"Midnight Judges," 55.

Missouri Compromise, 86, 88, 89, 159, 163.
Monroe Doctrine, 93.
Morgan, William, 103.
Morris, Thomas, 137.
Morton's Amendment, 230.
Muhlenberg, F. A., 19, 31.

NAPOLEONIC WARS, 60, 65.
National Bank (see *Bank*).
National Party (see *Greenback Party*).
National Republican Party, 96, 103 (see *Whig Party*).
Negro Exodus, 243.
Non-Intercourse Act, 68, 70.
North, Lord, 5.
Nullification, 105, 108, 112.
Nullification Proclamation, 113, 183.

OATH, IRON-CLAD, 191.
O'Conor, Charles, 219.
Office, Tenure of, 53, 105, 141, 203.
Orders in Council, 65, 73, 77.
Ordinances of Secession, 182.
Ordinance of 1787, 57, 86, 144, 195.
Oregon, 138, 144, 145, 147, 235.
Orr, Jas. L., 175.
Ostend Manifesto, 174.

PANIC OF 1837, 126.
Party Names: American Whig, 5; Federalist, 14; Anti-Federalist, 14; Republican (Democratic-Republican), 26, 97; Quids, 61; National Republican, 96; Democratic ("Jackson's Men"), 97; Anti-Masonic, 102; Whig, 120; Loco-foco, 120 (note); Abolitionist, 123; Conservative, 127; Liberty, 130; Hunker, 148; Barnburner, 148; Free Soil, 148; Anti-Nebraska, 159; American (Know Nothing), 160; Republican, 162; Constitutional Union, 181; Union, 187;

Radic..., 193; Copperhead, 194 (*note*); Liberal Republican, 219; Greenback or National, 231.
Patrons of Husbandry, 224.
Patterson's "New Jersey Plan," 10.
Pawnee Constitution, 163.
Pendleton, George H., 194, 195.
Pennington, William, 178.
Personal Liberty Laws, 154.
Pet Banks, 116, 125.
Pierce, Franklin, 156, 157, 164.
Pinckney, C. C., 41, 49, 58, 59, 66, 68.
Pinckney, Thomas, 39.
Pocket Veto, 108.
Political Parties, Origin of, 3.
Poland Committee, 220.
Polk, James K., 120, 126, 131, 138, 140.
Popular Sovereignty, 4, 152, 180.
Potter Committee, 240.
Presidential Elections (see *Electoral Counts, Disputed Elections*).
Protection, 21, 88, 99, 104, 185.

QUIDS, 61, 66, 74.

RADICAL MEN, 193.
Railroad Strikes, 239.
Randall, S. J., 236, 239, 242.
Randolph, Edmund, 10, 20.
Randolph, John, 61, 74, 89.
Reconstruction, 202, 210, 212, 228.
Republican Party of 1791 (see *Democratic-Republican Party*).
Republican Party of 1856: origin, 162; first great success, 182; manages the War against the Rebellion, 187; quarrels with Johnson, 200; accomplishes Reconstruction by Congress, 202, 210, 228.
Resumption, 227, 241.
Returning Boards, 221, 234, 239.
Riders, 149, 162, 202, 216, 242.

Rush, Richard, 101.

SALARY GRAB, 220.
San Domingo, 213, 223.
Schurz, Carl, 217.
Scott, Dred, 170, 180, 185.
Scott, Winfield, 156, 157.
Secession, 182, 188.
Sedition Law, 44, 99, 214.
Seminole War, 85, 127.
Sergeant, John, 111, 114.
Seward, William H., 162 (*note*).
Seymour, Horatio, 207.
Silver, Demonetization of, 239.
Slaughter House Cases, 223.
Slave Power, 172.
Slavery, 86, 122, 155, 172, 191, 195.
Slave Trade, 11, 174.
Smith, William, 101.
South Carolina, 182, 233, 238.
Specie Circular, 121, 125, 127.
Specie Payments, 227, 241.
Squatter Sovereignty, 152, 180.
Stanton, E. M., 204, 206.
State Bank System, 119.
Stephens, A. H., 185.
Stevenson, Andrew, 100, 106, 109, 117, 118.
Straight Outs, 219.
Strict Construction, 1, 14, 97, 162, 206.
Sub-Treasury System, 118, 119, 126, 129, 133.
Sumner, Charles, 165, 216, 227.
Sumter, Fort, 187.

TANEY, R. B., 116, 118.
Tariff, 20, 84, 87, 93; (of 1824), 94, 98; (of 1828), 100; (of 1832), 110; (of 1833), 114; (of 1842), 136; (of 1846), 145; (of 1857), 168; (of 1861), 185, 189, 191.
Taylor, John W., 89, 97.
Taylor, Zachary, 142, 147, 150, 154.
Tazewell, L. W., 131.
Texas, 85, 122, 136, 137, 139, 142.
Texas v. White, 210.
Third Term, 232.

Thomas, Lorenzo, 205.
Tidal Wave, 229.
Tilden, S. J., 232, 234, 237.
Tompkins, D. D., 82, 91.
Topeka Constitution, 164.
Tory, 5.
Trumbull, Jonathan, 25.
Tyler, John, 113 (note), 120, 124, 129, 131, 132, 138, 194 (note).

UNION PARTY, 187.

VAN BUREN, MARTIN, 109, 110, 111, 114, 120, 123, 131, 138, 148.
Varnum, Joseph B., 69.
Virginia Resolutions: (of 1798), 46; (of 1799), 47.

WALKER, R. J., 168.
Walker, William, 174.
Warner Silver Bill, 242.
Washington, George, 10, 18, 27, 29, 36, 38, 43.
Webster, Daniel, 120, 123, 133 (note).

West Virginia, 192.
Wheeler, W. A., 226 (note), 232, 234, 237.
Whig, 5.
Whig Party: origin, 120; first great success, 130; quarrels with Tyler, 133; decline, 151, 156, 166.
Whiskey Insurrection, 34.
Whiskey Ring, 227.
White, Hugh L., 119, 121, 123.
White, John, 133.
White, League, 212 (note).
Whitney's Cotton Gin, 86.
Wilmot Proviso, 144, 146, 151, 195.
Wilson, Henry, 219.
Winthrop, R. C., 146.
Wirt, William, 111, 114.
Wright, Silas, 138.
Wyandot Constitution, 177, 179, 185.

X. Y. Z. MISSION, 42.

YAZOO FRAUDS, 56.

www.ingramcontent.com/pod-product-compliance
Lightning Source LLC
Chambersburg PA
CBHW030014240426
43672CB00007B/943